Setting the Record Straight

Copyright 2021 Hany Longwe

All rights reserved. No part of this publication may be reproduced, stored in a retrieval system, or transmitted in any form or by any means, electronic, mechanical, photocopying, recording or otherwise without prior permission from the publishers.

Published by
Luviri Press
P/Bag 201 Luwinga
Mzuzu 2
Malawi

ISBN   978-99960-66-42-9
eISBN   978-99960-66-43-6

Luviri Press is represented outside Malawi by:
African Books Collective Oxford (order@africanbookscollective.com)

www.mzunipress.blogspot.com
www.africanbookscollective.com

Editorial assistance: Hope Kaombe

Cover Picture: Meeting called to draft the Salima Baptist Association Constitution at Senga Bay in the middle of the 1960s.

Setting the Record Straight

Essays on Ecclesiology, Missiology and Evangelism

Hany Longwe

Luviri Press

Mzuzu

2021

"Kusadziwa Nkufa Komwe"

Lack of Knowledge
is like Being Dead

Contents

Chapter 1
A Baptist Church Does Not Need a Pastor: A History of Theological Training for Convention Baptists in Malawi — 7

Chapter 2
Theological Education in Baptist Churches in Eastern and Southern Africa — 27

Chapter 3
Theology & Religious Studies and Development with Malawi in Mind — 54

Chapter 4
Missions across the Border: Baptist Convention of Malawi's Expansion into Neighbouring Countries — 75

Chapter 5
The *Matchona* Contribution to Early Baptist Church History — 91

Chapter 6
Kusadziwa Nkufa Komwe: The Baptist Theological Seminary of Malawi Fighting against HIV/AIDS — 115

Chapter 7
Achewa Providence Industrial Mission: African Independent Church or Baptist? — 127

Chapter 8
The Church, the Laity, and the Priesthood — 149

Chapter 9
The Ordination of Women in the Baptist Convention of Malawi — 167

Chapter 10
Baptist Churches in Africa — 183

Chapter 11
The Contribution of "Fellowships" in the Evangelization Process in Malawi   196

Chapter 12
Post-Classical Missions' Missionary Affair in Malawi   208

Chapter 13
Zimbabwe, Zambia and Malawi   243

Chapter 14
A Pictorial Essay on the Early Life of the Baptist Convention of Malawi   261

Bibliography   **281**

Chapter 1

A Baptist Church Does Not Need a Pastor:
A History of Theological Training for Convention Baptists in Malawi

If a pastor is understood as one looking after a congregation full-time or part-time, one does not find that office in the New Testament (NT). The word pastor occurs only once in Ephesians 4:11-12, and that is in the plural. A related word "shepherd" gives further insights. There is nowhere in the NT where one reads that one person was a shepherd of a certain congregation. Where the word shepherd occurs in the singular, it always refers to Jesus Christ who speaks of himself as the Good Shepherd (Jn 10). He is also called the Great Shepherd (Heb 13:20) and the Chief Shepherd (1Pet 5:4). The NT speaks twice of the elders of a church (again in the plural) as shepherds (Acts 20:28) and as overseers (1Pet 5:1-4).[1]

Ephesians 4:7-5:2 pictures the risen Christ as giving gifted persons to the church "to prepare God's people for works of service, so that the body of Christ may be built up" (4:12). Some people are gifts to the church! The elder/pastor is one of the many gifts. The Bible portrays the church as a living body or organism in which every cell contributes. Members of the church are to build up the body, "until we all reach unity in the faith ... and become mature" (4:13). The whole body "grows and builds itself up in love as each part does its work" (4:16). Historically, both pastors and laypersons, without making much distinction between the two, have led Baptist churches. In an ideal situation, pastors and laypersons work together in harmony for the sake of Christ and his kingdom.

Generally, Baptists have viewed theological training as a way of making God-called men and women disciples of Jesus Christ. It transforms them

---

[1] Klaus Fiedler, *Baptists and the Ordination of Women*, Zomba: Lydia Print. no. 5, 2008, pp. 3, 4.

by renewing their minds with biblical truth, impacting their hearts with ministry passion, and enriching their souls with deepened Christ-likeness. Trainees are those who are committed to preparation for the practice of ministry, which emphasizes sharing the Gospel of Jesus Christ with others so they can come to know and receive him as personal Saviour and experience him as Lord of their life. Ministry also includes attending to the physical, emotional, mental and vocational needs of others.

Theological training for Malawian Baptists began with the training in 1897 to 1899 in the United States of (USA) of John Chilembwe, who had been taken there by Joseph Booth, a Baptist from Melbourne, though not a Baptist missionary.

Chilembwe, the founder of the famous "PIM,"[2] was the first Malawian missionary to his own people and is better known as a national hero who fought for the liberation of Malawi from colonial rule that led to what has been dubbed the Chilembwe 1915 Rising.[3] His disciple Daniel Malikebu was invited to study in America by Emma DeLaney, the second National Baptist missionary to work at PIM. When Emma DeLaney left, his family refused him to go, but not much later Malikebu slipped out of the country and arrived in New York in 1905,[4] and by 1915, he had started training at Meharry Medical College, Nashville in Tennessee,[5] the same medical school where Kamuzu Banda was trained later, a fact which Banda seemed to have always steered clear of.[6] In 1917, he briefly attended the Moody Bible Institute in Chicago, and in the same year, joined the University of

---

[2]   Providence Industrial Mission, whose official name since 1966 is African Baptist Assembly, Malawi Inc. It is the oldest Baptist church in the country.

[3]   For a history that emphasizes both the spiritual and the political aspects of John Chilembwe's ministry, see Patrick Makondesa, *The Church History of Providence Industrial Mission*, Zomba: Kachere, 2006.

[4]   D.L. Saunders, "A History of Baptists in East and Central Africa," PhD, Southern Baptist Theological Seminary, 1973, p. 27.

[5]   G. Shepperson and T. Price, *Independent African*, Edinburgh: University Press, 1987, first paperback edition, reprinted Blantyre: CLAIM-Kachere, 2000, p. 142.

[6]   Klaus Fiedler, "Africa's Evangelical Turn," in Klaus Fiedler, *Conflicted Power in Malawian Christianity: Essays Missionary and Evangelical from Malawi*, Mzuzu: Mzuni Press, 2015, p. 364, footnote 82.

Pennsylvania where he studied tropical medicine and took his internship at Mudgett Hospital until 1918.[7] Malikebu passed on Chilembwe's legacy.[8] In 1926, Malikebu and his American wife, Flora,[9] reopened Providence Industrial Mission which the colonial government had banned from 1915 to 1924.

Bible Study and Sunday School, the Priesthood of all Believers and Evangelism

One cannot talk of theological training for Baptists, without a discourse on Bible study and Sunday school, the priesthood of all believers, and evangelism. It has been a general practice for Baptists to use Bible study and Sunday school as tools for evangelism that lead to church planting. Through these they assist converts to grow in their relationship with God. Once a Bible study fellowship was established, some preaching was soon introduced. All beginning efforts were directed to evangelism and church development. Whether the group was officially constituted or not, Sunday school was introduced in which the Bible was taught to help the people not only to grow in their faith, but also to know and assimilate Baptist beliefs and practices.

One of the fundamental beliefs of Baptists is the priesthood of all believers that rests on the foundation that all believers are priests and have direct access to God through Christ, who mediates for the believer. Baptists believe that no bishop, no priest, no pastor is mediator between God and people. There is no distinction made between the clergy and the laity. All are equal. The role and function of each believer as a priest is understood in a functional sense. Priesthood of all believers is an expression of the belief that the individual ultimately must answer only to God, not to human authority. The priesthood of believers affirms important truths about the

---

[7] Mekki Mtewa, "Tribute to Dr Malikebu," *The Enquirer*, Vol. 1 No. (6 September 1993), p. 5.

[8] See Hany Longwe, *Identity by Dissociation - A History of Achewa Providence Industrial Mission*, Mzuzu: Mzuni Press, 2013, pp. 26-28.

[9] Flora Ethelwyn G. Zeto was born in Congo, but brought up by missionaries in America.

individual, but it does not overlook the corporate nature of the Christian priesthood; it has to do with the individual as it has with the community. Every Baptist is to share the gospel of Jesus Christ and to bring those who profess their faith in Jesus together into local congregations. The priesthood of all believers is "a spiritual privilege, a moral obligation, and a personal vocation. The privilege is access to God. The obligation is to the church which teaches priesthood. The vocation is the arena where priests serve. Being a priest is both a gift and a demand."[10] Each person is competent in religious matters and each believer is a priest. Some Baptist groups that have established themselves in Malawi include the Central African Conference of Seventh Day Baptists, Baptist Convention of Malawi (BACOMA), Independent Baptist Convention of Malawi and Evangelical Baptists.[11]

Baptists are characterized by evangelism at all levels: individual, congregational and institutional, which has led to a considerable expansion of BACOMA. Nevertheless, individual witnessing has remained central. They work diligently and compassionately among the people. The individuals were ready to work against the grain of traditional church membership, and were happy to apply the "born again" ("BA" in short) principle. BACOMA members are free to evangelize and begin churches whenever and wherever they find people. In the process of evangelizing, BACOMA expresses the gospel they experience to those outside their churches.[12]

The Beginning of Theological Training in BACOMA

For BACOMA, theological training began in the 1960s soon after the establishment of a couple of congregations that later became Baptist Convention of Malawi (BACOMA) through the influence of the Baptist Mission in Malawi (BMIM), an agent of the Southern Baptist Convention (SBC from the United States of America. The only actors, who had

---

[10] www.baptisthistory.org/baptistorigins/priesthood.html [13.6.2018].

[11] For an overview of Baptist denominations in Malawi see: Rendell Day, "From Gowa to Landmark Missionary Baptists: One Hundred Years of Baptist Churches in Malawi", PhD module, Kachere Document no. 52, Zomba: Kachere, 2008.

[12] Hany Longwe, *Christians by Grace – Baptists by Choice: A History of the Baptist Convention of Malawi*, Mzuzu: Mzuni Press; Zomba: Kachere, 2011, p. 232.

theological training and were of influence in the earliest BACOMA churches, were the SBC missionaries. That soon changed with the involvement of some of the earliest Malawian "co-workers" of the SBC missionaries, such as Stephen and Mary Galatiya.

Although BACOMA began in the cities of Blantyre, Zomba and Lilongwe, it remained basically a rural church. As a result of the growing work, there was need to train more workers. Consequently, in 1962, the Southern Baptist Convention (SBC missionaries organized the first short-term lay pastors' institute. Some of the men in attendance included Stephen Galatiya from Mwanza, Kachaso Gama and Gwembere from Zomba, McDonald W. Kaduya from Chiradzulu, Makhaya and James Zuze from Luchenza and Huckson William Bonzo from Lilongwe. They were joined by the Achewa PIM leadership that comprised of Aaron Kamkalamba, Mathew Ndalama, Fenias (Peter) Kalonga and Yosofati Ndege.[13]

This first lay pastors' school was held for four weeks in one of the rented rooms behind Kadongo's grocery shop at Falls Estate between April and May 1962. The teachers included missionaries LeRoy Albright, Gene Kingsley and Bill Wester, and Abel Nziramasanga, pastor of Waterfalls Baptist Church in Harare. Nziramasanga was not just brought by the mission to teach in the school, but also to discuss with Malawians what it meant to be a Baptist,[14] that is one must understand the core beliefs of the Christian faith. Galatiya proved to be the best student of that class.

As a way of helping in the development of more church leaders, Albright bought five plots in a row on a road south of Kawale Post Office. One side of the first plot was along the main road into Kawale. The idea was to develop the plots into a leadership training centre. Although the congregation was meeting at Falls Estate, Albright was looking to a day when the Mission would construct a training centre and a church building in the same area. A couple of buildings were erected on the plots, and the larger building was used as a classroom. For a while all leadership-training sessions were carried out there until the construction of the Bible School campus at

---

[13] Hany Longwe, *Christians by Grace – Baptists by Choice*, p. 51.
[14] Gene Kingsley, a note to Hany Longwe, Fort Worth, nd.

Falls Estate.[15] In 1965 they finished the construction of the first permanent buildings. Classes were started using short term courses of six to eight weeks "between crops" to allow the students who were mainly subsistence farmers to attend classes. The courses were taught in the local language since many of the students could hardly read and write let alone speak English.

Graduates from the BBS contributed to the establishment of the BACOMA local churches throughout the country. They used Bible Study and Sunday school and Bible Way Correspondence school materials as tools for church planting, and these tools became popular in BACOMA. Consequently, church planting resulted in many churches that needed theologically trained leaders. The answer was sending more people to the Bible School. Many BACOMA pastors and church leaders have been BBS graduates. In 1998, the last group of 30 students graduated from the Baptist Bible School. That made a total of approximately 631 graduates trained at the School since 1962.[16]

To give opportunity to more men and women who qualified to study the Word of God in their areas, BACOMA introduced regional or localized Bible schools. Localized Bible schools later gave some seminary graduates opportunities to teach, which in turn helped them to learn more the Word of God in order to teach effectively.

Seminary Training

In 1963, the Southern Baptist Convention (SBC sent Stephen Galatiya and his wife Mary, as members of Ndalama church, for further theological training at the Baptist Theological Seminary of Zimbabwe at Gweru. and in 1965 they returned to Malawi. In those days, a Baptist seminary only accepted students who were certified members of Baptist churches. In the same year, Dafren and Joanna Makhaya went to Gweru seminary and in 1966, MacFerron Njolomole and Elizabeth Phiri followed. H. and Elestina

---

[15] Int. Ruben Nkhata, Lilongwe, 23.6.2003.

[16] From BACOMA 1997 Annual Report. Probably 70 of them were serving as pastors. Many of these later received further training at Lilongwe Seminary.

1: A Baptist Church Does Not Need a Pastor

Baduya went to Lusaka in 1966 and moved to Gweru in 1967 until 1969. In the same year, Bamusi P. and Martha Kanowa, and Ruben and Raika Nkhata went to the Baptist Seminary in Lusaka and were back in Malawi in 1972. The training was basically to meet the needs of the local BACOMA churches whose main concern was evangelism.

Between 1971 and 1989, the Baptist Convention of Malawi (BACOMA), with the support from the Baptist Mission in Malawi (BMIM), sent approximately 25 families to Gweru and Lusaka seminaries, with the majority going to Gweru. All but Fletcher Kaiya, George Mwase, Akim Chirwa, Peter Maseko, Hany Longwe and Molly Longwe who were awarded diplomas from Gweru seminary, received certificates in Christian service, ministry or theology. Of those who received diplomas, only Fletcher Kaiya's Diploma was with music although all who went to Gweru seminary studied some music and conducting as part of their programmes. Early in 1989, Blantyre Baptist Church called Fletcher Kaiya as Music Director. The church choir continued to grow and improve under his capable leadership.[17] Throughout the country, Fletcher Kaiya's involvement in church music was a witness in itself.

It was only Emmanuel and Jane Chinkwita Phiri who went to Arusha Baptist Seminary in Tanzania from 1983 to 1985. While studying for a diploma in theology at Arusha,[18] Günther Wagner, a visiting professor from the Baptist Theological Seminary of Rüschlikon in Switzerland, invited Chinkwita Phiri to study at Rüschlikon. He considered Chinkwita Phiri to be an outstanding student and thought him capable of doing degree level study at the European Baptist Seminary in Switzerland. BACOMA also recommended him for training in Rüschlikon.[19] In January 1985, Rüschlikon seminary accepted Emmanuel Chinkwita Phiri as a BDiv student. Jane did not qualify to be a seminary student; instead, she attended classes suitable for those with limited education that were not graded on the same level as those with university type backgrounds. After four years of study

---

17 Report Patricia and Lonnie Quillen – Baptist Mission in Malawi, 1989.
18 Sam Upton – Chinkwita Phiri, 9.6.1983.
19 W.A.C. Chisi – Baptist Theological Seminary, Rüschlikon, 3.8.1984.

Chinkwita Phiri received a Bachelor of Divinity degree in December and he was officially welcomed by BACOMA on 5 January 1988. In the same year, he became the Bible School director.

Though BACOMA did not issue a public statement of any kind in 1992, nevertheless, they were one of the signatories of letters by the Christian Council of Malawi (CCM) addressed to the president demanding a referendum and criticizing some abuses of power, and that fairness be applied to the referendum process, that all harassment should be stopped and that all prisoners of conscience be released. Emmanuel Chinkwita Phiri as the Convention President signed the letter on behalf of BACOMA.[20] The Convention Baptists were proud that during the course of the political changes in the country, they had not been spectators through the significant roles that members such as Chinkwita Phiri and others played. Like Akim and Martha Chirwa, Chinkwita Phiri and many other members of BACOMA, were involved in building bridges between political leaders and the general public for a common cause, the introduction of a democratic form of government. In 1994 Chinkwita Phiri was Malawi's ambassador to Mozambique up to 1996, when he represented Malawi in Zambia. In both Mozambique and Zambia he took every opportunity to preach when it came, and combined well his roles of ambassador for Malawi and ambassador for Christ.[21] Apart from politics, Chinkwita Phiri organized and led Bread of Life, an evangelistic group that was instrumental in winning many people to Christ, some of whom became Baptists. The group had members from different Christian denominations.

The last group that was sent to seminaries outside the country comprised Graham and Agnes Chipande from Zomba, Samuel and Linesi Mwale from Kasungu, and Hany and Molly Longwe from Dwangwa, who went to Gweru in 1989 All women who were sent to the seminaries outside Malawi, except for Molly Longwe, did so on their husbands' tickets. The Baptist Mission in Malawi (BMIM) sent Hany and Molly Longwe to Lusaka Seminary to upgrade their diplomas to BTh degrees to teach at BTSM on

---

[20] Hany Longwe, *Christians by Grace – Baptists by Choice*, p. 462.
[21] Hany Longwe, *Christians by Grace – Baptists by Choice*, p. 466.

their return.[22] They received financial support from BMIM to pursue first-degree level studies because it was part of the BMIM plan. No one else has received financial support from BMIM to study for a first-degree award. It was considered unnecessary. BMIM then did not see any need for training more people at that level or beyond. The reason given was that there were no positions for trained Malawians in BACOMA churches and institutions. Hany and Molly Longwe were the last people to receive official support to study outside the country. In December 1995, they were both awarded a BTh, and started teaching at the Baptist Theological Seminary in Lilongwe from January 1996.

Baptist Theological Seminary

Since then, most of the church leaders came out of the Baptist Theological Seminary (BTSM) in Lilongwe. While the BTSM was designed to provide pastoral training, it has not been specifically a pastors' school, but its task was to train "men and women called by God for ministry." While they trained for ministry, it was the local congregation that called someone to be a minister. Candidates from the Lilongwe seminary formed the largest segment of seminary trained BACOMA leaders. Several have been women. The Lilongwe seminary used the decentralized form of theological education (DTE). The students travelled from their various homes to the seminary many times during the course of study. Since the Seminary training was designed for men only, the student's spouses attended a separate programme from their husbands. For the first four years of its operation the seminary offered only a certificate in theology.

The first Diploma level class at the BTSM began because of a demand from serving pastors who had been to Gweru and Lusaka seminaries, and were Certificate in Theology holders. In 2000, the first Diploma in Theology class at the Baptist Theological Seminary graduated. Members of this class were Kapalamula Banda, Christopher Butao, W.A.C. Chisi, Gunya, Dickson Kamanga, Fraser Makhuwira, Andy Namalima, Ruben Nkhata, Benard Alifeyo Phiri and Misinde Phiri. The quality of education offered by BTSM

---

[22] Report BACOMA, 1994.

was accepted by the University of Malawi through the Department of Theology and Religious Studies and the Faculty of Humanities.

In 2009, the BTSM introduced a first degree programme using the part time approach. However, the response was not good. As a result, in 2010, the BTSM enrolled three full time Degree students: Rustin Kalenga,[23] Napolo Alexander Chimombo, and Chrispin Mzumara. Unfortunately, Chrispin Mzumara dropped out because of lack of financial support. In 2012, the seminary had graduated four BTh degree students, two of whom were women.

Women at the Lilongwe Baptist Seminary

Since the original purpose of BTSM was to train men for ministry, no woman was qualified to attend classes there let alone to teach theology, but, in 1996, things changed with the arrival of Molly Longwe as a lecturer. She was a lecturer at the Lilongwe seminary for nearly twelve years. She paved the way for not only women to teach at the seminary but also to study at diploma and later degree levels. The seminary has been deliberately attempting to enroll female students. The reason was to refute the idea that the institution was for training pastors while it was to equip "God called men and women for Christian ministry."[24] However, that was a difficult move to be accepted amongst the majority of the membership of BACOMA and some of the missionaries. Unfortunately, the response of women enrollment has since remained slow. For example, in September 1996, Liddah Kalako was the first woman to be enrolled at BTSM. She was the only woman in a class of thirteen students. Many pastors and church members including her fellow women asked questions such as whether she was going to be a pastor after completing the course. Despite all challenges

---

[23] Rustin Kalenga was the BACOMA President from 2013 to 2019.

[24] Molly Longwe, "Engendered Theological Education: A Case of Women Theological Educators in the Baptist Convention of Malawi," in Isabel Apawo Phiri (ed), *Journal of Constructive Theology*, Pietermaritzburg: Centre for Constructive Theology, 2010, p. 85.

faced, Liddah Kalako graduated with a Certificate in Theology in the year 2000. Unfortunately, she died the same year.[25]

In 2002, the second woman, Nellie Phiri, graduated with a Certificate in Theology.[26] Nellie Phiri went on to study at diploma level. After Nellie Phiri, there followed four other female students who did not finish because of different reasons. Daina Mhango, a teacher at Bhive Private School in Mzuzu, came after these dropouts in 2007. She was the only female student amongst twenty men. Daina Mhango graduated in 2010 with a certificate in theology. She finished her studies when Mary Kagwa was in her second year of studies. She was a pastor's wife ministering in Mangochi.

In 2009, Amess Mwamdaza enrolled with the Lilongwe seminary with her husband, Maiden. While her husband was in the Certificate class she was studying for a Diploma.[27] For the first year, Amess Mwamdaza was the only female student in a class of ten. In 2010, Lydia Chinkwita Phiri and Annie Mkandawire joined the Diploma class.

Annie Mkandawire and Amess Mwamdaza continued to first degree level studies. Annie Mkandawire was the Director of Hope Missions Ministries and wife to Francis Mkandawire, the General Secretary of Evangelical Association of Malawi (EAM). They were the first Baptist women to study for the first degree at the Baptist Theological Seminary of Malawi. There has been a great change though slow on women's enrollment at BTSM.[28] By 2017, eleven women had graduated from the seminary in Lilongwe.

Upgrade from Diploma to BA in Theology

A discussion between Emmanuel Chinkwita Phiri, then President of BACOMA and Klaus Fiedler, a German Baptist and missionary who was

---

[25] Hany Longwe, *Christians by Grace - Baptists by Choice*, p. 291.
[26] Hany Longwe, *Christians by Grace - Baptists by Choice*, p. 291.
[27] The husband died before Amess completed her training.
[28] Amess Mwamdaza, "The Relationship between the Baptist Convention of Malawi (BACOMA and the Baptist Mission in Malawi (BMIM) and the Nationalization of the Baptist Theological Seminary of Malawi (BTSM)," BTh, Baptist Theological Seminary of Malawi, 2012.

lecturing at Chancellor College of the University of Malawi, led to the creation of a new partnership in theological studies. The most urgent thing was to upgrade some from Diploma (obtained at Gweru and Lusaka Baptist seminaries) to BA in Theology at Chancellor College.

Akim Chirwa and Peter Maseko were the first to benefit from this partnership. In 1996, the University of Malawi awarded them a BA in Theology. Peter Maseko's BA was with Credit. Akim Chirwa was pastor of Zomba Baptist Church before becoming the first full-time General Secretary of the Baptist Convention, a post he held until 2002. It was during his tenure as General Secretary that BACOMA set up home missionaries in districts where Convention work was weak or did not exist. In November 1997, Akim Chirwa accompanied by Ruben Nkhata as President of BACOMA, signed the partnership agreement between Malawi and Oklahoma during the Oklahoma annual assembly in Oklahoma City.

Peter Maseko served as head of the Senga Bay Baptist Clinic before he left and established, together with his daughter, Dr. Anne Alaniz, Pothawira, meaning "Safe Haven" in Chichewa, a clinic to meet the medical needs of the district of Salima. At the time of writing, it was an outpatient clinic which treated more than 300 patients during busy days, many of them mothers and young children.[29] It served as a lifeline for thousands of people connecting them to lifesaving medical treatment. It was expected to grow into an established inpatient hospital. In 2014, the clinic began construction of a new maternal surgical unit, thus ensuring that women in the region have access to safe birthing services. Pothawira also partnered with the Ministry of Health and Salima District Hospital. Apart from the busy schedule, Peter Maseko with his wife Emma pastored Salima Baptist Church.

On top of health services, Pothawira had children's homes that provided wholistic family-based care. Each family included a house mother and 10-12 children of varying ages that lived in duplexes. Five duplexes were originally constructed to house 100 children. Those numbers quickly rose to 113. With assistance from other partners, Pothawira was able to

---

[29] Int. Angela Maseko, Salima, 7.8.2018.

construct an additional duplex in 2015 that was completed in 2016. By 2018, 127 children were able to call Pothawira home.[30]

Fletcher Kaiya followed Akim Chirwa and Peter Maseko to enroll for the BA in Theology and Religious Studies at the University of Malawi, and he graduated in 2008. In addition to pastoring, Fletcher and his wife Clara have been running the 'Agape' Orphanage in Blantyre. The original orphans ranged in age from 5 to 13 years. The project is funded mainly from Fletcher and Clara's own finances and some donors from the West. Despite the fact that it was a Christian orphanage that taught Christian values, 'Agape' welcomed orphans from other faith backgrounds. Fletcher Kaiya has also been the European Baptist Mission (EBM International) regional representative for Southern Africa based in Malawi. He manages EBM International's projects in Malawi, Mozambique, Zambia and South Africa.

The upgrading programme of diploma to BA did not only benefit those from Gweru and Lusaka seminaries. Those from BTSM also benefitted. Christopher Butao was top of the class and supported by the seminary to study at Chancellor College of the University of Malawi, and he later graduated with a BA in Theology. He was followed by Dixon Kamanga from the same diploma class to graduate with the same qualification from the same university in 2005.

Women also benefitted from the BACOMA – Fiedler partnership. The first was Martha Chirwa, Akim Chirwa's wife. The Department of Theology and Religious Studies recommended Martha Chirwa to join the BA programme, but the College refused. Fiedler put her then into the ICI BA correspondence course, which has links with the Assemblies of God School of Theology in Lilongwe, but it did not really work out. In 1997, she joined Zomba Theological College on a full-time basis, and received a Bachelor of Divinity Degree in 2001.

She went to the USA and for four years, she was a housewife waiting upon her husband who was studying for a Master of Divinity degree at Mid-America Baptist Seminary, a 'conservative' institution that did not allow

---

[30] Int. Angela Maseko, Salima, 7.8.2018.

women to pursue theology degrees. Mid-America Baptist Theological Seminary claimed that it does not discriminate students on the basis of race, colour, national, or ethnic origins. But they did discriminate on the basis of gender. They believed that certain courses are for men only because they were convinced that the ordained pastor of a church must be male according to 1 Corinthians 11:3 ff and 1 Timothy 2:9-15.[31] Since their return, Martha Chirwa has been a lecturer at the Baptist Theological Seminary in Lilongwe.

Another woman to benefit from the partnership was Rachel Banda. She was the first lay woman to undertake theological training in her own right. Klaus Fiedler supported her in Australia where she was studying for her BTh with Christian Missionary Alliance College in Canberra. She was in Australia accompanying her husband, Jande, who was studying at Australian National University on a scholarship through the University of Malawi. Rachel Banda had wanted to enter BA (Theology) at Chancellor College in the first year, but the College refused because, according to the University rules (at that time), she had had her chance to study at Bunda College of Agriculture and could not take another course in the University on the same level; she could only continue with agriculture. Instead she enrolled with Zomba Theological College as a "private" Baptist candidate. Within two and half years she was able to get a BTh. This was only possible through her husband's extension of study leave by half a year, and financial support from Klaus Fiedler and Hughes Baptist Church in Canberra, where the Bandas were members.[32]

First Degrees in Theology from other Institutions

Outside this partnership, Grace Matupi had been to Lusaka seminary with her husband, Oscar. She joined the African Bible College in Lilongwe, and in 1999, she graduated with a BA degree in theology. She was the wife to the pastor of Zomba Baptist Church, and taught at the church's primary school.

---

[31] Mid-America Baptist Theological Seminary Catalog 2000-2002, pp. 53-54.
[32] Klaus Fiedler, reminiscences to Hany Longwe, Zomba, August 2003.

From 1997, Rutherford and Marrie Banda were part of the full-time teaching staff at the BTSM. They obtained their degrees from Anderson Theological Seminary. Marrie died in 1998 and Rutherford left the BTSM in 2000. He started a ministry under Grace Baptist Church, a ministry that he has led since.

A few BACOMA Baptists received their first degrees from South Africa. George Mwase, the last Malawian director of the Bible School, graduated with a BTh from Randburg Baptist Theological Seminary. Titus Nkhata was next to graduate from the same institution. Apart from being a pastor, Mwase has been involved in the leadership and oversight of Jimmy Hodges Ministries International from Oklahoma that began working in the country from 1992. The ministry established many BACOMA churches in many parts of the country. Titus Nkhata became a part-time seminary lecturer for some time before he pastored Living Stones Baptist Church in Blantyre. He later left and went to Tanzania. He has since come back. Another person who received a first degree in South Africa was Ollen Khumbo Sosole. After being a pastor for a brief period in Mzimba, he became a lecturer and the registrar of BTSM in Lilongwe at a time when he was studying for his MA with Mzuzu University.

Through the years, several Malawi Convention Baptists, both men and women, graduated from the African Bible College (ABC) in Lilongwe. These included: Funwayo Mafuleka, John Mastern (1999), Aubrey Kanyama (2004), Alice Kanyama, Aubrey's wife (2006)[33], and Jimmy Phiri 2007, who were members of Capital City Baptist Church (CCBC).

In 2004, sisters, Malla Kaiya and Grenna Kaiya, graduated with a BA from African Bible College. Malla has two MAs; one from Diakonhjemmet University College, Norway (2008) in social services, and the other (2017) from the Eastern and Southern African Management Institute (ESAMI) in Arusha, Tanzania in Management. Grenna Kaiya, on the other hand, gra-

---

[33] Alice Kanyama got an MA in Christian Leadership in 2015 from ABC. The topic of her dissertation is: "Leadership Studies, Social Policy and Community Development."

duated from the Diakonhjemmet University College in Norway with an MA.[34]

MA & PhD Studies

In April 1991, Sandress Msiska joined Student Christian Organization of Malawi (SCOM) as General Secretary. In 1997, he took leave to study theology at Nairobi Graduate School of Theology in Nairobi, Kenya, for two years where he obtained an MA in Christian Education in 1999. In 2001 he left SCOM and between 2001 and 2004, he served as BACOMA Deputy General Secretary and later briefly as head of Baptist Publications. On 4 January 2004 he joined World Relief as Deputy Country Director and in January 2006 he was appointed Country Director for World Relief in Malawi, a position he held till end of May 2012. On February 24th, 2008 Capital City Baptist Church and BACOMA ordained him as pastor, and on October 11, 2009 CCBC he became an associate pastor at Capital City Baptist Church. The following year, Sandress Msiska became the Senior Pastor.

Funwayo Mafuleka went on to be the pastor of Zomba Baptist Church before he left for MA studies in the USA. In 2007, Funwayo Mafuleka graduated from Gordon-Conwell Theological Seminary with an MA in Urban Ministry Leadership. John Mastern worked for African Leadership (BTCP) as National Coordinator for about a year and then moved to World Relief as the Programme Coordinator for about 7 years. He graduated from RTS in May 2010 and joined EAM as the Central Region Church Coordinator under a programme for Billy Graham Evangelistic Association and then joined CCBC up to July 2018, from where he became the General Secretary of the Baptist Convention of Malawi. During the period, Mastern has also served as a volunteer lecturer at BTSM and Logos Institute.[35] In 2014 Jimmy Phiri and his wife, Wezzie and their family went to Liberty

---

[34] The title of her MA is: "The Role of the Churches in Human Rights Advocacy: The Case of Malawian Members of Jehovah's Witnesses, Their Accounts of Stories and Memories as Victims of Religious Persecution from 1964 to 1994."

[35] John Mastern, Baptist Convention General Secretary, email to Hany Longwe, Lilongwe, 7.8.2018.

University in Virginia, USA, where he graduated with a Master of Divinity in Theology. He is currently serving with Capital City Baptist Church as Missions Pastor.

The desire for further theological training being fulfilled, BACOMA looked forward to having more Baptists trained at MA and even PhD levels. Klaus Fiedler also promoted further studies on MA and PhD level. BMIM missionary, Rendell Day registered for PhD, but he did not finish because he left Malawi.[36] Hany Longwe was the first BACOMA Baptist to get an MA from the University of Malawi in 2000. His dissertation is: "Identity by Dissociation: The First Group to Secede from Chilembwe's Church: A History of Peter Kalemba and the Achewa Providence Industrial Mission. It was later published as: Hany Longwe, *Identity by Dissociation - A History of Achewa Providence Industrial Mission*, Mzuzu: Mzuni Press, 2013. Rachel Banda was second and her dissertation is: "Liberation through Baptist Polity and Doctrine: A Reflection on the Lives of Women in the History of Women in the Baptist Convention in Southern Malawi," MA, University of Malawi, 2001. It was published as: Rachel NyaGondwe Banda, *Women of the Bible and Culture: Baptist Convention Women in Southern Malawi*, Zomba: Kachere, 2005.[37]

Vincent Chirwa graduated from Cape Town Baptist Seminary with an MA in 2001.[38] He had ministered alongside Victor Covington, an interim African American from UBIA (United Brethren in Action) pastor who returned to the United States in 2003. From then on, Vincent Chirwa became the resident pastor of Blantyre Baptist Church, a predominantly Malawian church with a few expatriates from Africa and White people from

---

[36] One of his PhD modules is useful for the study of Baptists in Malawi: Rendell Day, "From Gowa to Landmark Missionary Baptists: One Hundred Years of Baptist Churches in Malawi," PhD module, Kachere Document no. 52, Zomba: Kachere, 2008.

[37] In addition the last chapter was published as: Rachel NyaGondwe Fiedler, *Coming of Age. A Christianized Initiation among Women in Southern Malawi*, Zomba: Kachere, 2005.

[38] The title of his dissertation is: "The need for counselling as a major in the pastor's scope of ministry and theological education in Malawi in light of HIV/AIDS". He pastored alongside Victor Covington an African American from UBIA (United Brethren in Action) until 2003 when Covington returned to the United States of America

Africa and abroad. Blantyre Baptist Church is very much involved in formal education of children and young people in the City of Blantyre.

Molly Longwe got an MTh in African Christianity with the University of Natal and Akrofi-Christaller Memorial Centre for Mission Research and Applied Theology in Akropong, Ghana, under Dr Kwame Bediako. She was there through a scholarship from the African Theological Fellowship (ATF) in Ghana. Klaus Fiedler was only involved as Molly Longwe's local adviser. Her dissertation is: "*From Chinamwali to Chilangizo*: The Christianization of Pre-Christian Chewa Initiation Rites in the Baptist Convention of Malawi," University of KwaZulu Natal, 2003. It was published as: Molly Longwe, *Growing Up: A Chewa Girls' Initiation*, Zomba: Kachere, 2007, and is, like Rachel Banda's book, also available through African Books Collective, Oxford.

In 2002 Akim Chirwa left for the USA, and by 2007, he had earned a Master of Divinity degree from Mid-America Baptist Theological Seminary. Before studying theology, Owen Mkandawire had a Bachelor of Education degree from the University of Malawi. In 2010, the University of KwaZulu-Natal, in South Africa awarded an MA in Theology to Owen Mkandawire. His dissertation is, "An Ecclesiological Discussion of the Recent History of the Baptist Convention of Malawi (BACOMA) 1989-2005." Both Chirwa and Mkandawire have served as lecturers at the Baptist seminary in Lilongwe.. Akim Chirwa until his death (as Principal) in 2020. Owen Mkandawire is no longer with the institution.

Klaus Fiedler also supported Bright Kawamba's entry into the MA (Residential) University of Malawi programme, and became his supervisor. Kawamba graduated in 2013. His dissertation is: "The Blantyre Spiritual Awakening 1969 to 1986: an Antecedent of the Charismatic Movement in Malawi."[39] Brighton Kawamba worked for World Vision for about twenty years before Orchard Grove Community Church in Michigan (USA) called him to be an Associate Pastor for the church.

---

[39] Published as: Brighton Kawamba, *The Blantyre Spiritual Awakening and its Music*, Mzuzu: Luviri Press, 2018.

Concerning PhDs in Theology in BACOMA, Christopher T. Nkhoma is recorded as the first holder. With the help of a few friends he left Blantyre Baptist Church for Dallas, USA in 1988. About three years later, Christopher Nkhoma graduated with a PhD, after which he decided to stay in the USA.[40] He taught at Dallas Baptist University for some years before he died in 2008. The next BACOMA PhD in Theology is that of Hany Longwe. In 2008, the University of Malawi awarded him the degree of PhD. His dissertation is: "Democratization of the Christian Faith: The Influence of the Baptist Doctrine of 'Priesthood of All Believers' on the History of the Baptist Convention of Malawi (BACOMA)," 2007, which was published as Hany Longwe, *Christians by Grace- Baptists by Choice: A History of the Baptist Convention of Malawi*, Mzuzu: Mzuni Press; Zomba Kachere, 2011.

In 2011 Rachel NyaGondwe Fiedler received a PhD from the University of the Free State, Bloemfontein, South Africa. Her dissertation is: "The Circle of Concerned African Women Theologians (1989-2007): History and Theology." Based on the cutoff point of her PhD research, a book was published as: Rachel NyaGondwe Fiedler, *A History of the Circle of Concerned African Women Theologians (1989-2007)*, Mzuzu: Mzuni Press, 2017. In 2012, Molly Longwe was awarded a PhD in Gender and Religion from the University of KwaZulu-Natal in South Africa. Her dissertation is: "A Paradox in a Theology of Freedom and Equality: The Experience of Pastors' Wives (Amayi Busa) in the Baptist Convention of Malawi (BACOMA)," published as Molly Longwe, *African Feminist Theology and Baptist Pastors' Wives*, Mzuzu: Luviri Press, 2019.

Apart from participating in and contributing to the life of BACOMA and other non-profit organizations, Rachel, Molly and Hany have been lecturers in academic settings. Rachel and Molly have been concerned with the empowerment of women and girls (not forsaking men and boys) through the Circle for Concerned African Women Theologians.

---

[40] A copy of his thesis has not been found yet.

Conclusion

In the Baptist context, theological training is not aimed at pastoring a church, but equipping a person for spiritual growth and ministry that results in the salvation of souls and the gathering of these people into a regenerated local community, called church. It is true a person's call to ministry has little to do with formal training; nonetheless, they believe training is important. If Jesus took time to train his disciples, training must be essential for effective ministry whatever the ministry may be. The Bible talks about a Christian in ministry to be "qualified to teach. "All Christian workers must be capable of disproving error. One must be able to come alongside and pastor, that is "shepherd," and help and encourage according to the gifting from the Holy Spirit. All of that assumes something happening in the person's life. It could come through formal schooling, or it could come through informal experience and training.

Because of the belief in the priesthood of all believers, there is no distinction made between the clergy and the laity among Baptists. Every believer, with or without theological training, is called to be a priest; the role of each believer functioning as a priest is understood in a functional sense. The priesthood of all believers has as much to do with the individual as it has with the community. Therefore, a Baptist church does not need a pastor for it to be a church. It is the task of every follower of Christ to make disciples of all ethnic groups, which include women and children.

Theological training is there to prepare people for what they are already doing and will continue to be doing. So, when God calls someone to be a pastor or to work in a Christian organization or teach in a Christian academic setting, the studies are to help them for that.

Chapter 2

Theological Education in Baptist Churches in Eastern and Southern Africa[1]

Although Baptists are the largest Protestant denominational family worldwide, they are a relatively small group that is active and influential within Africa. Comparing to other denominations, Baptists work had a slow start in West Africa, a weak one in Southern Africa, and a late beginning in Eastern Africa. Apart from missionary work, Baptists are heavily engaged in theological education in many parts of Africa.

Concept of Theological Education

Many Baptists in Eastern and Southern Africa seem to understand theological education as a preparation for ministry of a mature regenerate church member, one who is born again; in other words, one with a genuine conversion experience.[2] The major textbook for such preparation is the Bible. Very few know that preparation for ministerial vocation includes other subjects such as systematic theology, apologetics, counselling and church history.

The New Testament verb translated "to minister," is "to serve." Baptists in this region would view ministers or pastors as they are commonly known, primarily as servants. The basic distinctive that distinguishes the Baptists from mainline churches is the concept of a *regenerate church membership*, a congregation of people with personal faith committed to serve Christ as their Lord. In this local congregation, all believers are priests, and this produces the distinctive of *the priesthood of all believers*.[3] Since Christian ministry is doing something of service like Jesus did, Baptists affirm that

---

[1] First published in Isabel Apawo Phiri and Dietrich Werner, *Handbook for Theological Education in Africa*, Oxford: Regnum, 2013. ISBN: 978-1-908355-195.

[2] Gottfried Osei-Mensah, *Wanted: Servant Leaders, Theological Perspectives in Africa No. 3*, Achimoto: Africa Christian Press, 1990, pp. 22-26.

[3] Klaus Fiedler, *Baptists and the Ordination of Women*, p. 1.

every Christian is called to minster in the name of Jesus Christ. Although they may not be able to articulate the doctrine of the priesthood of all believers, many Baptists understand the church as a priesthood, a "royal priesthood" (1Pet 2:9) that ministers corporately in the name of Jesus. Someone who has received theological education is viewed as a minister among many, a priest among priests.[4] Therefore, theological students and graduates are expected to serve. Academic requirements are of value if theological students contribute directly to the work of serving others.

Nevertheless, theological education has been understood as concerned with developing church leaders; leaders in ministry, a more or less "professional" ministry.[5] Almost all seminary students study to become better leaders in Christian ministry. They are expected to become leaders who lead by serving others. For one to become a leader, one must be trained in the areas of intellect, skills and spirituality. Many Baptists view theological education primarily as "spiritual formation." It is a formation whereby one's inner character is developed so that the person experiences more of God, reflects more of God's characteristics in everyday relationships and increasingly knows the power of God in ministry,[6] and that it is a process.[7] That is why many Baptist seminaries encourage or require students to be actively involved in ministry through local congregations while attending seminary. The Baptist distinctive of *the autonomy of the local church* recognizes the local congregation as the highest authority. This calls for the need for voluntary cooperation between local churches as it is expressed in the concept of associations and conventions, and in some cases, unions or fellowships.[8]

---

[4] John Stott, *The Cross of Christ*, Leicester: Inter-Varsity Press, 1989, p. 263.

[5] H. Wheeler Robinson, *The Life and Faith of the Baptists*, London: The Kingsgate, 1946, 104, 105.

[6] J. Robert Clinton, *Making of a Leader: Recognizing the Lessons and Stages of Leadership Development*, Colorado Springs: Navpress, 1992, pp. 214, 215.

[7] J. Robert Clinton, *Making of a Leader*, pp. 14-16.

[8] Klaus Fiedler, *Baptists and the Ordination of Women*, p. 2.

Two Perspectives of Theological Education in the Region

While theological education is understood as preparation for ministry, the theological institution has been understood as a "pastors' school". After winning people to Christ, Baptist missionaries brought the converts together into groups that later became local churches in many areas of the countries where they were found. While this was and probably still is the primary objective of Baptist missionary agencies, the initial step in accomplishing this task required, in addition to this primary task, the setting up of supportive ministries in order to achieve these aims. That included the establishment of some type of theological training institutions such as Bible schools and seminaries. Anyone who has been to one of these was automatically called a "pastor."

Many people, including Baptist men and women, have been made to believe that only men can be pastors. For example, the Baptist missionary conviction has been that the ordained pastor of a church must be male.[9] The argument has been that Scripture prohibits a woman to serve as a pastor of a church. Women have been perceived as homemakers because Baptist missionary wives were not called 'missionaries', but 'wives of missionaries.' They were on the mission field to support their 'missionary' husbands. Though some single women have been accepted as missionaries, they still played supportive roles. As a result, African women accepted the homemaking role as part of their Baptist faith.[10] Women have been admitted to theological schools on their husbands' tickets, and a few as individual students. They have been allowed to study courses specifically designed for women, leaving those intended to prepare students to serve as ordained pastors for male students only. Of late, some institutions have allowed female students to audit or take full credit for any individual course offered in the curriculum for which they are otherwise qualified. The erosion of the priesthood of all believers to the priesthood of men only, has led to some theological school denying women to study theology and or

---

[9] Sam Turner, *Baptist Beliefs and Customs*, Nairobi: International Publications, 2004, p. 55.

[10] Suzan Rakoczy IHM, *In Her Name: Women Doing Theology*, Pietermaritzburg: Cluster, 2004, p. 234.

become pastors. Although the concept of freedom is the bedrock from which Baptists have come off, they have denied some local congregations' members of academic freedom.[11]

While to the north of the Limpopo River, Baptist theology has been confined within male Baptist missionary perspective, to the south, particularly in the Republic of South Africa, Baptist theology has all too often been confined within a white, male, middle class and clerical perspective.[12] Although the white Baptist missionaries formed a Baptist union in 1811 and began work among black South Africans in 1816, Coloured in 1888 and Asiatic Indians in 1903, compared to other theological training facilities within Southern Africa, Baptists took their time to discuss full-time training for pastors because of the influx of foreign pastors.[13] The first Baptist Bible School in South Africa was formed in 1926.[14] From 1930, Black ministers were trained separately at an institute specifically for "Native Ministers and Evangelists" as they were called. The first Baptist theological college in South Africa, whose aim was to train ministers of the gospel, missionaries and Christian workers excluded blacks and women given the nature of South Africa and the missionary agency.[15] Like many Christians, South African Baptists were quick to advocate ideas of freedom but often just as quick to forsake that heritage for mean causes.

There were two obvious reasons why Baptists operated racially separate theological institutions. The first one was that due to unequal economic and political circumstances, naturally it was difficult for black Baptists to obtain

---

[11] Alexander Strauch, *Biblical Leadership: An Urgent Call to Restore Biblical Church Leadership*, Littleton: Lewis and Ruth Publishers, 1995, pp. 51-66.

[12] Louise Kretzschmar, *Privatization of the Christian Faith*, Legon: Legon Theological Studies Series, 1998, p. 7.

[13] The German Baptists in the Eastern Cape ("Kaffraria") until after World War II received almost all their pastors from Germany or America. Fritz Haus, the last of the German pastors there, wrote his PhD on the history of the first pastor, Fritz Haus, *Carl Hugo and Mary Gutsche and the "German" Baptists of the Eastern Cape*, Mzuzu: Luviri Press, 2019.

[14] Reinhard Ludwig Frey, *History of the Zambia Baptist Association 1905-2005*, Zomba: Kachere, 2009, p. 65.

[15] Louise Kretzschmar, *Privatization of the Christian Faith*, p. 252.

even basic education. The admission requirements effectively excluded most of the black Baptists. Looking back, the colleges could have, for example, catered for black students by offering a bridging course which, on successful completion, would have enabled them to pursue their theological education alongside their fellow white students. It can be argued that the white Baptists in South Africa accepted the "separate development" ideology of the apartheid government policy of separate education by skin colour.[16]

The second reason for the separate theological education was that, despite the belief in the separation of the Church and the State and the freedom of religion, Baptists permitted the government to decide how they could train ministers. Black students were excluded from an institution that was in a white-only area. The Baptists did not even consider that that was a law which they ought to disobey. The white Baptists were also encouraged by the government to close an institution in one area because of the view that blacks were not to be regarded as permanent residents in the "white" urban suburbs. The missionaries defended themselves by describing themselves as "law-abiding South Africans," as a result, they considered an alternative remote site for an institution that would accept black students.[17] Although it was in the middle of the 1970s that the missionary agency opened doors to all racial groups to study together,[18] black students were still at a disadvantage. An attempt to work towards a united, relevant and credible theological Baptist education in South Africa was not accepted by the white dominated Baptist executive bodies.[19]

Why Theological Education

Why should the church teach? The answer has been because Jesus specifically asked the church to teach and make disciples. Baptists

---

[16] Louise Kretzschmar, *Privatization of the Christian Faith*, p. 253.
[17] Louise Kretzschmar, *Privatization of the Christian Faith*, p. 253.
[18] Louise Kretzschmar, *Privatization of the Christian Faith*, p. 252.
[19] Louise Kretzschmar, "The Ethos and History of the Baptist Convention of South Africa's Winter Schools of Theology, *Winter School 1998*, Johannesburg: Baptist Convention College, 1998, p. 12.

understand that God did not ask them to make converts, but disciples, learners or followers of Jesus Christ. Discipleship has been perceived as endeavouring to seek and grow like Christ; it is a continuous process. It should begin when one accepts Jesus as Lord and Saviour of one's life and finishes off when one is at Christ's feet. Discipleship costs and it pains; it is joy and happiness. It is an initiation in, and a willing embrace of, a certain form of life in obedience under God, revealed in and through Jesus Christ.[20] The responsibility of theology is to help God's people to be what God wants them to be. A mature disciple is expected to win and teach someone else.[21] In theological education, the institutions are to teach God's called men and women to observe all things.

It has been argued that theological education and church growth go hand in hand. There is no church growth if there is not theological education. The only way to ground the churches in the faith is to put the leaders under theological education. The purpose of theological education is to develop leaders. In a broader sense, Baptists understand theological education as a way to equip the churches to participate in God's mission in the world; it is about following Jesus and learning from him. The greatest theological challenge has been to communicate the gospel in its fullness in order not only to build up believers who will impact their societies as salt and light, but also enhance and enrich their own lives.[22]

Many people have believed that a habit of personal Bible study makes the study of theology unnecessary. A Bible study student penalizes oneself by not studying theology, for theology, which is in fact an overall grasp of Bible teaching, enriches Bible study enormously. Theological education enables one to see more of what is there in a biblical passage. All things being equal, one sees further into the meaning and implications of Bible passages than one would do otherwise. Good theology then grows by induction out of

---

[20] Parush Parushev, a response to, "Challenges to Christian Mission," in *Proceedings of the Summit on Baptist Mission in the 21ˢᵗ Century*, Fall Church: Baptist World Alliance, 2003, p. 28.

[21] Sam Turner, Baptist *Beliefs and Customs*, p. 22.

[22] Stanley J. Grenz and Roger E. Olson, *Who Needs Theology? An Invitation to the Study of God*, Downers Grove: Inter-Varsity, 1996, pp. 138-148.

Bible study and must always be taught with reference to its biblical base. The converse is that Bible study is informed by theology.[23]

Theological Training Methods

Theological education can be done in two ways: informally and formally. The informal aspect is expressed in sermons, songs, popular literature, hymnbooks, Sunday school and Bible study materials, church documents, booklets, etc., while the formal aspect is expressed through theological education institutions.[24] There are a number of ways in which this is done throughout the Eastern and Southern Africa region.

The need for theological education has called for a whole spectrum of training programmes. The call for every Baptist to be a learner and the cost of training, among other factors, has made some education to be available to the masses and other programmes for a few. The triangle below represents how theological education has been conducted. The triangle shows that more people have been trained at a low level of education and very few at high level. The challenge has been to develop leaders, both pastors and laity, from the local church to national structures.

The broad area at the base of the triangle represents lay-workers within the local church, with training programmes usually being part of a church theological education curriculum. This is where many people are theologically trained. Topics that are studied include: who are Baptists? Baptist beliefs and practices, which include Baptist understanding of church membership, baptism, the Lord's supper, evangelism, the local church, association and convention, Sunday school, family life, and so on. This prepares the person to be able to lead a group of new converts or Christians into a local church.

The next segment represents pastors and lay-leaders that would lead or are already leading mainly vernacular speaking churches. Many of the leaders will often be somehow bi-vocational. To a certain extent, they support

---

[23] Bruce Milne, *Know the Truth: A Handbook of Christian Belief*, Nottingham: Inter-Varsity Press, 1998, p. 10.
[24] Louise Kretzschmar, *Privatization of the Christian Faith*, p. 251.

themselves financially. They would learn how to prepare and deliver sermons and leadership skills on top of what is taught in the first group. A lot of emphasis is given to local church leadership development and evangelism that leads to the establishment of local churches.

The third segment represents pastors who are generally trained through seminary or a theological college programme. Although Baptist institutions pick from a range of subjects what to teach, the Bible is central to their theological programmes. Since the focus of many schools is to produce pastors or pastor related leaders, the courses are designed to equip students with understanding of what the Bible teaches on fundamental subjects of Christian doctrine, and how to apply these truths to one's life and to the cultural context in which one ministers.

The small segment at the top of the pyramid represents persons who are prepared to fill other specialized roles in denominational life or become seminary teachers. These positions often require advanced academic training, either in their own country or in some other country. A few have received theological training outside of Africa.

- Seminary Teachers and Denominational Leaders' training
- Seminary Training
- Bible School Training
- Local Church Training

Local Church Training

Few men are gathered together, mainly lay-preachers, for some theological education at a local place. One of the ways would be to begin by just teaching the Bible. All beginning efforts were directed to evangelism and church planting and development.[25] One of the Baptist theological convictions is from the New Testament teaching about the need to share the Good News of Jesus with those without Christ (Acts 1:8). Evangelism is defined as, "telling others about Jesus." It is seen as the work of all Christians, both as individuals and as a group such as a local congregation. Baptists teach each other the various ways of how to share the Gospel. One can tell others about what Jesus has done for one. A person can proclaim or preach the gospel. One can talk to others about who Jesus is. One can discuss with others the meaning of the Christian faith.

Baptists believe the life of a witness should prove that one has been changed; if one does not, it can prevent others from accepting Christ. Every area of a Christian's life needs to prove that one has been changed, or regenerated, or born-again. This is seen in one's business affairs, with family, with community and even in the church. Being born-again is the first qualification for who can be a member of a Baptist church. An emphasis upon regenerate church membership has historically been dominant in Baptist life that some Baptist leaders have contended that this theological tenet is the core distinctive for Baptists.[26] Anyone who has been born-again may become a church member. A church is a fellowship of believers. One should not conclude that the Bible teaches that the churches are sinless (1Jn 1:8). There is tension between the ideal and the actual holiness of the members of the churches of Christ.

In the beginning, apart from using the mission station approach, some missionaries began by just teaching the Bible in the process of making early contacts. All beginning efforts were directed to evangelism and church development. Bible studies led to the beginning of Sunday schools, the

---

[25] Hany Longwe, *Christians by Grace – Baptists by Choice*, p. 35.

[26] R. Stanton Norman, *The Baptist Way: Distinctives of a Baptist Church*, Nashville: Academic, 2005, p. 47.

effort that would materialize in many cases into local congregations. The missionaries also prepared Bible notes to equip the early co-workers or local leaders. They taught the local leaders during the evenings. In turn, the leaders used some of the biblical materials they had studied in evangelistic meetings so that they had on the job training. The training was so important to the development of theological understanding that the missionaries brought the leaders to a central location for in-service training, after which they awarded the trainees with certificates. The length of training sessions increased from a few evenings a week to several weeks per year, and that went on for several years.[27]

Although in some cases, single missionary women taught the men,[28] local women were not included in the local leadership programmes.

Bible School Training

The local church training programmes in many ways had direct influence in the establishment of Bible schools. Though the training of evangelists and lay-leaders in short courses worked well, people realized that it was not enough. As the numbers of local congregations that the evangelists had opened increased, the requirement for church leadership also increased, therefore, the need to establish Bible schools.

Depending upon the need and design, some schools started courses ranging from two to four years long. Though at first many schools conducted their course in local languages,[29] many later adopted English as the medium of communication. A few schools have continued to teach in the local languages with some transliteration of certain theological terms.

Some training programmes were designed with students in mind. For example, in Malawi the missionaries brought together pastors and lay-leaders for brief intensive courses of study "between crops," that were

---

[27] Reinhard Ludwig Frey, *History of the Zambia Baptist Association*, p. 58.
[28] Reinhard Ludwig Frey, *History of the Zambia Baptist Association*, p. 58.
[29] Reinhard Ludwig Frey, *History of the Zambia Baptist Association*, p. 65.

planned to avoid interfering with their work since many of them were subsistence farmers.[30]

Most of the Bible schools in the region were opened basically for training pastors and lay-leaders.[31] The need for a course of study specifically designed for a particular country also resulted in the opening of Bible schools.[32]

Residential Seminary/College Programme

Baptist seminaries in the region have been offering theological courses for ministers at different levels. Some have been offering a three-year course for primary school graduates, and an advanced course for high school graduates.[33] The majority of participants have received Bachelor of Theology, Diploma and Certificate for those with little or no college education.

Some institutions have served students from a number of countries. For example, the seminary at Gweru, for a number of years trained ministerial students from Malawi, while the one at Arusha served all East Africa.[34] That remained so until it was soon apparent that theological seminaries within the countries were necessary.

Some institutions began with student bodies that were composed of men and women.[35] The female students were not expected to be pastors, but were trained as Christian workers. Some colleges have trained women and their conventions have ordained them into ministry. An example is the Baptist Convention of South Africa.[36]

---

[30] H. Cornell Goerner, "Africa," in Baker J. Cauthen et al. (eds), *Advance: A history of Southern Baptist Foreign Missions*, Nashville: Broadman, 1970, p. 165.

[31] H. Cornell Goerner, "Africa," p. 161.

[32] H. Cornell Goerner, "Africa," p. 163.

[33] Frank K. Means, *Advance to Bold Mission Thrust: A History of Southern Baptist Foreign Missions 1970-1980*, Nashville: Southern Baptist Convention, 1981, p. 379.

[34] H. Cornell Goerner, "Africa," p. 161.

[35] H. Cornell Goerner, "Africa," p. 167.

[36] Baptist Convention of South Africa 36th Annual Assembly, p. 32.

Decentralized Theological Education (DTE) Programme

A couple of seminaries have used a modified residential approach to theological education – decentralized theological education (DTE). This approach was as a result of the concept to train the largest number of qualified applicants in the most economically efficient avenue available for the greatest likelihood of effective ministry in the country.[37] The students were never at the seminary for more than a month at a time and generally not more than two weeks at a time. The students used 90 workbooks by the time they graduated after four years at certificate level. While at home the students were expected to send their books and seminary reports.

The seminaries offered certificate (secondary level in vernacular language), advanced certificate (secondary level in English), and diploma (post-secondary level) awards. After two years in advanced level work, a student might qualify to work for a diploma.[38]

TEE and Theological Training

Within a few years of providing theological education, the task of developing leadership centred in seminaries, Bible schools and local churches. Later it became apparent that those institutions prepared only a proportion of the leadership needed for rapid multiplication of churches and the indigenous strength. Without appropriately trained leaders, the churches would not be able to nurture new converts or train sufficient leaders. The rapidly growing movement for theological education by extension (TEE) supplemented what was being done in more formal theological institutions. TEE was well-recognized as part of Christian leadership training in many countries.[39] Some Baptists introduced TEE as early as 1974 to help those who studied the Bible at home.[40] In some

---

[37] Baptist Theological Seminary of Malawi Handbook, 2003, p. 32.

[38] Baptist Mission and Baptist Convention of Malawi, "Report and Proposals of the Seminary Feasibility Study Committee," 1988, p. 18.

[39] Winston Crawley, *Global Mission: A Story to Tell. An Interpretation of Southern Baptist Foreign Missions*, Nashville: Broadman, 1985, p. 311.

[40] Baptist Convention of Zimbabwe, *Programme Design*, Bulawayo: Baptist Publishing House, 1984, p. 19.

countries, TEE gained a wide acceptance. TEE combined with a strong discipling programme focused on obedience and, with hard work, the result was churches.[41]

TEE does not remove students from their normal productive environment; instead, it brings the resources of theological education to the functioning and developing leaders of the congregation. Its material helps the students to reflect cognitively on a biblical lesson, and then act in response to their reflection, and finally bring the results of their actions to the discussion seminars and reflect on the consequences of their actions to refine and better their ministries.[42] Records have shown that some students as they did Christian service eventually left secular employment for full-time Christian ministry. I am one such person. I was a mechanical engineer with a sugar company, and during the process of TEE studies, I felt the call to ministry, which I did and went to a Baptist seminary. Though I have not used much of the TEE material in training others, it is because of TEE that I have been able to be a theology lecturer in a seminary and universities.[43]

Regional Bible Schools

Certain Baptist groups started regional Bible school programmes within their countries in an effort to train more leaders or give opportunities throughout the country to more people who qualified to study the Word of God in their areas. An example is Malawi. The teachers taught the lessons for several days, for example four days – Thursday through Sunday.[44] Another regional Bible School developed a curriculum for a two-year programme of four weeks of study per year. The quarterly sessions of one week duration began with classes on Monday morning through Saturday morning. Teachers were expected to teach of the three courses for at least

---

[41] Ralph D. Winter and Steven C. Hawthorne (eds), *Perspectives on the World Christian Movement: A Reader*, Pasadena: William Carey Library, 1981, pp. 601, 602.

[42] Stewart G. Snook, *Developing Leaders through Theological Education by Extension: Case Studies from Africa*, Wheaton: The Billy Graham Center, 1992, pp. 7, 8.

[43] I have taught at the Baptist Theological Seminary of Malawi in Lilongwe, and at the University of Livingstonia under the Faculties of Education and Theology, and at the Mzuzu University under the Department of Theology and Religious Studies.

[44] Reinhard Ludwig Frey, *History of the Zambia Baptist Association*, pp. 80, 81.

two hours per day, Monday through Friday, with Saturday reserved for reviewing and testing. Seminary graduates taught in the Bible schools. Although the schools were not designed to train pastors, the output has been more of vernacular-speaking pastors. The numbers of women trained through the schools increased mainly because some felt called to be pastors, therefore the training, while many went to improve their understanding of God's Word.

Winter Schools of Theology (WST)

In South Africa they also have had what they call Winter Schools of Theology (WST). The WST is similar to conferences in which papers are presented and they are collated and discussed in the WST Book. They are different because the WST seeks to create a context in which all participants are leaners and teachers, that is to say, they share their various insights and experiences as a group so that all the participants have the opportunity to listen and speak. Built into this is time for small group reflection and evaluation, worship and stories.[45] The WST is also a part of a wider process within the Baptist Convention of South Africa (BCSA) and the Baptist Convention College (BCC) in which they aim to more fully understand and live out their Mission Statement. The educational task is only completed when members read, digest and apply the contents of the booklets. The WST is more than an academic conference, it is a life changing encounter. It is also seen as a place of theological formation for those members of the BCSA who regularly attend. As a result, theological education is understood as intimately linked to personal discipleship, ecclesiastical renewal and social transformation. It is seen as part and parcel of their salvation through Jesus Christ who is the Living Word.[46]

Baptist University

In the Western tradition, theology has been known as the queen of the sciences and therefore has been one of the subjects offered at the

---

[45] Louise Kretzschmar, "The Ethos and History," pp. 2, 3.
[46] Louise Kretzschmar, "The Ethos and History," pp. 4-8.

universities.⁴⁷ However, in other traditions theology has been regarded as the province of churches and therefore, has been kept out of the universities. As a result, churches had had seminaries. People have thought the reason seminaries exist was to form people for Christian ministry. Many people still hold that what the seminary does is or should be as different from what a university department does. Nonetheless, looking at the definition of theology, there should be no distinction. Whereas people always talk as if theological education necessarily must lead to becoming pastors, it should equip men and women for Christian ministry to the world.⁴⁸ There has been one Baptist University in the Eastern and Southern Africa region – Mount Meru University (MMU) in Tanzania, formerly known as the International Baptist Theological Seminary of Eastern Africa (IBTSEA), which for about 40 years met the spiritual needs of Christians. In 2002, the nationals took full responsibility of the seminary, and in the same year Mount Meru University began operating as a fully-fledged university when it embarked on meeting the intellectual and social needs of the region. It became an accredited university in 2003. MMU's mission is "to equip students with Christian, ministerial and professional skills to improve their quality of life and that of their communities, nations and the whole world." This is carried out through training, conducting research and offering consultancy services to the public.

On this basis, Mount Meru University strives to:

1. Sustain training programmes which focus on spiritual and physical needs;
2. Become a leading provider of high quality consultancy and community service; and
3. Conduct high quality research and disseminate research findings to the users.⁴⁹

---

[47] Bruce Milne, *Know the Truth*, p. 9.

[48] John S. Pobee, "Theological Trends in Africa Today," in J.S. Pobee and J.N. Kudadjie (eds), *Theological Education in Africa: Quo Vadimus?* Accra: Asempa, 1990, p. 60.

[49] Mount Meru University, www.mmu.ac.tz, [4.7.2007].

Like a seminary, MMU has been producing men and women for education-related occupational roles, church-related occupational roles such as pastors and other church leaders, academically-oriented occupational roles, and a more diffused group of occupational roles such as mass-communication, welfare work and adult education. This was in line with the university's vision which is to be a fountain of knowledge and wisdom that produces "excellent, God-fearing, visionary, skilled, proactive, hardworking and transforming servant leaders."[50]

The Concept of Servant Leader

Like in many movements, Baptists confuse the metaphor of servant leader with the popular pressure toward making ministers "enablers" or "equippers" or "conflict managers." This picture has also a biblical base, Ephesians 4:12. Theological institutions need to educate the churches that, though that may provide peace and unity in the churches, the calling of ministers as leaders is to project a vision, to offer directions and to exercise oversight as well as to participate in congregational life.[51]

Residential and Non-residential Programmes

Some interpreters and missionaries in some countries fell into the trap of polarizing institutional leadership training and theological education by extension. That was sometimes followed by a pendulum swing between two emphases. A "both-and" approach would have been more constructive.[52] Baptists in the region worked on the adoption of a workshop or laboratory approach whereby students performed more in the learning process rather than merely sitting in a class like a sponge to soak up the teacher's knowledge. Theological education being a dynamic process, the concern was with attitudes rather than just information. The concept of having approaches which combine residential with non-residential studies was viewed as a

---

[50] Mount Meru University, Arusha, Tanzania, http://emica.org/projectEAhighlight_9066.shtm [4.7.2007].

[51] Donald E. Messer, *Contemporary Images of Christian Ministry*, Nashville: Abingdon, 1991, p. 98, 99.

[52] Winston Crawley, *Global Mission*, p. 311.

more effective way of doing theological education. In any case, Baptists in the region agreed that the personal relationship between teacher and student was more important than the information the teacher passed on.[53] This is why students of any programme were required to have practical experience during their training if they were to be considered for positions of leadership within the local churches or national bodies.

Partnerships and other Options in Theological Education

For the purpose of training church leaders for various degree levels, several Baptist seminaries/colleges have had to go into partnerships with other like-minded accredited universities or seminaries on the continent or overseas. The students are trained in several different capacities (i.e., theology, religion, religious education, and so on) while they serve in different leadership roles in their community and surrounding communities (i.e., pastor, youth minister, music minister, teacher, administrator, and so forth). The degrees, certificates and diplomas are offered for the purpose of seeing the growth of pastors/ministers. The colleges have been offering accredited or validated diplomas and degrees through partnership with both secular and Baptist universities and other theological seminaries or colleges in the region. Many Baptist students of theology have programmes offered by other secular colleges and universities in the region to study at MA and PhD levels, and those who joined faculties of Baptist colleges have brought other perspectives into the life of the institutions.

Women and Theological Education

Baptist theological education has offered no real place for women. Many theological institutions had separate women's theological schools some of which have since integrated into the theological institutions. As it is in many countries, women organized meetings where they learned and discussed biblical topics, apart from home making.[54]

---

[53] Gerald Wright, "Theological Education as Ministerial Formation: A Response," in *Theological Education Consultation*, Cisurua, Foreign Mission Board, 1990, p. 2.
[54] Reinhard Ludwig Frey, *History of the Zambia Baptist Association*, p. 80.

In some theological institutions there were "men's courses" and "women's courses."[55] That was so because women went to the seminary as wives of seminary students. They were not students in their own right.[56] That was to change. Southern Baptist history and their rural background had forged strong ties of loyalty to traditional cultural values,[57] which also influenced the Africans' theology and women. Almost all of the women who went to the seminaries with their husbands never thought of themselves as becoming pastors in their own right, but pastors' wives playing a secondary role to that of their spouses. When asked, almost all said that they went to the seminary on their husbands' tickets. They described themselves as being lucky and thankful to the local churches that called them to be trained alongside their husbands. Even those who were admitted on their own tickets to study at the seminaries, did not think of themselves (at first at least) as training as pastors.[58] Though the population of women is greater than that of men in almost all churches in this part of Africa, women have often not been allowed to stand before men, that is, to preach or teach, although Baptists believe in the priesthood of all believers.[59] Yet, in many communities in Eastern and Southern Africa, it is not their culture that bars women from standing before men and teach in public places, but the missionary Baptist culture.[60]

Though white Baptist women in South Africa served as missionaries and engaged in evangelistic work, they were not offered any formal theological education by the colleges whose aim was to provide not only for ministers, but also missionaries and Christian workers. On the other hand, black Baptist women were the core of the churches, particularly in the rural areas. Their situation was even worse than that of the white women because they did not have the educational opportunities that the white women enjoyed.

---

[55] Baptist Theological Seminary of Zambia Handbook, 1985, pp. 18, 35.
[56] Baptist Theological Seminary of Zambia Handbook, 1985, pp. 14-15.
[57] John Lee Eighmy, *Churches in Cultural Captivity: A History of the Social Attitudes of Southern Baptists*, Knoxville: University of Tennessee, 1987, p. 55.
[58] Hany Longwe, *Christians by Grace – Baptists by Choice*, p. 260.
[59] Hany Longwe, *Christians by Grace – Baptists by Choice*, p. 263.
[60] Ibid, p. 288.

Within the white dominated Baptist union, theological education was essentially offered only to men.[61]

Women to the north of the Limpopo River have had more freedom to study theology than their counterparts to the south. Some women have taken advantage of their husbands' study leave and used the time to study theology at colleges and universities within and outside their countries. Almost all of the institutions these women had gone to, were non-Baptist. That has been for many a way to upgrade their lives and find employment, especially in non-governmental and para-church organizations. Several non-South African women have earned MAs and PhDs in theology from universities in the Republic of South Africa. All of them did not receive denominational sponsorship. Some had to pay for their education, while others benefitted from scholarships from theological fellowships and other small grants from various sources. Their families provided moral support and encouragement for them to keep going.

In the face of hostility against women, several Baptist women have been teaching in Baptist theological institutions and in national universities throughout the Eastern and Southern Africa region. In the region as a whole, very few women have graduated from Baptist theological institutions let alone from other theological institutions. Although issues pertaining to women have received some attention, the position of women in the Baptist theological education system still leaves much to be desired.

Baptist Theological Education and Socio-religious Issues

Some of the missionary understanding and practices of theological education were severely flawed by their conception of the Christian faith which did not make an effective or fully Christian contribution to the myriad of problems facing the people of Africa.[62] They understood theological education as being there to meet the "spiritual" needs of the churches alone, and did not address the physical, social, economic and practical needs of the wider society. After the establishment of theological

---

[61] Louise Kretzschmar, *Privatization of the Christian Faith*, p. 256.
[62] Louise Kretzschmar, *Privatization of the Christian Faith*, p. 6.

institutions, there was no potential of establishing strong leadership teams in the conventions that were able to theologically address contemporary issues. The theological systems were there basically to produce preachers who could evangelize and plant churches wherever they went, with less regard for physical needs of the people they preached to. In many parts of the region, theological education was not able to provide a basis for socio-ethical analyses for strategies to achieve genuine church unity across racial and cultural divides. African Baptists have not been able to critique their diluted version of the gospel and, thereby, develop a more wholistic perception of the Christian faith. Baptist seminaries and colleges did not adequately equip black ministers to develop the necessary skills and confidence to challenge the white version of Baptist faith and principles.[63]

The theological colleges gave little attention to the theological debate which had been taking place within the region especially in South Africa. While they were claiming to be training ministers for work within the South African Baptist context, the colleges offered no courses that included the social dimension of these subjects. While some African Christians were vigorously debating how Christians should respond to their African context, Baptist colleges did not offer theological education that reflected such issues. Baptist theological perceptions remained tied to Western theological models and were abstract, conservative and privatized in their emphasis.[64]

Quest for Relevant and Credible Theological Education

The African church has largely grown as a result of the obedience of foreign gospel workers. Though many Africans have continued that work by planting and leading churches, many still lack proper training as they lead churches with their self-taught knowledge. Though Baptist seminaries and colleges are striving to train as many leaders as possible, their capacity has been inadequate. By 2008, there were 13,292 in East and Central Africa,[65]

---

[63] Louise Kretzschmar, *Privatization of the Christian Faith*, p. 255, 256.
[64] Louise Kretzschmar, *Privatization of the Christian Faith*, pp. 288, 289.
[65] Baptist World Alliance, 2008 Yearbook, pp. 141-143.

but the number of trained ministers was estimated to be far less. To make things worse, because of their evangelistic zeal, Baptists started hundreds of new churches each year, a few of which will never have theologically trained leaders. Clearly, the greatest need facing Baptists is to train new and more leaders. Training of leaders is not anywhere near that of the need. Quality leadership is required to nurture and disciple members who will also disciple others. If leadership training is not increased significantly, it will negatively impact church growth opportunities. There is the challenge of the leadership pool which has been shallow, while the costs and facilities of training qualified leaders are not easily available.

Though some heads of institutions have wanted to make their colleges to be academically credible, they been hampered by the limited vision of their colleges. Many pastors trained in the Baptist theological institutions in this region have not been able to assist their members to make a contribution to the vast social needs of their communities in which they live. What is more, by perceiving Western theology teachings as "the truth," the institutions have not been able to train Baptist pastors to relate the Christian faith to the entire African life. As a result, Baptist theology became inextricably linked to the white self-interest at the expense of the needs of black Africans.[66] Baptist theological education in this region for a long time remained at the watchful eyes of foreign missionaries who wanted it to remain "Baptist," meaning what suited their interpretation and purpose. That did not allow theologians of every nation to develop their own theology that was appropriate to their culture.

The All Africa Baptist Fellowship (AABF) organized a Theological Educators conference that aimed at moving Baptists in southern Africa towards united, relevant and credible Baptist theological education.[67] Baptists realized that there was need to transform the entire understanding of theological education. For theological education to be a life changing encounter, theological education institutions have to be places of theological formation. Theological education has to be sufficiently oriented

---

[66] Louise Kretzschmar, *Privatization of the Christian Faith*, p. 306.

[67] Andre Bokundoa and Frank Adams, "All Africa Baptist Fellowship," in *Baptist World Centenary Congress Official Report*, 2005, p. 132.

towards the new paradigm that it would open students' hearts, minds and souls to the new realities which demanded new solutions for missions.

A rationalistic understanding of theology, history and biblical studies without a spiritual dynamic would turn out students incapable of reaching their society. Head knowledge without heart knowledge leads to emptiness, and vice versa. Theological education in this region is also the key for missions. One practical recommendation for encouraging and stimulating the worldwide missionary effort of all Baptists was to support the establishment of, at least, one major University on every continent. The purpose of such a university would be to challenge and equip students intellectually, lay and ordained, to confront secular and pagan worldviews with the gospel of Jesus Christ in their own contextual and cultural settings.[68]

It calls for the rewriting of the curriculum to include not only the appropriate contexts in which the skills of social interrelationships and communication are shared and experienced, but also the economic and political structures which sustain and enable the community. Today these structures have both global relationships and international references and therefore the theological student must learn how to live, function and witness in this new reality. Therefore, effective theological education demands the integration of academic knowledge and the skills for ministry. The undertaking demands time, energy, commitment, collaboration and interdisciplinary teaching, adequate funding and maybe even a reconfiguration of the delivery of theological education.

Concept and Understanding of Accountability[69]

Theological enterprise remains a most sacred responsibility for the churches. Baptist churches encourage every denominational theological institution in this region to understand that they do not exist for self. To be true to God, theological institutions must have purpose in organizing

---

[68] Denton Lotz, "Paradigm Shifts in Missiology, in *Proceedings of the Summit on Baptist Mission in the 21st Century*, Falls Church: Baptist World Alliance, 2003, p. 62-64.

[69] I developed this section from some notes from material presented to representatives of theological institutions and national conventions from Eastern and Southern Africa, Nairobi, 1993.

theological education. This speaks of accountability to God for it is his work, and to the churches because it is for their benefit that the institutions exist. Accountability to the churches includes that for students, results, good will and prayer support, and finances. It is understood that by being accountable to the churches in these areas, the churches are able to carry the institutions where God wants all of them to go.

Accountability for Students

The primary purpose for Baptist theological institutions has been to train leaders for the local churches and denominational organizations. Theological institutions understand themselves as servants of the churches through denominational channels of associations and conventions/unions/fellowships of churches. The denominations depend upon churches for their leadership. Therefore, the local church is understood as the necessary base for recruitment for students in theological training. There are two sides of recruitment, and these are, quantity and quality. The church should understand its responsibility in recruiting leaders in training and making sure that these are quality leaders. Too many failures in theological training are the result of churches not supplying the quality persons for training.

Fundamentally, Baptists insist on the autonomy of the local church. For many this means that each church has the freedom to choose and call its own leadership. Many Baptist churches have no restriction in the selection of leaders other than those restrictions that they impose on themselves under God and his word. That includes the amount of training required. However, the requirements from church to church vary from no training to the other extreme of multiple degrees as well as years of experience on the job.

Since many churches in Eastern and Southern Africa are young and are really tuned to the Great Commission, their primary interest is to start new churches. Always the question was: Where are we going to get leaders for those new church-type groups that evolve out of our new work of evangelism? Non-growth or slow growth churches are defeated by this thinking that they can begin work only with satisfactorily, theologically trained leaders. Multiplication-growth churches either provide lay leaders from their churches or adopt the Acts 13 and 14 model of taking new converts in the group to be the leaders for those groups.

Some new Christians and new as well as old churches may be slow in patronizing theological training for their leaders. A definite part of the accountability of theological institutions is a responsibility to conceive and implement ideas and methods of instilling a sense of need and value in both leaders and churches for training. This sense of need causes churches to be co-enlisters in theological education. Also, there is the responsibility to enable both parties to know what training opportunities are available as well as the benefit of each.

Many local Baptist churches and their leaders in Eastern and Southern Africa have been struggling to reach the point of seeing the value of sacrificing in order to buy Christian books, Sunday school materials, and, too often, a personal Bible. That has made it difficult for them to understand the greatness of the need for theological training. As a result, in order to succeed well, theological institutions have been compelled to acknowledge the responsibility to help their communities to understand the need to make this training a high priority item.

Accountability for Results

The local congregations had held the theological institutions accountable for the results of their training. Many young men who have gone to the theological institutions have done so because they were willing to study to become ministers. Too many times, in their minds, it has been a means to be in employment for which there has been a vast need in most parts of the region. Those responsible for establishing theological training programmes have seen the need to be accountable to God and the local churches. Attempts have been made to train those in ministry rather than training those who someday would become ministers, and most important, emphasis has been put on quality training for students without taking them out of their ministry, culture, support base and their accountability to their own local churches. Having students of this kind has not been easy.

Baptist theological institutions in Eastern and Southern Africa are responsible to the local churches to teach their leaders how to find needed information, how to break that information down, how to design something useful, more effective, and how to evaluate most effectively that which is produced or done. This helps the churches to adapt the changing societies and an increasingly complex world. Theological institutions are responsible for the type of ministerial leadership they turn out.

Baptists in this region have the responsibility to develop their leadership capacity. Strategies to develop leaders by providing opportunities for quality education have been extremely weak. Baptist theological institutions have not yet developed into viable centres of excellence. Baptists have made it extremely difficult for some of their best minds to serve in the theological institutions as the churches continue to rely on foreign personnel because the conventions/unions do not pay them. The Baptist autonomous heritage has to some extent inhibited the capacity for the conventions/unions to work together as a region to develop joint institutions for capacity building. Instead of every country trying to build a college they can hardly run, Baptists should pull their meager resources together and support a few strong institutions for national, regional and continental leadership. It is the responsibility of the churches to pull their resources together and invite Baptists who are serving in non-Baptist institutions who wish to join the vision of developing indigenous leadership in the region and move on.[70]

Accountability for Good Will and Prayer Support

The purpose of theological education is also spiritual. The work of churches is primarily a matter of volunteerism, built around spiritual values and ideals. Most of the church leaders are volunteer leaders, which means that many of the students in theological training programmes have little or no material support from their churches. Realizing that the whole work of the theological institutions depends on volunteerism, the churches and the

---

[70] Douglas W. Waruta, "Celebrating Christ: The Hope of Africa," All African Baptist Theological Educators' Conference, Ibadan, 2000, p. 9.

institutions have to watch carefully how they enlist more volunteers and how they encourage those already enlisted.

Spiritual development has two aspects: personal relationship with God and relationship with others. Spirituality is not merely an academic exercise. The theological institutions have to structure programmes so that the students have adequate time and energy for their own spiritual growth. The task of spiritual formation, however, has always been loaded with difficulties. There are meaningful differences in the way people understand spirituality. Besides, there is always tension between individuality and conformity in spiritual discipline. As a spiritual venture, theological institutions are expected to undergird themselves with prayer.

Prayer support will relate to good will. Theological institutions have had to build good relations that mean good will towards the organizations in order to succeed. That has only been true where the leaders and the local churches have seen the theological institutions as "our Bible school, "our seminary," or "our university." Good will is a result of good communication. It can be won or lost as a result of communication. Volunteer participation and volunteer support is determined by the amount of good will that has been generated through the institutions expressing their dependence on and accountability to the churches, while demonstrating their value to the local congregations.

Accountability to Finances

In the early days the mission organizations carried the primary burden of theological education. For many years the churches depended upon the mission boards overseas. They supplied the theological institutions with missionary teachers that went together with the money. That tremendously affected the ability to support the institutions locally.[71] Of late, Baptist theological institutions in the region like in many others in different parts of Africa were increasingly looking to local churches in regard to support for training their leaders. The preparedness of the churches has had to

---

[71] Lothar Engel, "Funding of Theological Education," in J.S. Pobee and J.N. Kudadjie (eds), *Theological Education in Africa*, Accra: Asempa, 2000, p. 136.

experience how it feels to be responsible for the theological institutions under their conventions. It does not matter whether the money comes in the form of student fees, direct, regular contributions from the churches to the institutions, or contributions through the associations or conventions/unions/fellowships, or endowment funds. Because it is right for the institutions to look to the churches for their support, it makes the institutions more conscious of their need for accountability to the churches and of the need for the right kind of results in theological training.

Stewardship is understood as a responsibility for the whole of what one is and has. Theological institutions have a responsibility to reach local congregations through the leaders whom they train what Christianity really is. God set the pattern – he gave his one and only begotten Son. Christ carried on the pattern – he gave his life that people might live; that the church might be born. Anyone who has Christ within has a spirit of giving. It is in this spirit that one is more Christ-like. The local church needs this responsibility for supporting theological institutions. Theological institutions have to lead the way in creative brainstorming to come up with new ways for teaching this original principle that Christianity is a life of giving rather than of receiving. If people's value system is changed, the institutions will be adequately funded. The churches will embrace theological institutions as theirs only when they fund the institutions to a degree. Then the institutions will see themselves as accountable to the local churches. If churches commit themselves to the struggles of the theological training, that would be sustainable.

Conclusion

In general, Baptists understand theological education as a spiritual pilgrimage. As a result, Baptist success is only possible as they place themselves at the disposal of the Holy Spirit because the challenges in theological education are great.

Chapter 3

Theology & Religious Studies and Development with Malawi in Mind

A part of the many things that Christianity has contributed to the development of the modern world, is the establishment of schools that have taught reading, writing and other skills. Without the work of the Church in establishing schools, the development in many countries of Sub-Saharan Africa would have been delayed. At the same time, the colonial and independent governments would not have been able to build and maintain all the schools in the countries, let alone the quality of education that has been celebrated in these nations. The educational system owes a great debt to the churches.

Yet, some members of the Ministry of Education and universities in Malawi, for example, have time and again publicly spoken against the continuation of Theology and Religious Studies in public universities as well as in primary and secondary schools in this country. Some have discouraged students to major in or even take Theology and Religious Studies (TRS) courses in their degree programmes citing lack of its usefulness in a world of science and technology. But they forget that science alone does and will never solve every human need. This article aims at correcting this wrong view and showing the development of theological education courses and their contribution to national development. For a student who wants to study TRS, it is their human right and should not be discouraged. For those in employment, it is their right to practice one's religious beliefs in the workplace. The education system in this country, as is in many countries of Sub-Saharan Africa and the world, is linked to the development of intellectual pursuit that began in church monasteries and cathedrals.

Early African Christianity and Intellectual Pursuit

Africans have made significant contributions to the development of theology and its influence on education. Theological giants such as

Augustine, Athanasius, Cyril of Alexandria, Clement of Alexandria, Tertullian, Cyprian and Origen, were Africans. These Church Fathers led in the articulation of the Christian faith in a different idiom as Christianity encountered the Greek language and philosophy. Alexandria in Egypt was at that time the leading centre of Greek philosophical thought and learning. As such, some early and formative expressions of Christian thought in Greek philosophical language developed here.[1]

The Catechetical School established at Alexandria probably in the second century, was located in the heart of the intellectual activity in the East where there were three other centres of learning: the Museum, the Serapeum and the Sebastion. Consequently, it became the first Christian institute of higher education. It dealt with the interface between Greek culture and philosophy and the Christian faith. The school also taught a wide range of subjects. The anti-intellectual sentiments among some evangelicals and secular scholars prevalent in Malawi and Africa are foreign to early African Christianity. The African Christianity is not averse to intellectual pursuit and rigorous enquiry. Therefore, the idea of a university that many in African Christianity promote now is like a recovery of this heritage.[2]

Christianity's disappearance from much of North Africa in the seventh century is one of Christian history's darkest absurdities. With it went advancement in higher education. The Arab conquest and the spread of Islam in North Africa ultimately prevented the spread of Christianity as well as of higher education from reaching the rest of the African continent. Instead, higher education began to develop in closely neighbouring Christian Europe with their rich doctrinal legacy thanks to African Church Fathers such as Augustine and Cyprian.[3]

---

[1] James Tengatenga, "Early African Christianity," in Isabel Apawo Phiri and Dietrich Werner, and Chammah Kaunda and Kennedy Owino (eds), *Anthology of African Christianity*, Oxford: Regnum, 2016, p. 16.

[2] James Tengatenga, "Early African Christianity," p. 16.

[3] Rosino Gibellini (ed), *Paths of Africa Theology*, London: SCM, 1994, p. 2.

The Schoolmen

In Europe between 1050 and 1250 there was a surge of intellectual life which produced a succession of great theological teachers who were known as "the Schoolmen," the greatest of whom is Thomas Aquinas. They were called" Schoolmen" because they belonged to the "Schools" or colleges which had begun to flourish at that time in some of the monasteries, and still more in the cathedrals.[4] It was from the Church that there appeared a new system of schools; those in the monasteries had been begun for boys who were to become monks. Though it was exceptional, monastery schools sometimes gave the chance of education to sons of kings and nobles, and so had great influence upon the outside world.

Cathedral schools grew out of the instruction given in the bishop's household to only boys who were to become clergy. When the schools were transferred from the monasteries to the cathedrals they came to belong to the whole diocese and by the ninth century, many were taking on the work of schoolmaster. Such a man was not just teacher, but also an "education officer" for the diocese, and, next to the bishop himself, one of its most important figures. In the twelfth century, closely connected to the cathedral schools, there followed a revival in learning which led to a form of education which became of worldwide influence, the rise of universities.[5]

Just before 1200, some of the centres of learning began to develop into universities. The schoolmen were the products of this movement, and the movement was produced by these men who included such people as: Anselm, Peter Abelard, Peter Lombard, Albert the Great and Thomas Aquinas.

Around 1066 Anselm, an Italian, took his place as a theological teacher who was to be the first important theologian to become Archbishop of Canterbury. He stood for the rights and liberties of the Church and to act

---

[4] John Foster, *Setback and Recovery: Church History 2: AD 500-1500*, London: SPCK, 1991, p. 112.

[5] John Foster, *Setback and Recovery*, p. 101.

for its reform. His most famous work is, *Cur Deus Homo* ("Why did God become Man") which has remained of permanent value to the Church.

Peter Abelard, a French, in his best-known work, *Sic et Non* (Yes and No) deals with questions about science, ethics and religion, and gives as answers quotations from Scripture and from the Church Fathers. The book was meant to stimulate logical reasoning since he had been educated in the new Aristotelian logic. Abelard did not exalt reason above faith, but he also believed that faith and reason belonged together.

Peter Lombard, an Italian, taught at the Cathedral school in Paris. His famous book is, *The Sentences*, which is in four parts: (1) God, the Trinity, God's attributes, Predestination, (2) Creation, Man, Sin, Free Will, Men's need, (3) Redemption, and (4) The Seven Sacraments: Baptism, Confirmation, Eucharist, Penance, Extreme Unction, Ordination, Marriage. The Bible and The Sentences were often the only books which a theological student owned at a time when books were scarce and expensive.

Albert the Great, a German, studied in Italy and became a famous lecturer at Paris University, and later at Cologne. His interest was in science, and he made full use of the works of Aristotle as an aid to Christian thought about the universe and the human life.

Another Italian Schoolman, Thomas Aquinas, while at Naples university, completing his studies in arts, came to know his calling: to be a Christian leader. His family opposed this and confined him in one of their castles for fifteen months, but he escaped and became a Friar. He studied theology at Paris and moved to Cologne. After teaching in several Italian cities, including Rome, he was appointed adviser to three Popes, and did his most influential teaching in Paris. Aquinas wrote theological works, commentaries and joyful Latin hymns. His most famous work is the *Summa Theologica* (i.e. systematic theology) which took him nine years to write; imagine! Dealing with the basic question of faith and reason, Thomas Aquinas gives great scope to reason, holding that even apart from revelation, people may arrive at belief in God, his eternity, oneness, creative power and providence. Even so, the ground of his Christian belief was not reason but revelation through the Scriptures, and the Church Fathers.

These he argued were accepted by faith, which is an act, not of people's intellect, but of will and is therefore a moral decision. Thomas Aquinas not only understood Aristotle, but positively admired his powers of argument, his method of scientific enquiry and emphasis upon human beings as rational beings.[6]

The Rise of Universities

Centres of learning had grown up in a number of the leading cities of the West in many cases from the monastic and cathedral schools. Towards the end of the twelfth century a few claimed to be of more than merely local importance. These began to be called *studium* and subsequently *studium generale*, (Latin for a place for "study of every kind"), or places to which scholars resorted from all parts of Europe. The specific term *universitas* was confined to the scholastic guild within the *studium*. The *universitas* often meant simply the student body, usually called the nation, organized for the communal protection of the foreign student body, men who otherwise, being aliens, were at the mercy of local inn-keepers and tradesmen. The fusion of the *universitates* into a single *universitas* was a gradual process.

The gradual and almost unnoticed growth of a university may best be illustrated from Paris, the city that had an exceptional number of teachers. Early in the eighth century the school at the monastery of Denys, to the north, was famous enough for the ruler of France to send his two sons there. Within the city, the cathedral of Notre Dame had its school, and to the south the churches of St Victor and Ste Genevieve each had one. As a result of the numbers of schools and teachers, students flocked to Paris.

The teachers or masters, many of whom were not from Paris nor even French, felt it necessary to combine together, just as at this time members of different crafts or trades were combining in "guilds" in order to protect their rights. Their connection with the Church freed these teachers from control by the city. However, connection with the Church placed them under the bishop, who through the cathedral chancellor or education officer, was the authority who gave or withheld the right to teach. Masters

---

[6] John Foster, *Setback and Recovery*, p. 113-119.

of more advanced studies wished to be free from all local interference, so they appealed to the Pope, who took them under his own protection. That meant that there was no authority but these masters themselves to fix standards for teachers and students. They had become a new institution, a *studium generale*, a university. Fortunately, Popes continued to regard universities as rivers of knowledge which fed and fertilized the universal Church. Such independence became the accepted right of universities, and many of them were founded by a charter from the Pope. The city fully recognized the university's importance. When the king of France visited Paris, the rector of the university was there to read a Latin address of welcome, his colleagues with him in their gowns and hoods. On the death of a rector the city gave him the burial of a prince.

Paris grew to be a city of student youth. Being young and vigorous, the students would be the group that made its presence felt. Students came to Paris from every province of France, from many European nations, from as far east as Syria and Egypt. There were, of course, occasions when students were noticed in the city's life because they interrupted its peaceful flow, especially at night.[7]

University Studies

University studies were divided into four faculties: theology, law, medicine, and arts which was by far the biggest. Theology was given an honoured place in every university and was called "Queen of the Sciences". Many of the teachers and students of a medieval university were clergy because throughout the Dark Ages learning had been preserved and passed on by the Church. The clergy were no longer the only educated people, but they were the best educated.

Students came to the university from the age of thirteen onwards, with seven years of *trivium* (Latin for "three ways"), that is, grammar, logic, rhetoric (i.e. style), and *quadrivium* (Latin for "four ways"), that is, music, arithmetic, geometry and astronomy, to complete.

---

[7] John Foster, *Setback and Recovery*, pp. 119, 120.

At the end of the arts course a man became a "Bachelor of Arts. "Bachelor" was a term first used in the military, not an academic qualification. It meant a young knight serving under a senior knight's banner, not yet having one of his own. Academically it meant a man who had specialized in one department of knowledge but was not yet adequately independent to teach. Later he became "Master," which meant that the university's chancellor gave the right to teach.

Beyond the arts course, a student might choose to go on to theology or law or medicine, which were, as is said today, post-graduate courses. The Church did not require postgraduate theology training for its pastoral ministry. Only a few parish priests had been to university. The equipping of many was simpler – Latin from the grammar school, and at the cathedral school some acquaintance with parts of the trivium and quadrivium, to which were added, by the bishop or one of his more capable clergy, exposition of the Bible and some practical training.[8]

University Organization

The University of Bologna in Italy began in conditions which were different with those of Paris. Bologna was the finest law school in Europe. There, many of the staff members were local citizens. Students who came to study law at Bologna were those who had had art studies in other countries. As foreigners, they felt it was them rather than the teachers who needed to combine art and law to protect their rights.[9] As men on their way to become lawyers, they combined very effectively forming a body that possessed the supreme active power. The professors formed themselves into a college of masters isolated from the students. It was from the student end that a university began to take shape. This went on until the city fathers interfered and set up an organization more worthy of a *stadium generale*.[10]

In 1167, because of a quarrel with the king of France, King Henry II of England ordered English teachers and students at Paris to return home. By

---

[8] John Foster, *Setback and Recovery*, pp. 120-121.

[9] John Foster, *Setback and Recovery*, p. 121.

[10] John Foster, *Setback and Recovery*, p. 122.

1185, Oxford had its own recognized *stadium generale*, and went on to develop colleges much on the same lines with Paris. In 1209 some students from Oxford moved to Cambridge, which was already a centre of learning, and which in turn became a university by 1233.

Between 1200 and 1451, about 27 universities had been founded in Europe. The teaching fraternities of both Oxford and Cambridge universities and those of northern France and Germany dominated after the model of Paris. To a much greater degree, students who tended to be older men than those commonly found in the northern universities, controlled universities in Italy, Spain and southern France following the lead of Bologna.[11] The combination of various features from each model was by no means uncommon however, and this was shown most clearly in the universities of France in the fifteenth century.[12] Nineteenth century universities were often the product of provincial civic pride, and owed their existence to a growing desire for education, rather than the production of gentlemen.

Today the growth of universities has been both accelerated and extended beyond expectations, and has become an important factor in the life of every country in the world. On the surface it may seem that the states have taken the lead which in the Middle Ages belonged to the Church. However, a closer examination shows that in this modern period of universities' world-wide development, the way for many universities has been prepared by Christian schools and colleges, and Christian-educated teachers have played a part worthy of being compared with that of Christians of the medieval Church.[13]

Organization of the Universities in Malawi

During the early 1950s, Malawians who desired for learning and had the will to work for it began to raise funds for a "Nyasa College" when the University College in Salisbury was the only institution of higher education of the Federation of Rhodesia and Nyasaland. Long before the government

---

[11] Friedrich Herr, *The Medieval World*, New York: Mentor, 1963, pp. 242, 243.
[12] Denys Hay, *Europe in the Fourteenth and Fifteenth Centuries*, p. 362.
[13] John Foster, *Setback and Recovery*, p. 122.

of Malawi had taken any formal action to establish a university, a "Malawi University Association" was formed to collect funds from people in the villages.

Malawi had an unusual opportunity to create a university which would meet the economic and cultural needs of the country. The country's institutions of higher and further education under the Government, the Institute of Public Administration at Mpemba, the Soche Hill College of Education and the Malawi Polytechnic in Blantyre and the Undergraduate Campus at Chichiri in Blantyre, Bunda Agricultural College in Lilongwe, were all in the early stages of development, and it was the government's policy to combine them into one university. The Malawi Parliament passed the University of Malawi (Provisional Council) Act on 20 October and the Vice–Chancellor, Dr Ian Michael, took up his post on 3 November 1964. In October 1965, a few months after independence, the government established the University of Malawi (UNIMA). Teaching started at Chichiri campus on 29 September 1965 after the Chancellor, who was also the Prime Minister, had given the inauguration lecture to mark the opening of the University.

Academic Subjects in the University of Malawi

In 1965, the main subjects taught in the University of Malawi were grouped as follows: Natural Resources, Science, Technology, Social and Administration, and Arts. Religious Studies was not included under any of these groups. By 1974, Religious Studies was a new department with Dr J. Parratt from the United Kingdom in charge. He was the only lecturer in the department responsible for training those who would be Religious Education teachers in Secondary schools. The department offered Biblical Introduction and Theology, and Religions in Africa. From 1974-1975, Religious Studies became part of the Education Department. Later, after its introduction, the Faculty of Humanities comprised eight academic departments: African Languages and Linguistics, Classics, French, Fine and Performing Arts, English, Language and Communication Skills, Philosophy, and Theology and Religious Studies. The establishment of the Department of Theology and Religious Studies within the state system represented a significant change in state policy.

Theology and Religious Studies: Engagement and Benefits

Many people of all walks of life do not want to talk about or bring God into their life. However, according to the *World Christian Database*, the proportion of the world's population that claims membership in the four largest religions—Christianity, Islam, Buddhism and Hinduism was and is actually increasing. Failure of any society to understand religions poses one of the great challenges to international relations. Whether one likes it or not, religion is an inescapable part of politics, as well as an inescapable part of economics, foreign policy, social values and domestic interactions. Religion has a public role.[14]

World events have led many to a new appreciation of the importance of knowledge about religion and to a vivid awareness of the dangers that emerge when people fail to recognize religion as a potent source of motivation and behaviour. In a world shaped not merely by 9/11 but by Iraq, Afghanistan, Syria, Israel and the West Bank, Bosnia, Kashmir, Somalia, Egypt, Libya, Nigeria and Myanmar; not merely by abortion, but by gay marriage, euthanasia and stem cells—one increasingly needs to accept the idea that people need better to understand the diverse range of religious phenomena. Basically, adherents of religion create it. Billions of worshipers and hundreds of thousands of local religious communities shape and are shaped by the religious meanings of their traditions. Religious studies offer unique opportunities for students to engage in the large issues of life's meaning and to think critically and responsibly about the issues' role in the world.[15]

The study looks at what people believe, why people belong to particular religious traditions, how they practice their beliefs and what all of this has meant for our world in the past, and what it means for societies today. People from all walks of life study theology and related disciplines. TRS is a gateway to knowledge that has assisted people to understanding and

---

[14] www.aacu.org/publications-research/periodicals/religious-studies-major-and-liberal-education [17.12.2018].

[15] www.aacu.org/publications-research/periodicals/religious-sttudies-major-and-liberal-education [17.12.2018].

engaging with the Bible, church, culture, history, and societies which includes politics, economics, education, environment and climate change. Through the study of TRS, people have become familiar with lots of other academic subjects such as philosophy, history, literature and languages plus other mainstreamed fields of study such as gender that analyzes the power relationships that exist between women and men, which lend itself to a multi-disciplinary mode of study, and HIV/AIDS. TRS helps one respect, evaluate and make sense of other people's values and actions. It is unmanageable to deny the impact of religion on the world. A full understanding of any society requires an inclusion of knowledge about religion and beliefs. Religion has continued to shape the societies, their politics and the way people interact with each other.[16]

Theologians and National Development in Malawi

One of the most respected theologians in the country and Africa is Bishop Patrick Kalilombe, who was a visionary and progressive Roman Catholic bishop, a member of the Missionaries of Africa, and probably the most accomplished and important theologian Malawi has produced. He engineered the establishment of the Small Christian Communities (SCC's) or "grass roots communities"(*miphakati*) in Malawi through the Lilongwe Diocese. In fact, the communities have less to do with size, but with participation of the laity in the analysis of and Christian response to their own life context.[17] The *miphakati* emerged from traditions of local kinship and lineage as indispensable condition for life itself, unlike the SCC's of Latin America that grew up in the context of Liberation Theology.[18] It is a change of the way of being and doing church. Kalilombe wanted the Church, through the SCCs, to be self-reliant in financial needs of the Church, self-propagating in the nurturing of the faith, and self-ministering

---

[16] www.researchgate.net/publication/265634000_Why_Study_Theology_and_Religious_Studies [4.6.2018].

[17] Hubert Reijnaerts, Ann Nielsen and Matthew Schoffeleers, *Montfortians in Malawi: Their Spirituality and Pastoral Approach*, Blantyre: CLAIM-Kachere, 1997, p. 402.

[18] Hubert Reijnaerts, Ann Nielsen and Matthew Schoffeleers, *Montfortians in Malawi*, p. 436.

through formation of lay leaders and ministers in these small communities of the Church.

Kalilombe's reforming ideas were not only unpopular with some of the Catholic hierarchy in Malawi, but more significantly with President Hastings Kamuzu Banda who considered them potentially threatening to his own authority due to the possibility that they would mobilize communities that were not controlled by the government and which might foster seditious convictions. Against the backdrop, the government accused Kalilombe of being a communist and the emerging *miphakati* were banned. The one-party regime wrongly associated the naming of these communities with a political figure, Attati Mpakati, a Malawian dissident in exile in Zimbabwe. They thought these communities were grass-root machinery of promoting the rebellious intentions of Attati Mpakati.[19] In 1976, government officials interrogated Kalilombe for over six hours after which the MCP pressured the Catholic hierarchy to advise their colleague to leave the country. Kalilombe left the country to attend a conference and was detained at Lilongwe airport upon his return and refused entry into Malawi.

He spent the next twenty years in exile during which Kalilombe studied in Jerusalem and then began doctoral studies at Graduate Theological Union in California, where he obtained a PhD in 1983. His dissertation analyzed his own attempt to promote SCCs in Malawi: "From 'Outstation' to 'Small Christian Community': A Comparison between Two Pastoral Methods in Lilongwe Diocese." In 1979, he officially resigned as bishop and began teaching at Selly Oak Colleges in Birmingham, England in 1980, first as a fellow, then as lecturer in Third World Theology. He was the director of the Center for Black and White Christian Partnership until 1996. The Center was an initiative to reach out to African and Afro-Caribbean independent churches in the West Midlands in Britain.

During this period, Kalilombe also maintained his spiritual and theological connections with the Majority World through active involvement and leadership in the Ecumenical Association of Third World Theologians

---

[19] Maximian, Khisi, *The Church as the Family of God and the Care for Creation*, Mzuzu: Mzuni Press, 2018, p. 62.

(EATWOT), which had been founded in Dar es Salaam in 1976 as a forum for non-western theologians concerned with issues that were critically relevant to their contexts, such as theological inculturation, justice, and liberation, but were rarely priorities for western theologians and church leaders.

In 1994, Kalilombe returned home when Kamuzu Banda's rule came to a humiliating end. From 1998 to 2008, he lectured in the Department of Theology and Religious Studies of the University of Malawi. He also involved himself in the Bible Society of Malawi's ongoing work of translating and producing commentaries on the Scriptures. In addition, he participated in the activities of the local parish in Zomba, and spoke in many places in the country. Although Kalilombe's death left a big gap not only in the Catholic Church and the academia, but also in the nation, his personal example and earlier attempts at reforms contributed to the leading role played by the Catholic bishops in the early 1990s in decrying the human and civil rights abuses of the Kamuzu Banda regime, and praying and petitioning for a peaceful transition to democracy.

Political Transition 1992-1994

Malawi, like other countries in Africa at the dawn of independence, relied heavily on the Christian churches for technical and material support since the country lacked material means, institutional capacity, knowledge and skills to manage the modern country. The former mission churches played a leading role in the provision of necessary skills, knowledge and training required to manage a modern economy. The new government forged diplomatic alliances with mission church leaders that provided technical assistance to nation building initiatives. Most mission churches had previously supported European colonial governments. The Malawi government and related institutions such as the civil service, colleges, health clinics, hospitals, university and industry were led mostly by products of mission churches when the country became independent. Leaders of the former mission churches inadvertently assumed positions of serving the nation as development partners, but their contribution to social development varied. For example, the mainline churches sought to address social concerns such as poverty, under-development, social injustice and human rights,[20] while Evangelical, Pentecostal and Charismatic churches focused upon personal salvation, private morality of the church and church planting to reach unreached souls.[21]

Vigorous attempts to reconcile the divided Christian churches were carried out in the post-independence period largely due to multiple socio-political challenges faced in this country. As it was in many African countries, these included dictatorship and human rights. Churches formed national church councils and associations through whom they forged inter-church fellowships and alliances along worldwide confessional family ties. The church realized that the dispossessed and disadvantaged sections of society cannot fail to operate as a powerful political dynamic in the drive for social justice.

The church through its theologians contributed immensely to the transformation of the landscape in Malawian politics. The 1992 Roman Catholic Bishops' Lenten pastoral letter criticizing Banda and his government was a bombshell that many were not prepared for. Particularly between March and September 1992, Malawians found courage in the context of the church. In support of the letter, students of the University of Malawi at Chancellor College and the Polytechnic joined in through protests and demonstrations. This forced the authorities to close the campuses. Many preachers echoed from their pulpits the prophetic critique the pastoral letter advanced. Such preachers were subjected to threats, harassment and, sometimes, detention. Rallying behind the call of the Bishops the Presbyterian Synods of Blantyre and Livingstonia were instrumental in the formation of the Public Affairs Committee (PAC) the church organized but included representatives of the Muslim community, the Malawi Law Society and the business community that became the engine of political reform in 1992-1993, and has remained engaged with the

---

[20] Matembo S. Nzunda & Kenneth R. Ross (eds), *Church, Law and Political Transition in Malawi 1992-94*, Gweru: Mambo, 1994.

[21] See for example Hany Longwe, *Christians by Grace – Baptists by Choice*; Klaus Fiedler, "The Smaller churches and Big Government," pp. 153-170.

ongoing political process. The opposition of the churches was a key factor in the downfall of the one-party system.[22]

Research and Publications in Theology and Religious Studies

Since the 1980s the challenge of publishing local theologies was taken up by Mambo Press in Zimbabwe. At the beginning of the 1993-1994 academic year, the Department of Law and the Department of Theology and Religious Studies at Chancellor College of the University of Malawi joined forces to organize a series of seminars which examined different aspects of the political transition in the country.[23] The papers presented during the seminars formed the basis of the book, *Church, Law and Political Transition in Malawi 1992-94*, intended to be for the benefit of a much wider audience than the 150 or so staff and students who participated in the seminars. It is an in-depth analysis of some significant aspects of the transition which was intended to be of assistance to those working for a better Malawi as well as to interested observers who sought a clearer understanding of the developments. The book was offered as one of the contributions to the formation of sound understanding of the political transformation experienced in the country between 1992 and 1994.

From 1995, Klaus Fiedler started and headed publishing as the editor of the Kachere Series,[24] the publishing arm of the Department of Theology and Religious Studies at the University of Malawi (Chancellor College, Zomba). The development of scholarship in Malawi stimulated the writing of many new books and the Kachere Series became the leading academic publisher in the country. Although religion has been the central interest of Kachere, many of their publications are of interest to many who include historians and political scholars. Kachere has produced Kachere books, monographs,

---

[22] Matembo S. Nzunda & Kenneth R. Ross (eds), *Church, Law and Political Transition in Malawi 1992-94*, p. 12.

[23] Matembo S. Nzunda & Kenneth R. Ross (eds), *Church, Law and Political Transition in Malawi 1992-94*, pp. 8-10.

[24] From 1992, Klaus Fiedler was a lecturer of Theology and Religious Studies, and from 1996 to 2008, an associate professor at Chancellor College of the University of Malawi in Zomba. From 2008 to 2019, he was a professor at Mzuzu University and Postgraduate Coordinator in the Department of Theology and Religious Studies.

texts and studies. Kachere has also published two academic journals: *Religion in Malawi* and *Malawi Journal of Biblical Studies* on behalf of Malawi Cluster of Theological Institutions, and *Sources for the Study of Religion in Malawi*. Mvunguti Series is another of the Kachere Series that publishes in languages of Malawi other than English. From 2008, Mzuni Press under the leadership of Klaus Fiedler has continued the work of publishing a body of literature which enables students and others to engage critically with religion, culture and society in Malawi. Mzuni Press is represented outside Africa by African Books Collective Oxford. Because of the academic publications from Kachere and Mzuni Press, many academicians outside Malawi and Africa have called on Malawians to publish alongside other world-renowned scholars. Pioneering Malawian scholars such as Patrick Kalilombe and Isabel Apawo Phiri have offered theological analysis that is engaged with local cultural and social issues.

As a "third world theologian," Kalilombe wanted to see the gospel inculturated in the African context, and this is reflected in many of his essays which are collected in the volume *Doing Theology at the Grassroots*.[25] He believed he was in step with the spirit of the Second Vatican Council. Patrick Kalilombe finds much to value in his people's traditional worldview, and laments its rejection by western missionaries and subsequent demise under the pressure of colonialization and then globalization.

Isabel Apawo Phiri's involvement with the World Council of Churches exposed her to women's issues. Isabel Phiri, a Presbyterian layperson, understands herself as one concerned about the oppression of people, animals and creation.[26] In her publications, Phiri has shown that she loves men as part of God's creation, and holds to the fact that God created men and women so that they complement and affirm each other. She also believes one cannot separate one's faith in God from the politics of the day. She affirms that the challenge is for African Christians to become active at

---

[25] Patrick Kalilombe, *Doing Theology at the Grassroots: Theological Essays from Malawi*, Gweru: Mambo, 1999.

[26] Isabel Apawo Phiri is Associate General Secretary for Public Witness and Diakonia of the World Council of Churches, and Honorary Professor in the School of Religion, Philosophy and Classics at the University of KwaZulu-Natal.

every level of the development process – from the development of economic and political theory to the formation and implementation of policy, and from the highest levels of government to the village.[27]

Isabel Phiri's first book encompasses the struggle of women for recognition of their own personal relationship to God and their attempts to achieve some public manifestation of this in ministry based on Chewa women in the Church of Central Africa Presbyterian Nkhoma Synod.[28] She points out sexism in the African culture and Church and proposes the need for a partnership between men and women. Like Patrick Kalilombe, Isabel Phiri advocates a new way of doing church since the church is aware of the women's perspective to church history and theology. There is need for male dominated societies and organizations to recognize women's full humanity, and to give women equal opportunities to higher education, both formal and theological. Women need to be motivated to accept their position as equal partners of men in the eyes of God. Phiri emphasizes sexism is as evil as racism.[29]

In 1994 Isabel Phiri could have gone into politics and made a difference as a Christian and as a woman. But she did not because of her principles in spite of being invited to join the proposed cabinet of the Christian Democratic Party in Malawi. Her church identity was questioned when she joined the women who were complaining that the Blantyre Synod was discriminating against them on the basis of gender in housing, pension and medical allowances offered to its employees. Although she did not work full-time for the church, Isabel Phiri joined what she called her sisters as a

---

[27] Isabel Apawo Phiri, "Stand up and be Counted: Identity, Spirituality and Theological Education in my Faith Journey," in Denise Ackermann, Eliza Getman, Hantie Kotze and Judy Tobler (eds), *Claiming our Footprints: South African Women Reflect on Context, Identity and Spirituality*, Stellenbosch: EFSA Institute for Theological & Interdisciplinary Research, 2000, pp. 152, 153.

[28] Isabel Apawo Phiri, *Women, Presbyterianism and Patriarchy: Religious Experience of Chewa Women in Central Malawi*, Blantyre: CLAIM, 1997.

[29] Isabel Apawo Phiri, *Women, Presbyterianism and Patriarchy*, pp. 140, 141.

sign of solidarity in helping them put the document together when it was already in its final form.[30]

In 1995 Isabel Phiri with other three female academics in other fields carried out a research in the University of Malawi after being traumatized by violence at work as a result of "cultural conservatism."[31] The University community was not angered because of the frequent sexual abuse and sometimes even rape that had taken place on campus, but because these women dared speak out about sexual matters, a taboo. The findings on rape and sexual harassment in the University nearly cost Isabel Phiri's life. Although this was a joint paper, she was attacked, primarily because she had presented it. Her house was stoned, her office was damaged, and her name came into disrepute. She was labelled a radical feminist. This was after the confrontation with the Blantyre Synod. Isabel Phiri's marriage had almost collapsed. Her health was equally poor after she had undergone a major gynecological operation which had not been successful. She felt oppressed and that threw her into a deep depression. She felt very little solidarity from other concerned women apart from the charismatic friends in the Department of Theology and Religious Studies.[32] Then Isabel Phiri wanted to continue with her desire to make a difference politically, not just as she was a woman, but because she had a mission from God.

She left the country. She spent more time praying with the oppressed of society, especially in hospitals. It was this time in her academic career she published most, because she wrote not from her head, but also from her heart. This is the time she started experiencing being at peace with herself, with God and with creation. Isabel Phiri's desire has not been just to talk about oppression of women but to do something about it.[33] Isabel Phiri is happy because since her experience at Chancellor College, more women are

---

[30] Isabel Apawo Phiri, "Stand up and be Counted," p. 156.

[31] Rachel NyaGondwe Fiedler, *A History of the Circle of Concerned African Women Theologians (1989-2007)*, Mzuzu: Mzuni Press, 2017, p. 82.

[32] Isabel Apawo Phiri, "Marching Suspended and Stoned: Christian Women in Malawi 1995," in Kenneth Ross (ed), *God, People and Power in Malawi: Democratization in Theological Perspective*, Blantyre: CLAIM-Kachere, 1996, pp. 63-105.

[33] Isabel Apawo Phiri, "Stand up and be Counted," p. 158.

able to stand and speak out against patriarchy, and men listen without being violent. The University of Malawi established a Centre for Gender Studies at the very campus where she was stoned as a radical feminist.[34] Mzuzu University later followed by mainstreaming feminist theologies, liberation theology and gender studies in its Bachelor's programmes under the Department of Theology and Religious Studies. It was only in 2013 that the government of Malawi assented to the gender rights.

One of the most rewarding aspects of recent writing on Christianity is its readiness to expand the frontiers of research not only into areas which previously had received little attention, but also into every area of interest, both past and current and of national interest. The focus has been on issues that are of real concern to the African. The publications have been to bring their contribution to grassroots level so that its impact is felt as it empowers people to eradicate some extreme social imbalances and injustices that are deeply entrenched within African societies and among Christians. Like other Africans, Malawian theologians and scholars have been popularizing their thinking on issues of gender inequality which is fueled by patriarchy, HIV/AIDS, destructive masculinity, corruption, poverty, oppressive and regressive governance, all forms of violence, and socio-political and economic injustice through publications.[35]

Conclusion

All key issues facing Malawi and the rest of the world raise theological and religious questions. By studying TRS, one is able to develop the skills and abilities to assist one to understand why people think and act in certain ways, even if those people live in contexts which are radically different to one's own. One is able to disentangle the complex layers of debates and to respond in an informed and balanced way to questions about important issues facing the nation and the world.

---

[34] Isabel Apawo Phiri, "Stand up and be Counted," p. 158.
[35] Isabel Apawo Phiri, "Introduction and Survey on Recent Research in African Christianity," in Isabel Apawo Phiri and Dietrich Werner, and Chammah Kaunda and Kennedy Owino (eds), *Anthology of African Christianity*, Oxford: Regnum, 2016, p. 10.

Apart from being church ministers as well as researchers and teachers at every level, TRS graduates move into a diverse range of occupations, particularly in development work, community-based roles, aspects of welfare, social care and counselling, plus local and central government policymaking and administrative departments. In the wider employment market, many commercial organizations welcome TRS graduates in human resources or general management roles, broadcasting and journalism, publishing, library and information management. Employers draw on their wide knowledge and expertise. TRS graduate will have and can show that they have the following skills that many employers look for: teamwork, communication skills – oral and written, willingness to learn, self-motivation and desire to achieve, rapid identification of key issues, problem solving, time management – producing work to deadlines, research and investigative ability. Through studying Theology and Religious Studies one can: absorb and retain complex information and identify key issues, sift and select relevant information and think logically, express ideas clearly through essay writing and discussion, and develop a critical approach to contemporary issues, develop a disciplined approach to problem solving, develop investigative, analytical and critical evaluation skills, understand and take a sensitive approach to different cultures and beliefs, and show a real curiosity in people and world cultures. Some graduates may also acquire other skills through extra-curricular activities or vacation experiences such as: fundraising and handling finances generally, setting up or developing organizations and IT competence. Theology has not only ascended to its own platform, but its position has attained higher levels of recognition and transparency. That theological programmes in universities are themselves accredited by the national regulatory bodies is, in itself, a statement of endorsement by society. Theology is respected as a significant contributor to the national grid and as an academic discipline in its own right as a result of the understanding that the environment in the universities encourages quality assurance, inspires research and emboldens engagement with knowledge.[36]

If the nation truly wishes for students to engage the tremendous variety of human understandings of life, death, suffering, love, and meaning, there is perhaps no more direct path than through Theology and Religious Studies. John Chilembwe and Martin Luther King were graduates of theology!

---

[36] James Kombo, "Role and Relevance of Theology for the Future of African Christianity," in Isabel Apawo Phiri and Dietrich Werner, Chammah Kaunda and Kennedy Owino (eds), *Anthology of African Christianity*, Oxford: Regnum, 2016, p. 1225.

Chapter 4

Missions across the Border: Baptist Convention of Malawi's Expansion into Neighbouring Countries

Mission and church belong together. There has always been a strong mission impulse in the life of Baptists from the very beginning. The Baptist Convention of Malawi (BACOMA) began by proclaiming the gospel from Blantyre to other parts of the country and filled people's ears with the teaching of "being born again." Later, BACOMA's missions across the border followed through individual members and teams into Zimbabwe, Zambia, Mozambique and South Africa, but not Tanzania to the north. This could have been because of Malawi's closeness to central and southern Africa as a result of colonial rule. However, some Malawian Baptists who had come back from Tanzania formed the core group in the establishment of churches in the Karonga and Chitipa area.[1] One BACOMA church situated on the northern corridor of Karonga near the border, traces its beginnings to a Tanzanian missionary.[2] To be involved in mission was an essential task and characteristic of early BACOMA members.

Ministry of Seminary Students in Zambia and Zimbabwe

Some of the missionaries were seminary students who were studying in Zambia and Zimbabwe. It was a must in both seminaries at the time for students to be involved in ministry as part of their training. The emphasis was on evangelism to all people. In spite of difficulties in speaking, let alone preaching, in foreign languages, many seminary students either started new churches or ministered through existing ones. That also involved the students' families. Here is a sample of how the students were involved in the expansion of BACOMA's ministry into neighbouring countries.

---

[1] Hany Longwe, *Christians by Faith – Baptists by Choice*, p. 82.
[2] Hany Longwe, *Christians by Faith – Baptists by Choice*, p. 86.

In 1969, Bamusi and Martha Kanowa began a house church for seminary students' children and missionary families on the campus of Lusaka seminary. Some of the students left children in the Kanowas' care when they went out for weekend ministry. During the weekdays Bamusi Kanowa, with the help of other seminary students, witnessed at Bauleni, a high-density area a couple of kilometres south east of the Seminary. Some of the converts joined the church for Sunday services that were held in Kanowas' house on the Seminary campus. After a couple of months, the Seminary allowed Bamusi Kanowa and his congregation to meet in the seminary chapel for Sunday worship services. The congregation grew and there was need to find an alternative place for the church to be meeting in and to call its own. The congregation chose Bauleni. A piece of land was soon acquired from the Lusaka City authorities, and a building was constructed. The church began meeting in the building in 1971.

Bauleni church established a preaching point at Good Hope Farm nearby. One member of Bauleni church who knew a few workers there was instrumental in encouraging Bamusi and Martha Kanowa and the Bauleni congregation to start a ministry at the farm. Bamusi Kanowa and a few members from Bauleni made regular visits to the farm to witness and lead Bible study classes there. The next students to minister at Bauleni were Andy and Florence Namalima. In 1994, Timothy and Pulikeria Simango were the last team of seminary students from Malawi to lead the church. The Simangos were back in Malawi in December 1995.

In 1950, July Maya walked to Zimbabwe with other young men in search of work. He did not stay long in Harare but proceeded to Bulawayo where he worked for the Cold Storage Company between 1951 and 1952. In June 1953, Maya moved to Kimberly where he worked as a house servant for one of the managers at the mine. It is while he was at Kimberly that he met his wife, Agnes, born to a Mozambican father and a South African mother.[3]

At the end of 1961, Maya was accepted to study at the Baptist Theological Seminary at Gweru. Both Mayas received certificates in theology from Gweru Seminary. In 1962, Torwood Baptist Church at Que Que called

---

[3] Int. July Maya, Pastor Mombe Baptist Church, Liwonde, 28.8.2003.

4: Missions across the Border

them to the pastorate, but they were there for about nine months only. A request came from Zambia for a seminary graduate who spoke Nyanja to work in Kabwe area where there were no Baptist churches. Maya was taken and sent to Kabwe where he and his wife began Baptist work with the help of the Baptist Mission in Zambia. Between 1963 and 1978, the Mayas started a couple of churches; one was Bwacha and the other was Ngungu. Both churches had church buildings constructed with the help of the mission. There were also several preaching points, some of which did not survive after the Mayas returned to Malawi in 1978. July and Agnes and their children settled in Chilomoni in Blantyre. Towards the end of the year Chilomoni church called July Maya as its first fulltime pastor.

Some men who included J. Ngozo and Mafupa, both from Ntcheu District, had been in Zimbabwe on their own accord, and just like Maya, chose to study at the Gweru Seminary in answering God's call for ministers of his Word. Ngozo served at Gaika Baptist Church at Kadoma, while Mafupa was at Highfields in Harare.

Also from the Lusaka seminary were Ruben and Raika Nkhata who went to Mandevu, later Sunnyside Baptist Church, as their field of ministry during training. In 1969, when they joined the church, there were fifteen members who met in the home of Miller Phiri where it all started. The Nkhatas served this congregation well such that by the end of 1972, when they were leaving for Malawi after graduating from the Seminary, there were nearly 110 members meeting in their own church building. The Nkhatas served at Chichiri Baptist Church in Blantyre for seven years after which Sunnyside church called them back to pastor the flock there.[4] During his ministry at Sunnyside Church, Nkhata served as the treasurer for the Lusaka Baptist Association for five years when Moses Chimfumpa was the President.[5] One of the Malawians living in Lusaka, Peacewell Ngwata, was in a group of people who committed their lives to Christ during the

---

[4] Int. Ruben Nkhata, pastor, Lilongwe, 18.11.1997. He had an opportunity to visit the church in 1994 and 1995. It was a flourishing church then under a Zambian pastor. Sunnyside church has been one of the thriving Baptist churches in Zambia

[5] Moses Chimfumpa later became the Vice Principal and Academic Dean at Lusaka Seminary.

Nkhatas' Ministry at Sunnyside Baptist Church. Ngwata later attended seminary in Lilongwe and became the pastor of Mthabuwa Baptist Church in north Kasungu near the border with Mzimba District.

In Zimbabwe, Wyford and Nellie Chisi assisted I.T. Tuwe at the Seminary Church in Gweru. Between 1973 and 1974, Wyford Chisi used to cycle to and from Zaroba alone every Sunday, and on some days of the week. He started the ministry when he first witnessed to some farm workers there. As time went on, a few people at a time joined the fellowship at Zaroba.[6] Soon the house in which the church met could not accommodate all who attended. The congregation began to meet under a tree. The church that was meeting at the Seminary became responsible for Zaroba as its preaching point. Out of that small congregation at Zaroba came a Mr. Phiri who later became a pastor and led a Baptist church in Harare.

Expansion into South Africa

In 1973, apart from seminary students' participation in neighbouring countries in evangelizing those countries, the Baptist Convention of Malawi was able, without financial help from the Mission, to send Lichapa as a missionary to the Nyanja-speaking miners on the Rand in South Africa. That was as a result of a letter that had been received from the operators of the mine. In that letter they requested the Convention to send someone who was going to work as a bi-vocational pastor. The mine company was going to make working hours flexible for the candidate to enable him to minister to the workers. Lichapa volunteered, and the Convention EC agreed to release him.[7] Apart from having difficulties to get to Johannesburg, Lichapa was not welcomed as he had anticipated, nevertheless, God saw him through three years of service. The mine operators later paid his salary having seen the service he was rendering to their employees. Three men seemed to have been deeply touched such that they wanted assistance to enable them to start churches in their home areas after returning from South Africa. One of them was from Chiyendausiku

---

[6] This is part of an area covered by large farms that white settlers formerly owned surrounding the seminary.

[7] BACOMA Minutes, 24.5.1973.

in Balaka, the other was from Blantyre, and the third was from Mozambique across the border from Lilongwe.[8] There is no record of what happened to these men, especially the ones from Malawi, whether they went home or not, and if they did, whether they attempted to plant churches in their areas.

Acts 1:8 encouraged BACOMA to go across borders and to witness Christ and make disciples of all nations. In December 2011, BACOMA launched a branch at Katlehong, Johannesburg.[9] In 2017, the leadership of the churches in South Africa attended the annual meeting in Blantyre, and they requested the Convention to assist them to have official work permits to allow them, not only to minister, but also receive training in South Africa, and for the churches to have official registration with the South African government. That would enable BACOMA churches to multiply freely. The Convention assigned Emmanuel Chinkwita Phiri to facilitate the process.

Ministry in Mozambique

As it was with the Free Baptist Union in Sweden who entered Mozambique in 1921, and the South Africa General Mission who took over an earlier mission work in 1939 out of which emerged the United Baptist Church in 1968, Mozambique has also been a fruitful field for BACOMA, especially around the south east, south and south west of the Malawi border with Mozambique. The country needed more than just a handful of workers stationed mainly in the coastal cities.

Another individual, this time a woman, was instrumental in the establishment of a Baptist church at Kavalo Village in Mozambique. It was the result of the marriage between a woman from Chikwawa, Miss Limitedi, and a man from Kavalo Village in 1977, just across the Shire River from Nsanje. Although there were other churches in the village, they did not impress Limitedi. She told her husband about the Baptist church she used

---

[8] Int. Stephen Galatiya, Baptist pastor Lilongwe, 13.06.1997. See also Minutes BACOMA, 10.6.1975.

[9] Report George Mwase, President of BACOMA, Annual Convention, Blantyre, 2017.

to attend at Chikwawa. She wrote a letter inviting Nsomo Baptist Church to assist her to begin a Baptist church at her new home at Kavalo.

W. Jim Kalenga and the team from Nsomo crossed the Shire River by boat into Mozambique, and then walked to Kavalo Village. Just as in the villages where they had been witnessing in Malawi, the children were the first to accept the good news of Jesus Christ. Slowly but surely the adults began to listen to the messages. One of the first converts was Mario Vizara. After several days of teaching, Kalenga asked Vizara to act as the leader of the church that had begun meeting at Kavalo Village.[10]

On their second visit to Kavalo Village, Stephen Galatiya accompanied the group from Nsomo church at their invitation. Galatiya preached on Friday night and on Saturday morning when he baptized 103 converts. On Sunday the congregation met for a service in which Stephen Galatiya preached again. The church from Malawi returned home the following Monday.

It was not easy for the church at Kavalo Village to survive. The civil war saw the destruction of the entire village by fire. The day when the village was attacked and set on fire, Limitedi, her family and others ran away to Malawi except for her five-year-old who had been sleeping in the house and they presumed burnt to death. The burning of Kavalo Village marked the end of the first Convention Baptist missionary church by Nsomo church in Mozambique.[11]

The Period of Civil War in Mozambique

While there were a lot of church activities to the east, south east and south of Malawi there were also records of Baptist churches being planted to the south west of the country into areas across the border from Ntcheu, Dedza and Lilongwe.

In June 1987, Luciano Phiri heard Timothy Kandawe and Samuel Chilokoteni preach to refugees at Ngalande village in Ntcheu. On the third day, Luciano Phiri professed faith in Jesus as Lord and Saviour of his life

---

[10] Int. W.J.H. Kalenga, Baptist pastor, Nsomo Village, pastor, 12.11.1997.
[11] Int. W.J.H. Kalenga, Nsomo Village, pastor, 12.11.1997.

and became a Baptist. He stayed close to Chilokoteni who also loved him. Phiri was able to go everywhere Chilokoteni went to teach. Soon Luciano was assigned to lead the youth group, and later he became the church treasurer, a post he held for only three years.[12] He accepted God's call to fulltime ministry, and from 1991 to 1992 he studied at the Bible School in Lilongwe. His wife, Patricia, also attended two sessions at the school during those two years. Luciano and Patricia Phiri were the first couple from this side of Mozambique to study at the Baptist Bible School in Lilongwe.

Zambezi Province

At a time when Zambezi Province was under RENAMO, Convention Baptist ministry in the area started as a result of three Mozambican Christians, Augusto Moises Namuko, Gusto'nio Sumaine and Real Fernando Malei of Murangala, T/A Pindu, Villa Milanje, as they pursued to understand more about "true baptism." For some reason they began to question the validity of their baptism and why candidates had to pay a fee to be baptized.

In the midst of their search they heard of Baptists and their teaching on baptism. One day when Gusto'nio Sumaine was at Sukasanje in Milanje District, he saw a signpost written, *Mpingo wa Baptist*. He stopped by and made inquiries. Namuko, Sumaine and Malei started a church based on Baptist doctrine at the beginning of August at Nansato. The church was made up of 33 people. On 15 July 1989, Migowi Association at one of its regular meetings, registered Nansato Baptist Church as a preaching point of Sukasanje.[13] In May 1990, Malei was baptized at Limbuli at a baptism ceremony that had been arranged for the Kalaiston church members only.

Namuko and Sumaine attended association meetings which were held once every 2 or 3 months at Migowi. It was not easy and it was risky business to walk so often to and from Malawi. Many times these man experienced humiliation and torture from the soldiers, but that did not dampen their search for truth and personal growth in Christ. Sometimes the soldiers

---

[12] Int. Nazare Luciano Phiri, Lilongwe, 9.11.2004.
[13] Int. D.M. Makonyola, pastor, Migowi Baptist Church, 12.9.1999.

forced them to carry the fighters' plunder and walked for days. In some instances, they were stripped of their clothes and left to go almost naked. As a result, Namuko and Sumaine normally walked at night to and from Malawi. In October 1990, pastor D. Nanthambwe baptized the two men at Naminjiwa Baptist Church in Migowi.[14]

During the civil war they chose to meet in the bush on the banks of Kanlulu stream that ran through a valley with small hills on the sides. Since the membership was between 80 and 90, they divided into two groups with one meeting between nine and twelve in the morning and the other between one and three in the afternoon. When one group was worshipping, men from the other group stood some distance around watching for any sign of soldiers. That was the way of life of Nansato church especially during 1991 and 1992, when things were really rough. When the situation was not so bad, a month or so passed without soldiers in sight. They only saw part-time soldiers who were not rough to the civilians. That is the time when the congregation met in its building.[15]

Beginning in January 1987 many people sought refuge in Malawi. Among them were deacons Biliyati, Chitini and Paulo Tsabola together with their families, and there were others from Simukwi church who left early in the year for safety.[16] Many people crossed into Malawi. Some of the people were taken by the refugee agencies to Makhwai in Phalombe, while others were housed at camps in Mwanza. Frank Muhosa and his family went and lived at Mandawala village under chief Nazombe, near Lake Chirwa. They became members of Domasi Baptist Church. Malei also left Chipinimbi, and he went and lived at Mandawala village. He met with other Baptists who included Paulo Tsabola and L. Mazumbi. Together they established Naminkhaka Baptist Church at Pangani.[17] Mazumbi and Chikomesa brought Baptist teaching to chief Kazimbi's area in Milanje District.

---

[14] Int. Gusto'nio Sumaine, Lilongwe, 16.3.1998.
[15] Int. Fernando Malei, Lilongwe, 18.3.1998.
[16] Int. Frank Muhosa, Baptist Bible School student, Lilongwe, 24.3.1998.
[17] Int. Frank Muhosa, Baptist Bible School student, Lilongwe, 24.3.1998.

In the same year a total of 58 converts were baptized at this first baptism ceremony at Kazimbi. After a year, Tsabola was elected secretary of the congregation. The church began to reach Mchivilivi, Chanemba, Nachanje and Nakoma. Within two years, the church elected Tsabola as a preacher. Malikebu of Thundu Baptist Church, Jali, Zomba, was also responsible for the church at Kazimbi.

In 1989, a preaching point was opened at Chief Kajama's area in Niassa. An evangelistic meeting was organized, and men only went on this mission because the war was at its peak. From Kazimbi to Kajama was a distance of 25 km by road, but it took them 12 hours for these men to walk. They had to be careful of the warring factions and that slowed them.

Malikebu contacted Rendell Day who organized a consignment of *Likuni Phala* (a brand name for a special porridge powder for malnourished children), 105 garden hoes, and 20 Bibles. The church at Naminkhaka shared the gifts among themselves as equitably as they could. The congregation continued to live and work together and there was no friction amongst the members.

After returning to Mozambique, the number of congregations increased to 25. Since there was an increase in congregations, churches were encouraged to choose shepherds among them. Churches chose Naminkhaka as a meeting place for large or association gatherings.[18] In 2000, there were 15 churches under Kazimbi Association in Mozambique.

From Nkhota Kota to Niassa Province with the Word

On the other side of Lake Malawi facing Likoma, is Ngofi Baptist Church in Mozambique. E. Liwembe began Convention Baptist work there. He was from Kasamba in Nkhota Kota district. Beginning in 1982, when he went across the Lake to Mozambique, he shared the story of Jesus with those he came into contact. Immediately E.N. Ngaunje on Likoma Island heard that Baptist work had started on Mozambique soil straight across from Likoma, he went there and baptized the first five converts in the Mkalawira River. They had no church building and these men were meeting in a home

---

[18] Int. Paulo Tsabola, Milanje, Mozambique, 24.3.1998.

belonging to Aidane Chaotcha. People of the area called it "men only" church because there was no women participation. In 1983, Ngaunje replaced Chaotcha as the leader of Ngofi church. Nevertheless, before the end of the year, some women had become Baptists. The first two were M. Gumbwa and L. Mizedi.[19]

In 1984 people discussed the idea of constructing a church building. They went to Chief Mapunda to ask for land on which to build, but he refused. He accused Baptists in the area as *wa mpatuko* (rebels) against the Anglican Church that had been the only church for many years since the arrival of missionaries in this part of Africa. Every person in the area was supposed to be an Anglican. If ever another church was allowed to compete for people of Ngofi, it would mean a decline in Anglican Church membership that the chief wanted to avoid at all costs. The congregation continued to meet in Chaotcha's home. When Baptists on Likoma heard what was going on, they sent P. Ng'ombayera over to Chief Chitenji. There he preached and three people accepted to join the Baptists. These were D. Katemesha, M. Banda and his wife. Ng'ombayera remained there; he didn't go back to Likoma.[20]

When the war intensified around 1985, many people were killed. People were scattered; some went to Likoma, while others crossed the Lake in small boats to Nkhata Bay and Nkhota Kota. Still others remained in Mozambique. Those who remained in Mozambique also continued to meet. Both groups met as house churches.

Post-Civil War Period in Mozambique

Many of the refugees went back to Mozambique after the cease-fire in October 1992. Moses went back to Chipinimbi on 12 August 1993. The other churches that Moses was instrumental in starting, Napiranje, Nabulanje and Isotole, came into life again with more witnessing taking

---

[19] Int. Aidane Chaotcha, church leader, Mambere Baptist Church, Nyasa Province, Mozambique, 17.3.1998.

[20] Int. Aidane Chaotcha, church leader, Mambere Baptist Church, Nyasa Province, Mozambique 17.3.1998.

place. Moses and three other church leaders were ordained as pastors in August 1994. Since then, Moses baptized 46 new converts at Chipinimbi, 62 at Napiranje, 103 people including the chief at Nabulanje, and 21 at Isotole. Two preaching points were started in 1995: one at Nandiye where 48 new converts were baptized, and the other at Manyala. In 1996 Moses was at the Bible school in Lilongwe. After his return, he began yet another preaching point at Masangano. The church at Isotole joined the Four Square Gospel Church because it was said that the Four Square Gospel Church gave its members money.[21]

Frank Muhosa and his family returned to Mozambique in 1994. Simukwi church began to gather again under the leadership of Tsabola and Muhosa. On 21 January 1996 Nikoroma baptized 57. Beginning 5 May, the congregation began moulding bricks. A few weeks later they burned the bricks. Construction of the church building was completed before the end of the year. On 10 April, Nikoroma and Makonyola, baptized and preached, respectively, at an evangelistic meeting at Simukwi. Sixty-one people were baptized during this meeting. On 26 October 1997 Simukwi church started a preaching point at Mikolimbo. The church chose G. Chakaya and L. Dedza as leaders of Mikolimbo preaching point. Simukwi church was a member of Migowi Association. It is a 3 to 4 hour ride by bicycle from Simukwi to Migowi.[22]

Ngofi Baptist Church

In 1994 some converts from Ngofi were baptized in Nkhata Bay. These included Aidane Chaotcha. When the war was over, Baptists, like many other people returned to their homes beginning from 1994. In the same year Ng'ombayera was chosen to be the pastor of Ngofi and Likoma. Also, the chief agreed to let the Baptists put up a structure. A pole and mud building was erected. As part of the opening ceremony, Ng'ombayera was also ordained. Nkhoma from Nkhata Bay presided over the ordination

---

[21] Int. John Moses, Lilongwe, 25.5.1998.
[22] Int. Frank Muhosa, Lilongwe, 24.3.1998.

ceremony, which many attended. From the preaching at the opening ceremony, many people declared that they had trusted Jesus Christ as their Lord and Saviour. Some of the people were Andrea and Charles Chaotcha, Tomas Maude, Chrissie and Maria Malaga, Tomas Nonie, Andrea Chambamkuya, Makelina Liwembe, Fere Juta, Joni Mwilaka and Esau Kalikowele. They were baptized on 20 March 1994 in Mkalawira River about 2 km from the church building.[23]

In May 1995 some members of Ngofi went to Mambere where they preached and witnessed to people of that area. A group of eight people began to meet regularly and soon they were baptized by Ng'ombayera in Lunyo River. These included Petro Antonio, Maria Mkasopa, John Mwenyeheri, Domingo Sukulu, Monika Mbwenda, Julia Chikoya, Molisi Chitungu, and Joseph Kamphambe. Ngofi church chose Malenga to lead and Chitungu to teach Mambere church.[24]

In 1996 Ngofi church, with the encouragement of the Baptist Bible School, chose Chaotcha to go for training at the Bible School in Lilongwe. Chaotcha went to the school in February 1997. He became the first Baptist leader from the Nyasa Province to study at the Bible School.[25]

After June 1997 Chaotcha and D. Banda began a church at Chigoma. By the end of the year there were three Baptist churches in the Nyasa province. These were Ngofi led by Ng'ombayera, Mambere led by Chaotcha and Chigoma led by Juta.[26]

From Ngalande to Mtengowambalame

After the war was over, Luciano and Patricia Phiri went back to Mozambique where they settled at Matope Village, Mtengowambalame which is Patricia's home. They were able to connect with other returnees who had been at Ngalande, and they began a church which they named Chipulumutso Baptist Church. Luciano Phiri became the leader and in 1998

---

[23] Int. Aidane Chaotcha, 17.3.1998.

[24] Int. Aidane Chaotcha, 17.3.1998.

[25] Int. George Mwase, Baptist Bible School Director, Lilongwe, 18.3.1998.

[26] Int. Aidane Chaotcha, 17.3.1998.

the church ordained him in the presence of several members from Malawi. The church quickly grew in numbers, and also became a strong church in the Villa Ulongwe area. They received much of their support from BACOMA, and not from the Baptist Convention of Mozambique because they were closer to Malawi than to Beira or Tete. The two conventions agreed to work with them, and Chipulumutso Church is registered as a member of the Mozambique convention, but is expected to receive more assistance from the nearest convention, BACOMA. Nevertheless, there were times they felt that they belonged neither to Malawi nor to Mozambique. Neither convention treated them seriously. Their yes was not always yes, the same with their no to requests from Chipulumutso Church. But one thing was given, a place for a member of Chipulumutso Church to study through the Bible School regional system.[27]

Luciano Phiri would have benefited most if both conventions had worked together as did the Free Methodists in Malawi and Mozambique. They did not just let their Bible School students do it alone, instead the church in Malawi continued to follow and help converts from the refugee camps who had gone back to Mozambique.[28]

Capital City Baptist Church: Mission to Mozambique

In 1997, Capital City Baptist Church (CCBC)'s missions' committee chose Timothy and Pulikeria Simango who were serving at Mchinji Baptist Church to be missionaries to Villa Ulongwe in the Angonia region of Mozambique. CCBC was not able to obtain residential permits for the Simangos, as a result, CCBC decided to rent a house for the Simango family at Dedza from where they could operate into Angonia. The Simango family moved to Dedza in 1998.

Every time Simango crossed the border the immigration officials threatened him with arrest if he overstayed in Angonia. So he made sure that he was out of the country before the end of time given for a short visit. He worked

---

[27] Int. Nazare Luciano Phiri, Lilongwe, 9.11.2004.
[28] See Henry Church, *Theological Education that Makes a Difference: Church Growth in the Free Methodist Church in Malawi and Zimbabwe*, Blantyre: CLAIM, 2002, pp. 64f.

behind Chipulumutso Baptist Church which was led by Luciano at Mtengowambalame. Simango still had no work permit to work in Mozambique in spite of the efforts of individuals at CCBC. Later CCBC bought a house along the Blantyre-Lilongwe road, and a motorbike to enable the Simangos to travel faster and go into places there with no good roads. They were able to begin churches at Villa Ulongwe which was the administrative centre of Angonia, at Chimvano and Mtengowambalame. In 1999 they also attempted to begin churches at Lifidzi, and Magwai which was a settlement established by those who had been in Malawi during the Mozambique civil war and had been assisted by Malawi Baptists across the border. In that same year Bible school courses were held at Ntcheu which also attracted leaders from Mozambique[29]

Several reasons contributed to the failure of some of these churches from growing and multiplying. One reason was that the Simangos did not have work permits for Mozambique so that they could not have open and large meetings. Instead they let the local people organize the meetings, and they went as invited guests for fear of being arrested. The second reason was that many of the leaders were of very little formal education; they could hardly read and write and that made life difficult for both the teacher and the students. Also, if the leader moved, the local body was left without a leader and in some cases the church stopped meeting. Another reason was that a couple of the churches were in the vicinity of well-established Roman Catholic churches. By 2000, only Villa Ulongwe, and Magwai churches that were credited to the Simangos' ministry, still existed.[30]

Ministry to Yao Muslims in Mozambique

The period from the late 1970s to the middle of the 1980s noticed major BACOMA evangelistic activities amongst Muslims across the border that resulted in churches in Mozambique.

---

[29] Int. Timothy Simango, missionary to Mozambique, Dedza, 15.9.2003.
[30] Int. Timothy Simango, missionary to Mozambique, Dedza, 15.9.2003.

In 1987 the Far East Broadcasting Association (FEBA) made a proposal to reach the Yao people of Malawi using media, primarily radio.[31] By 1990 the Baptist Convention of Malawi was one of the participating denominations in the Yao Project. Amos Phiri represented BACOMA. In the beginning of the project in the 1990s, Fletcher Kaiya prepared and recorded Scripture songs in Yao.[32] On 1-3 June 1990, Kaiya made a trip to Mangochi to initiate field recordings of Yao language materials. The purpose of the trip was to document traditional Yao music for study in the development of new Yao Christian music and to record existing Yao Christian music.

Although the programme at first targeted Muslims in Malawi, it did finally reach Muslims in Mozambique. Before the end of 1994, through the Yao Outreach, Amos Phiri and Francis Nkhoma visited Lichinga in Mozambique. God blessed the ministry. In 1995, Amos Phiri and others visited Mandimba, about 150 km from Lichinga from where they went to Majuni. In 1996, he visited these places again with the help of Mozambican pastors, Paulo Rozvi and Maulana. At Chepaundi Village, 51 people accepted Christ and were placed under the guidance of Maulana. Between 2015 and 2016 Amos Phiri was able to visit several churches that have benefitted from FEBA.

Conclusion

BACOMA influenced Baptist work in the neighbouring countries, especially in Mozambique. In Zambia and Zimbabwe, it was mainly by seminary students and in two cases, former seminary students starting churches or developing existing churches which resulted in growth in numbers of membership and also congregations.

---

[31] Michael Canady – Baptist Mission in Malawi, 12.12.1998. FEBA was a non-governmental, international, interdenominational, Christian organization, with short-wave transmitting facilities in the Seychelles. It provided a service of professional assistance and technical facilities for those churches and Christian organizations in the service areas to supplement their ministries by enabling them to speak to their own people in their own languages by means of broadcasting.

[32] Report Steve Evans – Baptist Mission in Malawi, Blantyre, 14.6.1990.

In Mozambique an association was formed with more than ten churches around Milanje. When they needed help, the leaders called on Malawi, especially in the area of Christian education. People in Mozambique were described by one BACOMA leader as "hungry for the Word." Anytime such a meeting was held, men, women and youths attended in large numbers. Some women would be breastfeeding mothers, and would not leave between lessons to attend to their children unless it was a must. Mozambican Baptists were very open to learning God's Word, and Malawian church leaders took advantage of that.

Across Dedza a committee was formed to work like an association although that did not come from the local congregations. It was an attempt by one of the former students of the Bible school in Lilongwe to set up an association of churches in Villa Ulongwe area. These churches participated in training sessions conducted at Ntcheu. Although there were no associations yet as was the case in Malawi, local Baptist congregations in Mozambique continued to receive help from individual BACOMA congregations. Baptists on both sides of the border felt that they were one people and therefore needed to continue to partner in ministry to the people in their areas.

Mission primarily is and should be the mission of the church. These individuals and teams were closely connected to local churches and engaged in missions as members of those churches.

Chapter 5

The *Matchona* Contribution to Early Baptist Church History[1]

Before and at the end of classical denominational missions in the 1960s, new churches came to Malawi and new non-classical missions began as an episode in a continuing story. The Southern Baptist Convention (SBC was one of the most visible examples. These churches obviously served Malawian interests because their beginning and development were largely due to Malawian initiative.[2] Christians of one nation have continued to hear the word from those of another. They have continued to share their faith, life and work. The expansion of Christianity often involved a period of cross-cultural transmission, followed by the emergence of a new local form of Christianity. All the local forms are provisional, part of the Christian missionary process.[3] One of the contributing factors to the provisional form of Christianity was labour migration.

Labour Migration

From at least the beginning of the nineteenth century, practically all peoples in Central Africa were involved to some degree in a variety of economic relations beyond the village level. In the late nineteenth century the Yao and the Tonga were in the process of becoming fully integrated into the world economy. The enterprise of Scottish Christians in Malawi was not confined to the missionary activities of their representatives at Livingstonia and Blantyre, but also comprised commerce. When commerce became

---

[1] Here *matchona* are people who went to work outside Malawi for a period and, either came back or stayed outside for good. The discussion centres on those who returned to Malawi. I write as one born of a *mtchona* and a Zimbabwean mother.

[2] Henry Church, *Theological Education that Makes a Difference: Church Growth in the Free Methodist Church in Malawi and Zimbabwe*, Blantyre: CLAIM, 2002, p. 43.

[3] Andrew F. Walls, *The Missionary Movement in Christian History: Studies in the Transmission of Faith*, Maryknoll: Orbis, 2000, pp. 239, 240.

practically an alternative to slave trade, a task too big to be undertaken by missionaries in addition to their other duties, the African Lakes Company was formed which in due course contributed a good deal to Malawi's commercial development through one of its best known trade names – Mandala – because one of first managers wore spectacles. The company relieved the missionaries of many of their worries about transport and supplies,[4] which soon included the shipping workers. In collaboration with Mandala, the missionaries organized a labour bureau, issuing written contracts and guaranteeing the return of workers when their time expired.[5] That later saw the introduction of Witwatersrand Labour Association (Wenela) that became responsible for labour migration to South African mines.

Failure to introduce agricultural and technical innovations in Malawi did play a crucial role in contributing to the creation of migrant labour system that became the central feature of Malawi's colonial economy. People working for white owned companies or institutions were paid regular wages, partly in cloth and beads, but also in British money that could be exchanged for articles at local shops. That contributed to the growing demand for European goods – a demand which could not be satisfied by the returns achieved from agricultural production or the low wages the institutions provided. The solution was for Malawians to seek work elsewhere.[6]

Although missionaries were successful in many cases in meeting the European demand for educated skilled labour for the companies and settlers in the country, the wages for the Africans were extremely low so that most men of determination eventually migrated to the south,[7] mainly to Zimbabwe and South Africa whose economic base created a constant demand for workers seeking employment for better cash. Although the

---

[4] John Weller and Jane Linden, *Mainstream Christianity to 1980 in Malawi, Zambia and Zimbabwe*, Gweru: Mambo, 1984, pp. 45-46.

[5] John McCracken, *Politics & Christianity in Malawi 1875-1940: The Impact of Livingstonia Mission in Northern Province*, Zomba: Kachere, 2008, p. 116.

[6] John McCracken, *Politics & Christianity in Malawi 1875-1940*, pp. 115-116.

[7] John McCracken, *Politics & Christianity in Malawi 1875-1940*, p. 155.

Protestant missions produced the initial impetus for the migration, it was H.H. Johnson and his successors who reinforced it through the tax and labour policies they followed, to satisfy Southern Africa's demand for Malawi labour, and the imperial and colonial authorities' willingness to comply deliberately or tacitly to those demands.[8]

Not only were many young men obliged to provide for their families, they were also eager to discover the world out there and looked forward to buying a lot of good things for themselves and their families.[9] Although some denominations tried to dissuade young people from going to the mines, the effort failed for the attraction of money and adventure was formidably powerful.[10]

Life in the Foreign Lands

Family life was threatened. In the foreign land, the mines and farms allocated the migrant labourers from Malawi living quarters designed for single people under what was known as the "one-man, one-room" system. The profit-minded failure to build family accommodation was an infringement on their workers social justice. Many migrant labourers were single, and if they were married, left their wives at home. As a result, prostitution was common in the compounds. The immorality as well as venereal diseases became rampant among the church's young adults, both male and female. By and by, many married foreign women and lived either in the single quarters, or in small houses that were later built for married people. Some, though not all, of those who left wives back in Malawi, lived a polygamous life.

Although some missionaries did and others did not encourage Malawians to take wage employment that led to the exodus, they both condemned the conditions that prevailed in the mines about 1904.[11] In 1903, the

---

[8] John McCracken, *Politics & Christianity in Malawi 1875-1940*, p. 342.
[9] Ulf Strohbehn, *Pentecostalism in Malawi: A History of the Apostolic Faith Mission in Malawi*, Zomba: Kachere, 2005, p. 40.
[10] Hubert Reijnaerts, Ann Nielsen and Matthew Schoffeleers, *Montfortians in Malawi: Their Spirituality and Pastoral Approach*, Blantyre: CLAIM, 1997, pp. 257-258.
[11] John McCracken, *Politics & Christianity in Malawi 1875-1940*, pp. 242-243.

missionaries in Zimbabwe agreed that it was a right principle that Africans should go away to work for cash wages. However, they were also concerned with the harsh conditions under which the African worked, and that needed a review. Though years later they achieved some success in improving physical conditions in the areas where African lived, they were also aware of the moral problems that arose from separation from family environment.[12]

Like in any other society that is growing, the established churches could not meet the many needs of the migrant labourers. One way was to issue Christian identity cards for migrant mine workers.[13] The missionaries also contacted their overworked counterparts in South Africa, Zimbabwe and Zambia who hardly spoke Nyanja to provide oversight on Malawian migrant workers. They were successful in having limited contact with the migrant workers in some places. Another way of serving was circulating an occasional pastoral letter among migrant workers. Faced by the bleak environment of the mining compound and the settler farm, Presbyterian Malawian migrant workers scattered far and wide and had established many independently organized, self-supporting congregations by 1907.[14] Many workers neither belonged to a church nor showed any interest in one, but some migrant labourers became active members of these churches. Others, inside and outside the compounds, formed Chewa or Tumbuka-speaking churches such as PIM in Soweto and several Presbyterian congregations in Zimbabwe that later became the Church of Central Africa Presbyterian (CCAP) Harare Synod.[15] Not only did the churches provide spiritual support, but also "home" fellowship and camaraderie even though the people came from different tribes and sometimes districts that were far

---

[12] John Weller and Jane Linden, *Mainstream Christianity*, p. 205.

[13] Hubert Reijnaerts, Ann Nielsen and Matthew Schoffeleers, *Montfortians in Malawi*, p. 236.

[14] John McCracken, *Politics & Christianity in Malawi 1875-1940*, p. 243.

[15] My family belonged to a Chewa-speaking Dutch Reformed Church in Sakubva Township in Mutare, Zimbabwe until 1964 when my parents moved back to Chintheche in Nkhata Bay.

apart such as Karonga and Nsanje. A good number converted to churches that were new to them.

The Return to Malawi

In the 1960 and 1970s, *matchona* and their families were a class of their own seen by many as above those who had not been outside the country. They spoke another African language, and they probably had more wealth than other Malawians at home. They had wives who were different in their outlook and could hardly speak local languages of Malawi, but some could speak good English. It was not easy to travel and so it was a challenge to go and come back alive and with a little more wealth, and in some cases with a wife and children. Later, the lifestyle of a few *matchona* tarnished that good image. The *matchona* influence on Malawian society, in many cases, has been very positive.

On their return to Malawi, they brought these churches with them. For example, Robert Chinguwo brought the Apostolic Faith Mission, while Moses Phiri brought the Free Methodist Church. There were a number of those who became Baptist as migrant workers and, on their return, did not bring with them a new church, but new found faith. For some, that new found faith landed them into being labelled *ampatuko*, while others where thought of as normal. These *matchona* later influenced the early history of the Baptist Convention of Malawi.

Stephen and Mary Galatiya

One of the *matchona* who has influenced the beginning and development of BACOMA from the early 1960s for almost 30 years is Stephen Galatiya and his wife Mary. They were probably the earliest "co-workers" of the Southern Baptist Convention (SBC missionaries in evangelism and church planting. When they arrived in Malawi, Stephen and Mary together with their children settled at his home at Chimbalanga Village in Neno where Galatiya began sharing his faith with his relatives, and also with other people. His parents and relatives at Chimbalanga perceived Galatiya as one who had deviated from the norm, which was Seventh-day Adventism.[16]

Steven was born in 1930 and grew up with his mother who was a single parent. Galatiya and his mother were members of the Seventh-day Adventist Church. Although they struggled because they did not have enough provisions, Galatiya was devoted to studying and managed to do standard 1 to 3 classes at Matandani SDA Mission School. Outside class hours Galatiya did piece work of hoeing and sold maize and beans for the family's sustenance and his school fees. In his later years Galatiya left home and went to Thyolo where he worked as a tea picker and a shepherd.[17]

While in Thyolo he was influenced by returnees to go and work in the mines in Zimbabwe. He travelled on foot to Blantyre where he registered with Mtandizi Employment Bureau that was responsible for recruiting Malawians to work in the mines of the Rhodesias and South Africa. Galatiya was sent to work in the mines of Orange Free State. From there he found his way to Cape Town where he worked as a waiter in one of the hotels. In Cape Town Galatiya became a Baptist. A workmate who was a member of Kenilworth Baptist Church in Cape Town witnessed to him and Galatiya chose to follow Christ in a Baptist church. The pastor (re-)baptized Galatiya after having found personal faith in Christ.[18]

Later Galatiya married Mary Phillips, a South African. Her father was Daniel Phillips, a Coloured from the Cape Province, and her mother was a Suthu. Galatiya describes his wife as a Suthu. Before she married Galatiya, Mary was a member of Somerset West Anglican Church. After marriage she followed Galatiya to Sommerset West Baptist Church. They were blessed with three children, two daughters, Endrina and Jane, and a son, Joseph. After working in Cape Town for several years the Galatiyas returned to Malawi with their three children.[19]

---

[16] Hany Longwe, *Christians by Grace – Baptists by Choice*, p. 36.

[17] Hany Longwe, *Christians by Grace – Baptists by Choice*, p. 36.

[18] Hany Longwe, *Christians by Grace – Baptists by Choice*, p. 36.

[19] Hany Longwe, *Christians by Grace – Baptists by Choice*, p. 36.

Back Home

Though no person responded to his teaching, Galatiya still believed that one day some would join him and begin a Baptist congregation in the area. The effort proved futile; the response was still negative. They were very opposed to the new denomination in the area, which was a Seventh-day Adventist monopoly.[20] Nonetheless, sometime early in 1960 Galatiya had established a small Bible study group.[21] Like most people in the area, Galatiya also spent time working on the land. He sold the bulk of his produce mostly to foreigners and upper class Malawians in Blantyre and Limbe. Sometime in 1961, while selling vegetables in Blantyre, Galatiya met Bill Wester, a Southern Baptist missionary. After some self-introductions, Wester invited Galatiya to help in establishing SBC work in Malawi.[22]

Involvement in the Establishment of the First and Second BACOMA Churches

The missionaries used Galatiya as the middleman between them and a Zion-type church, because the missionaries had not yet mastered enough Nyanja to have meaningful conversations with the local people who knew very little or no English at all. No one knew that this African Instituted Church that was led by Thomas Kachaso Gama at Ndalama village would transform into the first Convention Baptist church.[23] Kachaso Gama invited the missionaries and they, in turn, took along Galatiya to Ndalama Village where they taught about salvation and regenerate church membership. After several days of teaching, many of the people present were re-baptized, including Kachaso Gama. On September 1962, Ndalama became the first Convention Baptist church with 30 members. The congregation chose Kachaso Gama as their pastor. A further 24 people were baptized between September 1962 and April 1963.

---

[20] For the history of the SDA Church in that area see: Yonah Matemba, *Matandani. The Second Adventist Mission in Malawi*, Zomba: Kachere, 2004.

[21] Baptist Mission of Central Africa, Annual Report, Gweru, April 1963, p. 6.

[22] Hany Longwe, *Christians by Grace – Baptists by Choice*, p. 37.

[23] Int. Stephen Galatiya, Lilongwe, 16.4.2003.

In 1961, Stephen Galatiya was also involved in the beginning of what became the second BACOMA church. A group began to meet away from the missionaries' residence in buildings at Chichiri. These premises later became the first Malawi Congress Party Headquarters. Some of the members were Zimbabweans, both black and white, and Malawians. Several of the Malawians came from Mpunga Village where the Shoprite complex stands today opposite the national stadium. Stephen Galatiya and missionary Gene Kingsley witnessed in that village. The fellowship was interdenominational in nature, but the SBC missionaries expected it to become a Baptist congregation because the only members who had theological training and were of influence were Gene Kingsley and Bill Wester.

When the fellowship failed to become Baptist quickly, the Westers resigned from the group, and devoted their time to an attempt to start another fellowship, but the Kingsleys remained. Gene Kingsley was optimistic that the interdenominational, inter-racial church would one day turn into a Baptist congregation. Some members both black and white accepted the idea of an international Baptist church. Stephen Galatiya and Gene Kingsley made every effort and contacted English-speaking Malawians who worked at the Limbe Post Office and other offices in Limbe. They also made contacts with young people in secondary schools like Chichiri. Stephen Galatiya, Gene Kingsley and Bill Wester agreed amongst themselves for Gene Kingsley to pastor the multi-racial fellowship that was going to be meeting in Limbe Town. Some of those who were meeting at Chichiri moved and joined the Limbe Baptist Fellowship that was meeting outdoors. In October 1961 the multi-racial fellowship held its first service in a rented room in Cliccord House on the main Blantyre-Limbe highway opposite the market road in Limbe.[24] On 28 October 1962, Limbe Baptist Church was officially organized. This group later moved from meeting in Limbe to meeting at Chichiri Secondary School because the fellowship continued to grow, and later took the name Blantyre Baptist Church.[25]

---

[24] Hany Longwe, *Christians by Grace – Baptists by Choice*, p. 41.
[25] Hany Longwe, *Christians by Grace – Baptists by Choice*, p. 42.

The Establishment of Jerusalem Baptist Church in Limbe

Towards the end of his studies at Gweru, Stephen Galatiya asked for conditions of employment from the Baptist mission. The BMIM told Galatiya that the mission did not feel that it had a place it could use him for certain, and for sure, it did not pay pastors. Nonetheless, Stephen Galatiya became an associate pastor of the English speaking, multiracial Limbe congregation, with Gene Kingsley as the senior pastor.

The congregation was largely supported by the tithes of the missionaries and gifts of other white members of the church from which Stephen Galatiya also received monthly financial support. Early in 1966, Roy Davidson, then senior pastor, was not happy with Stephen Galatiya receiving support from mainly white members, and he suggested that Malawians support Galatiya, or Stephen Galatiya open and operate a bookstall in Mwanza (his home town); or better still to be a missionary to South Africa (his wife's home country). While the missionary claimed to follow the "indigenous church principle,"[26] Malawians viewed that as missionary racism toward black people. Stephen Galatiya decided to leave, and that is what he did, with the solidarity of his wife, Mary, even though she was breaking away from the close association with missionary women that they had enjoyed. The Galatiyas chose to forego status for the sake of the gospel, and they attained their freedom, too.[27]

Stephen Galatiya and his family held worship services at their home at Newlands, in Limbe, and some Malawian members moved from the Blantyre church to join this new Chichewa congregation. That contributed to their independence of missionary influence. On 5 July 1966, Stephen baptized the first group of new converts that included his daughter, Jane,[28]

---

[26] For more on the "indigenous church principle" see Klaus Fiedler, *Interdenominational Faith Missions in Africa. History and Ecclesiology*, Mzuzu: Mzuni Press, 2018, pp. 142, 187-189, 337, 400, 427, 462-467. He also shows the racist overtones.

[27] Banda, Rachel NyaGondwe [Fiedler], *Women of the Bible and Culture: Baptist Convention Women in Southern Malawi*, Zomba: Kachere, 2005, pp. 20, 29.

[28] She later became *Mayi Busa* Malabwanya. Samuel Malabwanya was a member of Jerusalem church where he married Jane, went to Lusaka seminary, and soon rose to position of prominence in BACOMA.

and the Ng'omas, J.M. and Helen, in the hired Imperial Tobacco Group (ITG) Assemblies of God Church baptistry. Stephen Galatiya spent time discipling new converts. Kaduya, who used to travel all the way from Chiradzulu, assisted him in discipleship.

In addition to Jerusalem church, Stephen Galatiya also pastored Soche at their invitation.

Evangelistic Ministry

In 1969, H. Sweet Chikanga, who sold Christian literature in the Lower Shire, invited Stephen Galatiya to preach in the area. The result was that a Baptist church was started at Domasi (Chikwawa). The seed was sown and the number of churches multiplied during the 1970 crusade in the Lower Shire where a number of people later became prominent pastors and denominational leaders, such as Jim Kalenga, whose son, Rustin Kalenga, is also a pastor and was, for two terms (6 years) the President of BACOMA.

In July 1973, Stephen Galatiya was back in the Lower Shire, this time at Nsomo church at the invitation of that church. At the meeting, Jim Kalenga's brother, Henford who later became Chief Mathotho, was one among many who professed Christ and was later baptized with 72 other candidates. Stephen Galatiya used to conduct regular discipleship classes for church members and their leaders in Blantyre and Chikwawa when he lived in Blantyre.

Mary Galatiya led women at New Jerusalem church in door to door witnessing. That set the ground for the revival meetings. That in a way put men and women equal as they all ministered together. Now and again women were given opportunities to lead in singing and preaching at New Jerusalem church.[29] Women's involvement in church worship services attracted more people to join the church.

During the first unlimited crusade of the 1970s that was described as national since the expectation was to reach as many areas as possible

---

[29] Int. Stephen Galatiya, Lilongwe, 15.4.2003. See also Rachel NyaGondwe Banda, *Women of Bible and Culture*, pp. 131f.

throughout the country, Stephen Galatiya led a team that witnessed in Ntcheu. When he preached, many people committed their lives to Jesus. He was also a member of the organizing committee for the national crusade. There was a great openness to the Baptist faith and message in many areas of the country that led to the growth of Convention Baptist work.

Many people have attributed their conversion to the Christian faith and to BACOMA to Stephen Galatiya's preaching, either at market places throughout the country, or in church services. One example are Nelson and Ethel Kuzalo of Utale. They became Baptists following the sermon Galatiya preached at *Msika wa Njala* (the market of hunger), a vegetable market at Kamba in Soche in Blantyre. Upon returning to Utale they narrated the story of their conversion experience to their children and relatives, and looked forward to a Baptist congregation being established in Kalambo Village. Nelson and Ethel later became *Mbusa and Mayi Busa* (pastor and pastor's wife).

Stephen Galatiya is credited with establishing Convention churches both in Chapananga in Chikwawa, and Mwanza Districts. Chapananga Convention Baptist work began with the establishment of Mphapa church from where the work spread. The first preaching points of Mphapa church were Kubalalika, Maleme, Kalambo and Thombo. During the late 1980s the Mphapa and Kalambo churches began two more preaching points. E. Chapsyinga from Kalambo, and S. Gabriel and Charles Changala[30] from Mphapa were instrumental in the beginning of the two preaching points. By 1996 there were nine churches that formed Chapananga Baptist Association.

In Blantyre, Stephen Galatiya was instrumental in establishing a church in South Lunzu. He witnessed to people in the area and a number of them became Baptists. For the years that he served at South Lunzu, Stephen Galatiya did not receive from the church the agreed financial support. South Lunzu was divided into 12 areas, and the church had members living in seven of those areas. In all but one of these areas there was a leader who

---

[30] Charles L. Changala, later attended the Lilongwe seminary and is a serving pastor of the Convention.

assisted Stephen Galatiya in visiting, passing out tracts and praying for the sick. Stephen Galatiya made every effort in training and using his leaders in the work of ministry throughout the community. Consequently, by the end of 1983 there were about 158 members, 190 by April 1984, 300 by June 1985, and 310 by December of the same year.[31]

From Blantyre, Galatiya went on to establish a congregation at Mwanza. He used a tract, *Ndichite Chiyani kuti Ndipulumuke?* (What must I do to be saved?) In 1989 Galatiya baptized a total of 28 converts from Kamchotseni II Village which was near the Mwanza trading centre. The converts named their church Mphatso (Gift) Baptist Church. They constructed the church at the *Boma*. In the same year Mphatso church planted a preaching point in Chief Mulauli's area, named Dzidala. Stephen Galatiya was the overseer for the two churches. After Stephen Galatiya retired from active ministry, other pastors from Blantyre stood in.

One special woman in BACOMA who attributed her meeting with Jesus to Stephen Galatiya was Liddah Kalako who later became the first woman to study at the Baptist seminary in Lilongwe. In May 1974, Liddah Kalako's life began to change when she attended meetings at which Galatiya preached at Lilongwe Baptist Church in Kawale. He preached from John 3:16, Romans 3:23 and 6:23. Kalako felt as if Galatiya was actually talking to her out of the crowd that came to hear him speak. Although she wanted to meet and discuss how she felt with Galatiya, she could not because there were many people wanting to meet with him after the meeting was over. She ended up by just being part of the crowd and left for home. When she got home, she explained her experience at the meeting to her husband whose interest in things of God was very low.

The second day Kalako prepared herself and the children early so that they could sit somewhere in the front rows. More people came to hear Galatiya preach than the previous day. The message for the day was taken from Luke 15. After preaching Stephen Galatiya gave an alter call, and Liddah Kalako immediately professed her faith in Jesus Christ that day. Kalako also decided that night to become a member of Lilongwe Baptist Church. Later

---

[31] Report BMIM 13.6.1986.

5: The Matchona Contribution to Early Baptist Church History

in that year, Pastor Gando baptized Liddah Kalako and she became a member of Lilongwe Baptist Church.

Immediately after her baptism she joined the church choir. Within two years Kalako had become a Sunday school teacher. She began with children's classes, and in 1979 she began teaching a new members' class. In the same year Liddah Kalako joined a group of young people who later formed the Baptist Crusaders, because she loved telling others the story of Jesus.

On the international scene, Stephen Galatiya has also had opportunities to preach at evangelistic rallies organized by Baptists in Johannesburg and Lusaka, Kabwe, Kitwe and Mfulira.

Prophetic Role

The establishment of Mphapa church in Chapananga was not without problems. During September 1978, Galatiya held several revival meetings in Chikwawa District. The next time Stephen Galatiya visited the area to encourage the new believers, the Malawi Young Pioneers (MYP) arrested him after he had finished preaching at Selemani and was returning to Gora where there was an MYP base. He was manhandled. The reason was that he was heard saying that "Salvation is found in no one else, for there is no other name under heaven given to men by which we must be saved" (Acts 4:12, NIV). That was against the belief of many in the country that there was no other saviour (*mpulumutsi*) for Malawi than Kamuzu Banda. Malawians were made to believe that without Kamuzu Banda the country would have not been freed from colonial bondage. No one would dare talk about another *mpulumutsi* during the one-party state.

With arms tied on his back, the two MYP took Galatiya to a nearby stream and threw him into the water. As he was struggling for his life, they pulled him out of the stream and rolled him on the ground. They also took soil and smeared it on his head and face. Galatiya had to keep his eyes closed because there was no way he could remove soil or any other foreign bodies which would have gone into his eyes. With their heavy military boots the MYPs kicked him left and right as they dragged him to the MCP offices.

Many people, men and women, shed tears as they watched Galatiya being tortured like a helpless drunk. It was getting dark and people were very fearful that Galatiya would not be seen again. Thank God for three men who were coming from a pub who suggested that Galatiya be deposited at the nearest chief and that the Pioneers would pick him up the following morning. After some exchanges the two parties agreed to leave Stephen Galatiya with one of the chiefs nearby. The chief kept Stephen Galatiya overnight and handed him over to the Pioneers the following morning who took him to their base, and soon after, the police arrived and they took Stephen Galatiya to their station at Chikwawa. The police asked Stephen Galatiya why he had said that the Ngwazi was not the *mpulumutsi* (saviour). In his reply, Stephen Galatiya quoted Acts 4:12. The police asked again, "*Palibe dzina lina: nanga Ngwazi?*" ("There is no other name: what about the Ngwazi?"). "That I do not know," Galatiya replied. The Police locked him up in prison until December of the same year.

During that period Stephen Galatiya appeared three times before a magistrate court. The prosecution failed to give enough evidence to warrant Stephen Galatiya to stay in prison. Christians from different denominations both inside and outside the country prayed for his safety and freedom. Many Christians petitioned for Stephen Galatiya's release because they believed he had not violated any law of the country, and he was not likely to do so. At the end of December, Galatiya was on bail. He had to report to the police station every Monday; later it was every month. Since the court allowed him to preach anywhere in the country, he had to report to any nearest police station when time was due depending on where he was in the country.

Other concerned persons went and met privately with the then Commissioner of Police, Kamwana, and briefed him of Stephen Galatiya's plight. He had an audience with Stephen Galatiya in Zomba. After presenting his case the Commissioner of Police put his arm on Stephen Galatiya's shoulder and asked whether Stephen Galatiya was a Christian. Before he could answer Kamwana asked another question, "Do you preach about forgiveness?" To both questions Stephen Galatiya replied *yes*. Kamwana immediately released him from police charge and closed the case.[32] Stephen Galatiya became even more zealous to preach the true Saviour that also saw more people becoming members of the Baptist Convention of Malawi.

Witnessing through Tape Recordings and Radio

Stephen Galatiya and other pastors such as Makhaya had sermons and Bible teachings recorded on tapes that were used in reaching people in rural areas. He also reached many people through the radio via MEMA studios in Lilongwe. MEMA was a scheme concerning audio-visual aids and radio broadcasting that the Dutch Reformed Church Mission (DRCM) fostered.

By mid-1965 half-hour programmes were being aired over Radio Voice of the Gospel. Member churches supplied programme materials, and the staff of MEMA Studio produced the programmes. The Christian Council of Malawi was satisfied by the way the Malawi Broadcasting Corporation (MBC) was using religious programmes Gospel Broadcasting Corporation (GBC) produced. The GBC gave the Convention Baptists opportunity to produce six programmes for use on MBC from November 1965. Stephen Galatiya and Makhaya were the first Convention Baptists to produce such programmes

Teaching Ministry

Apart from being an evangelist, Stephen Galatiya was also a teacher. In 1972, Stephen Galatiya was one of the Convention teachers at the Bible School in Lilongwe. The Bible School curriculum comprised preaching, evangelism, Christian living, the work of a pastor, and life and ministry of Christ based on Mark's Gospel. Stephen Galatiya taught evangelism. In 1973, as the treasurer of BACOMA, Stephen Galatiya spearheaded stewardship training in all the associations.

Early in the ministry, Mary Galatiya was an assistant pastor's wife to Blantyre Baptist Church which was basically an English-speaking church. She assisted the senior pastor's wife teach the women sewing and other

---

[32] Int. Stephen Galatiya, Lilongwe, 13.4.1997.

homemaking skills.[33] She also worked outside the church, a job that took her away from being available fulltime for the church. Mary Galatiya served at the first nursery school at Blantyre Baptist Church as she served with her husband pastoring New Jerusalem and Soche churches. The school was until the 1980s the only formal school for young children provided for by BACOMA churches. She was a teacher because of her ability to converse in English.

Leadership Role

Galatiya was one of the Africans who the Baptist Mission missionaries included in much of the planning of the mission in the early days. But later, the BMIM stopped listening to Malawian opinions seriously that led to Malawians deciding to constitute their own organization apart from and independent of BMIM. Almost all the BMIM missionaries felt they had the right to make decisions on behalf of the Malawian Christians. But that began to change with the arrival of a few Malawians, such as Stephen Galatiya, who had some theological training and foreign African influence. Stephen Galatiya was among the first group of registered trustees of BACOMA.

The real beginning of *Umodzi wa Amayi Abaptist aku Malawi* commonly known as *Umodzi wa Amayi* can be traced back to the assembly of Convention Baptist women that was organized as part of the leadership-training programme held on 8 May 1967 at the Falls Estate Bible School campus.[34] The organization of WMU in Malawi was to a greater extent a result of the influence of *matchona* wives that included Mary Galatiya. The first national leadership also included Mary Galatiya as the treasurer. The others were Elizabeth Phiri,[35] chairperson, and Hilda Mallungo as secretary.

---

[33] Rachel NyaGondwe Banda, *Women of Bible and Culture: Baptist Convention women in Southern Malawi*, Zomba: Kachere, 2005, p. 26.

[34] Maina a Azimai omwe Anadzachita Msonkhano pa Bible School, 8 May 1967, p.1.

[35] In 1971, Elizabeth Phiri and her husband, pastor MacFerron Njolomole Phiri, became the first BACOMA home missionary to the Northern Region where they founded the first BACOMA local church and latter pastored Mzuzu church. During the 1977 Baptist Women's Union of Africa (BWUA) conference held in Blantyre,

Representation in Different Forums

In 1967, two years after he had come out of seminary, Stephen Galatiya preached at an All Africa Baptist Fellowship (AABF) assembly. In 1974, Stephen Galatiya was part of the BACOMA leadership that participated in the training of national leaders from different countries at Arusha Baptist Training Centre, Tanzania. The other members were Njolomole Phiri and D.J. Makhaya. With Bamusi P. Kanowa and Samuel Malabwanya, Stephen Galatiya together with his wife, Mary, also attended the Baptist World Alliance in Canada representing BACOMA. Throughout his ministry, Stephen Galatiya represented the Convention in relationship discussions between BACOMA and BMIM.

Retirement

After he retired from active ministry, Stephen and Mary Galatiya settled at Senzani in Ntcheu District where several churches were organized as a result. Stephen Galatiya is one individual who is credited with the establishment of churches that later became the Baptist Convention of Malawi (BACOMA), an independent and Malawian Baptist Convention different from the American Southern Baptist Convention (SBC.

McDonald W. and Agnes Kaduya

Another family instrumental in the beginning and development of Convention work was that of McDonald W. Kaduya,[36] and his wife, Agnes, a Tswana from Francistown in Botswana, who made their home at Baluwa

---

Elizabeth Phiri was elected vice-president of BWUA for another term of five years. Elizabeth Phiri ministered alongside her husband who was the pastor of Mzuzu Baptist Church until the middle of the 1980 when they separated. Hilda Mallungo was also a pastor's wife. She was married to William Mallungo who was a director of the Baptist Bible School in Lilongwe. During the late 1980s. Hilda Mallungo taught spouses of the Bible School students who attended two-week programmes at the Bible School. Later, Hilda Mallungo and her husband pastored Mtendere Baptist Church in Area 25 in Lilongwe. She lost her husband in 1996, but has remained a member of Mtendere church.

[36] There is no direct relationship to the Kaduya of the Chilembwe Rising, but both men came from the same district and both lived close to Mbombwe Mission.

Village in Chiradzulu District. Kaduya met Agnes in Harare where she lived with her parents. They were members of the Baptist Convention of Zimbabwe congregation at Chitungwiza near Harare. Kaduya became a Baptist while living in Harare where he worked. Rev Isaac Chigede officiated Kaduya and Agnes' wedding at Chitungwiza. They left for Malawi around 1960.[37]

The Kaduya family was determined to start a Baptist congregation at Baluwa Village, about 22 km east of the PIM Mission in Mbombwe. I doubt whether they knew that PIM was Baptist, too. They shared the Gospel with their relatives and friends as they went about their daily work. Soon a group was gathered, which met for Bible study and worship. The Kaduyas contacted and asked SBC missionaries for help when they heard that the missionaries were in the neighbourhood. The Westers, later the Kingsleys, made several visits to Baluwa.[38] The missionaries later baptized all. Sometime in 1961 the BMCA hired Kaduya to work with Gene Kingsley in translation work in Blantyre.

At the end of 1962 there were ten baptized BACOMA Baptists in the village. Eight more were baptized on 17 February the following year. Under Kaduya's leadership and preaching, Sunday school and women's meetings were being held in the village. The fellowship met in a sun-dried brick and grass thatched building. The Mission spent approximately US$ 21.25 toward the cost of building the structure.[39] The church building at Baluwa was dedicated in the afternoon of 16 June 1963.

Evangelism Involvement

Agnes Kaduya began women's work at Baluwa village. During the 1970s crusade, Agnes Kaduya shared the Gospel with her relatives, friends and neighbours.[40] She was assisted by a couple of other women who were

---

[37] Hany Longwe, *Christians by Grace – Baptists by Choice*, p. 36.

[38] Int. Christopher Chimtengo, deacon, Baluwa 1 Village, Chiradzulu, 9.4.2002.

[39] Baptist Mission of Central Africa Annual Report, Gweru, April 1963, p. 6.

[40] For more detils on the crusade, see Hany Longwe, *Christians by Grace – Baptists by Choice*, p. 74ff.

already members of Baluwa Baptist Church, the first BACOMA church in Chiradzulu District. Like other women leaders, Agnes Kaduya played a key role not only in the development of *Umodzi wa Amayi*, in Southern Malawi, but also in BACOMA as a whole.[41]

Leadership Roles

McDonald Kaduya was one of the earliest lay people to begin and shepherd a local BACOMA church in Chiradzulu. Though he was doing the work of a pastor, he understood himself as an evangelist from the time he began ministering under Chigede in Harare.[42] He preached and led the congregation in the absence of a pastor. As an evangelist, McDonald Kaduya felt he could not baptize or lead in the celebration of Holy Communion; instead he called missionaries from Blantyre to administer the sacraments. It was after he had attended a five-month course at the Bible School in Lilongwe that McDonald Kaduya was comfortable to be called pastor, and was able, therefore, to administer the sacraments.

From 1 to 11 August 1972, Agnes Kaduya was among women leaders from 17 countries who attended the Baptist Women's Union of Africa (BWUA) Conference in Blantyre. Presiding over the conference whose theme was "Make Christ Known," was Joan Nyathi of Zimbabwe, President of the Baptist Women's Union of Africa.[43] One of the international dignitaries was Victoria Tolbert, wife of the then President of Liberia.[44] Agnes Kaduya's participation was as a result of her having had international exposure as well as fluency in English that was the medium of communication.

Agnes Kaduya continued to lead the Baluwa church after the death of her husband. The membership of the church recognized her as a gifted leader

---

[41] Hany Longwe, *Christians by Grace – Baptists by Choice*, p. 260.

[42] Int. Agnes Kaduya, Baluwa, Chiradzulu, 9.4.2002.

[43] *The Times*, 27.3.1972. To call Nyathi "President" was a bold move. Apart from the restriction, the foreign women were required to observe Malawi's dress code as it applied to women. Their dresses were to be long enough to cover their kneecaps.

[44] Both Tolberts were active Baptists in their home country, and Victoria Tolbert's husband was one of several Baptist World Alliance vice-presidents until he was ousted from power in Liberia and murdered.

who had ministered alongside her husband when he was alive. Though they did not call her 'pastor', she was the pastor of the church. She preached during Sunday services, and taught during leadership training sessions. She had a team of deacons who included women.[45] There could have been a very small minority that did not feel happy with a woman leading the church. The advantage was the she continued to live in the family's own house in Buluwa village close to where the church was. In addition, she did not lose any property. That in itself did not put strain on the church's meagre resources.

J.M. and Helen Ng'oma

This family can be called "Priscila and Aquila" of BACOMA because Helen outclassed her husband in terms of their contribution to the development of BACOMA. Very few people in BACOMA knew Mr. Ng'oma. The couple first appeared on the scene in relation to the early life of Jerusalem Church. Through the witness of Stephen Galatiya, J.M. Ng'oma, a Tonga *mtchona*, who was a Presbyterian and Helen, a Suthu, an Anglican rededicated their lives to Jesus Christ. Stephen Galatiya baptized them and they became members of Jerusalem Baptist Church, to which the Ng'omas had early given the name "Jerusalem Gospel Hall" before people settled for Jerusalem Baptist Church. The naming of the new church was an early sign of the leadership role the Ng'omas were to play.

Later the Ng'omas moved from Yiannakis to Zingwangwa where they had built a house. It then became difficult for the Ng'omas to travel to Jerusalem Church from Zingwangwa. They then decided to move their membership to Soche Baptist Church at a time when Stephen and Mary Galatiya pastored Soche and Jerusalem churches.[46]

Since the death of her husband in 2005, Helen Ng'oma lives in Blantyre with one of her sons, Mabvuto. She is a member of Soche Baptist Church, and a *mlangizi* (counsellor) for women and girls. She regularly attends

---

[45] Int. Joyce Tenewa, member, Baluwa Baptist Church, Chiradzulu, 9.4.2002.
[46] Int. Helen Ng'oma, Lilongwe, 1998.

Umodzi wa Amayi a Baptist meetings in Blantyre. She no longer attends meetings far from Blantyre because of her age.

Church Planters

One woman that has been instrumental in beginning churches in the three regions is Helen Ng'oma. She was instrumental in beginning Lilongwe, Ntcheu and Mzimba. She was involved in these places because of work transfers of her husband who worked for Southern Bottlers.[47]

The Ng'omas were instrumental in the establishment of a BACOMA church in Area 25 in Lilongwe City after they arrived in 1973 from Blantyre. The Ng'omas prayed in their home asking God to help them start a church in the area, and they opened their home for a church to meet there. For that to happen, they began witnessing to people close to them and later to those they met as they went about doing their daily business.

Though they struggled to speak good Chichewa, both Ng'omas were outgoing and very vocal, and could not stop at anything less than convincing some to think their way. So they started meeting outside their home but within their yard. That did not solve the problem either. As the group got bigger, they chose to meet under the shade of a mango tree not far from their home. The gathering attracted more people and the church grew, but not all the people in Area 25 were happy with that.

One leader of one of the denominations in Area 25 falsely accused the Ng'omas of stealing members from other churches. Immediately the Ng'omas were summoned to the Malawi Congress Party (MCP) office in the area and warned of the repercussions of their deeds. In effect they told the Ng'omas to stop meeting for prayer altogether. This anti-Baptist church leader was determined to see Helen Ng'oma deported to South Africa. He almost convinced the MCP official. The official did not make mention of her husband being banished to Nkhata Bay. Helen Ng'oma was more threatening than her husband because she spent much of her day witnessing

---

[47] Hany Longwe, *Christians by Grace – Baptists by Choice*, p. 267.

for Jesus while her husband was at work. In fact, she was the evangelist and church planter, and the husband helped when he was free.

Representative from BACOMA and the BMIM met with a senior MCP officer at the request of the Ng'omas. The District Party Chairman found out that the story was false and he warned the accuser for trying to disrupt the peace and religious freedom that existed in the country. The accuser asked for forgiveness, instead. That encounter led to more professions of faith in Jesus Christ.

A house was bought from a Mr. Nyirenda, and it was used as a church building. The congregation decided once more to meet in the open because the building was not big enough to accommodate all who came to church. They met in the open under the shade of a tree near the Area 25 market.

In 1977 the Ng'omas returned to Blantyre at a time when Area 25 church had called Mallungo as caretaker pastor because he had a fulltime job as the Director of Bible Way Correspondence School. In 1983 Area 25 Baptist Church bought a piece of land from the Lilongwe City Council and constructed a church building on it which they finished in 1986. In the same year the church called Mallungo to be its pastor, and he resigned from being the Director of Bible Way. The church also changed its name from Area 25 to Mtendere Baptist Church. The guest of honour at the dedication ceremony of Mtendere church was none other than Helen Ng'oma. In her speech Helen Ng'oma encouraged the members to spend more time on their knees than on their feet for it was power, the Christian's lifeline. Soon, Mtendere church opened new work at Chankungu, Mvera 1 and 2 in Dowa District, and Sinai at Mtandire near Area 47. The only church that more or less died was Sinai, which was later revived in 1997 under the name of Lingadzi Baptist Church.

Leadership Involvement

Helen Ng'oma was one of the earliest lay leaders who impacted the *Umodzi wa Amayi* as well as BACOMA as a whole. She was the one who introduced the idea of women's uniform in BACOMA. She said it was good and it showed women's unity; the uniform identified them as having come from one country at international meetings. Wearing uniforms was not a way for women to show off. According to Helen Ng'oma, since other WMU groups in Africa had uniforms, there was no reason for Malawian WMU not to do likewise.[48]

Helen Ng'oma also attended the Baptist Women's Union of Africa (BWUA) Conference that was held in Blantyre from 1 to 11 August 1972. It was made possible by the fact that she was one of the few leaders in *Umodzi wa Amayi* who would benefit from a meeting that was held in English.

The National Youth Committee (NYC) met for the first time at the Baptist Bible School in special sessions during the annual assembly of BACOMA. Helen Ng'oma was chosen a committee member representing the Southern Region, whilst Kapalamula Banda represented Central Region and Wilton Phiri, the Northern Region.

Helen Ng'oma was a founding member of *Umodzi wa Amayi*, a very active and forceful national leader not only for the youth group and women's guild, but also for the Baptist Convention of Malawi.

Timothy W. Kandawe – Minister to the Vulnerable Groups

Timothy Kandawe was married to a Zimbabwean woman. They became Baptists through the evangelism efforts of Stephen Galatiya. Timothy and his wife are remembered for their ministry to vulnerable groups such as refugees and farm workers. BACOMA was involved in meeting the needs of all people according to the Great Commission.

BACOMA sent Timothy Kandawe as one of the home missionaries working amongst refugees in camps along the border in Dedza and Ntcheu districts. He preached and discipled refugees from Mozambique, not only for them to become Christians, but also to be witnesses of Christ when they returned to their country. A couple of these started Baptist churches in Mozambique when the war was over.[49]

---

[48] Hany Longwe, *Christians by Grace – Baptists by Choice*, p. 249.

[49] Hany Longwe, *Christians by Grace – Baptists by Choice*, pp. 212, 213.

Although there were not as many farms as there were in the South and the Central Regions, nowhere in Malawi was BACOMA encouraged by an outsider to reach out to farm workers other than in the Northern Region. BACOMA heard the cry and responded by sending Timothy Kandawe. He did not endure farm life and under two years he was out of the area.[50] The South African manager as well did not stay long; he did not leave on his own accord as Kandawe did, instead he was dismissed. The church on the farm sooner or later stopped meeting.[51] Nonetheless, the time Kandawe was on the farm, BACOMA was able to minister to some of the vulnerable people in Malawi, and gave hope to many who were being oppressed

Conclusion

Though few, the *matchona* found in BACOMA have been very influential in the early history of the Convention. They were able to link up with the missionaries and served well as interpreters and associates in establishing the first BACOMA churches. Instead of developing English speaking churches, the *matchona* introduced Chewa speaking churches that has made BACOMA remain a rural type church though it also has churches in cities and towns. The *matchona* contributed in making BACOMA an organization of Malawian Baptist churches distinct from the American Southern Baptist Convention.

---

[50] Int. Timothy W. Kandawe, pastor, Lilongwe, 29.8.1997.

[51] Int. Gary K. Swafford, former SBC missionary to Malawi, Montgomery, Alabama, 17.10.2001.

Chapter 6

Kusadziwa Nkufa Komwe: The Baptist Theological Seminary of Malawi Fighting against HIV/AIDS[1]

"*Kusadziwa nkufa komwe*" (Lack of knowledge is death), said one of the Baptist Theological Seminary of Malawi (BTSM) students after he had noticed the quick change in his health after a long time he had struggled to get better to no avail. It was as if he was comparing himself with the man who had been sitting for over 38 at the pool of Bethsaida not knowing when he would be healed, or the woman who had been subject to bleeding for twelve years and had spent all she had. In both cases it was until Jesus came onto the scene that both were healed. It is written, "Then you will know the truth, and the truth will set you free" (Jn 8:32). Malawi has been struggling with the HIV/AIDS pandemic which was shrouded with stigma and discrimination. Information is not power until it is applied. When Malawi became a multi-party democracy freedom of speech was re-established that created a more liberal climate in which HIV/AIDS education could be carried out without fear of persecution. However, by this point HIV/AIDS had already damaged Malawi's social and economic infrastructure.

This article is an attempt to set the record straight on BTSM's contribution to the national fight against the HIV/AIDS epidemic which was the leading cause of death amongst adults and the major factor in the country's low life expectancy which stood at 38.5 in 2005. The Baptist Seminary understood HIV/AIDS education as critical to preventing the spread of the epidemic, that it also played a vital role in reducing stigma and discrimination. Both the Board of Governors and the seminary argued that there was no reason for anyone to die when drugs and other help were available.

---

[1] For the purposes of anonymity and confidentiality, no names of the affected and infected are mentioned in this article.

The Beginning of the Fight

By the time I became the principal of the Baptist seminary in Lilongwe in 1998, I had lost several members from my extended family, many of whom were young breadwinners who had died in mysterious ways. People could not openly talk about the cause because of the stigma and discrimination associated with it. One of the biggest challenges that Malawi faced at the time was the lack of human resources available within the country. Although the shortage of medical staff in Malawi had partly been caused by factors such as emigration and a lack of access to education, it was also directly aggravated by HIV/AIDS, as was the case in all other sectors of Malawi's workforce that included Lilongwe seminary students. HIV was a taboo subject in many communities; stigma and discrimination were common. As a result, few people living with HIV/AIDS made known their status; many had difficulty discussing the subject with their families, and some support groups did not meet openly. I was determined to see BTSM change that amongst its staff and students, and the surrounding community.

Neither I nor any member of the teaching staff at BTSM had had training in HIV/AIDS. Thank God that the Evangelical Association of Malawi (EAM), who was renting some office space on the BTSM campus, had an HIV/AIDS programme going on. I approached the General Secretary, Francis Mkandawire, who was very willing to help the seminary. He led me to Howard Kasiya, HIV & AIDS Programme Manager, who gave me some of the notes they had, and I sat down and planned a tentative course to suit the students' course load. Some students and teaching members of staff thought that I had lost sense of direction by introducing a course, "Understanding HIV/AIDS and Counselling," which was later called, "Biblical Approach to HIV/AIDS." It was a course some students did not want, and if they had the choice, they would not have attended such classes.[2] The problem was, it was a must for all students.

---

[2] Cesar Nkhoma, BTSM 4th Year Student, Christ Saves and Loves: Dowa Baptist Church - The Steps of Ladder (Achievement), Report, Baptist Theological Seminary of Malawi, February 2006.

When we started, I taught the facts about HIV/AIDS, and Kasiya taught the medical side of it because of his background. Through teaching I was also learning and making decisions as to the way forward for not only the students, but also for the staff, myself, my family and immediate community. I consulted the EAM notes and the internet for up-to-date research results and developments in information and treatment. An introduction course looked something like this:

HIV/AIDS MODULE 1: FACTS ABOUT HIV&AIDS

Aim of the module

To provide the student with facts about HIV&AIDS in wholistic and gender sensitive approaches that will enable them understand the disease process to appreciate the nature of the epidemic.

Learning objectives

By the end of each module, the students should be able to:

1. Define AIDS
2. Discuss causative agents
3. Discuss modes of transmission
4. Discuss immunity
5. Discuss cell destruction
6. Discuss stages of HIV infection and development of AIDS
7. Discuss signs and symptoms of AIDS
8. Discuss cultural and socio-economic factors impounding on HIV&AIDS
9. Impact of HIV&AIDS on humankind
10. Identify signs and symptoms of HIV&AIDS
11. Discuss management of HIV&AIDS
12. Describe HIV&AIDS prevention
13. Describe the relationship between Sexually Transmitted Infections (STIs) and HIV&AIDS
14. Examine some issues in a culture sensitive pastoral care

The last module, number 15, was the Ministry of Hope to Persons Infected and Affected with HIV/AIDS through pastoral care and counselling.

The other source of support for BTSM to teach the HIV/AIDS course was help from World Relief in Malawi in partnership with the Malawi Council of Churches (MCC) in Lilongwe. After I approached these organizations and told them of what the BTSM was doing, they provided the seminary with some teaching materials.

Later, the Malawi Interfaith Aids Association (MIAA) was also involved in one way or another. In 2003, on behalf of the BACOMA leadership, Molly Longwe and I attended in Johannesburg a World Vision Southern Africa Sub-Region leadership conference whose theme was: "The Church and Poverty, HIV/AIDS, Gender Issues, Peace and Reconciliation." In 2004, I participated in a seminar: "Mainstreaming HIV/AIDS," which World Relief in Malawi in partnership with the World Council of Churches (WCC) through the Malawi Council of Churches (MCC) organized in Lilongwe. And in 2007, I attended another seminar on "HIV/AIDS Counselling "that the Ecumenical Counselling Centre (ECC) in Lilongwe organized. In his official opening speeches at two separate HIV &AIDS training workshops, the General Secretary of the Malawi Council of Churches, Canaan R.K. Phiri,[3] argued that it was unfortunate that it was the Government of Malawi inviting the Church to join them in the fight against HIV&AIDS, instead of the Church inviting the Government. From the Bible, helping people is not an option, he emphasized, but the duty of every follower of Jesus Christ. The Church has no option of choosing whether or not to talk about HIV&AIDS or to counsel People Living with AIDS (PLWA). The training programmes organized by World Relief Malawi (WRM), the Ecumenical Counseling Centre (ECC), Malawi Council of Churches (MCC), Fellowship of Christian Councils in Southern Africa (FOCCISA), and other faith organizations, were to equip churches with knowledge and skills to help those in need.[4]

During the course of my leadership of the seminary, I also attended several seminars organized by MIAA and the MCC that helped me more in understanding and teaching of HIV/AIDS. I did not only understand and

---

[3] An HIV&AIDS Counseling Training organized by Ecumenical Counselling Center (ECC) at Msamba Catholic Parish, 1-6.10.2007; and HIV&AIDS Coordinators Training organized by FOCCISA-NORDIC Cooperation for member churches at Natural Resources College (NRC), Lilongwe, 15.10.2007.

[4] Canaan R.K. Phiri, Official Opening Speech, HIV&AIDS Counseling Training organized by Ecumenical Counselling Center (ECC) Msamba and NRC, Lilongwe.

teach, but I also challenged students and staff to know that no one was safe; therefore, all needed to do something about it.

Positive Developments

The first thing I and my wife, Molly, did was to lead in voluntary counselling and testing. I encouraged every staff member to go to the nearest counselling and testing centre on a regular basis, which might have been as little as twice a year if one had no symptoms and were coping well, or more frequently - perhaps four times a year if symptoms had started and antiretroviral treatment was being taken, or as frequently as required when very ill, daily or weekly. There was a lot of fear and anxiety amongst the BTSM family when it came to voluntary counselling and testing, especially at the beginning of the exercise. But later, members could easily talk about it. The second thing I did was to support those infected or affected. I encouraged students to talk to me individually in confidence and it was my duty to see to it that they got the necessary help they needed at the seminary and even after they had left the seminary. For some, I was able to follow them, and for others, we kept in touch through mail and connecting them to some support groups.

The Seminary Board of Governors also encouraged the institution to have all staff and students tested for HIV&AIDS so that appropriate assistance could be given. In one of his devotions during their meetings, the then Board Chair read from Job 23:17. He said that he read the book from the background of suffering – not justified or deserved suffering. People ask why they were suffering. He said he used the book to help people who were suffering. Though at the end Job met with God, he did not get the answer why he was suffering, instead God justified him. His friends were reprimanded by God. Verse 17 impressed the Chairperson more. He said there were times when we are covered by darkness.[5]

This was so frequent in Malawi – HIV/AIDS was an example of the times that people were living in. A faithful wife is found to be HIV positive by virtue of being married. In these circumstances people needed to help the

---

[5] Klaus Fiedler, Chairperson Board of Governors, Baptist Theological Seminary of Malawi, Meeting Minutes, Lilongwe, 9.7.2006.

woman not to succumb to the darkness. Being infected with HIV/AIDS might seem like a curse or a punishment from God, or a betrayal by a person one cared for or a pure bad luck that befell one. However terrible it might feel, God's grace and power may turn this darkness into light, this dying into a new life.[6] Job with all the theology thrown at him knew God would see him through. *Kusadziwa nkufa komwe* (Lack of knowledge is as being dead), and the opposite is true.

In the process of making known what the BTSM was doing, we developed partnerships that made BTSM's efforts productive. Staff members at the Light House at the Kamuzu Central Hospital were very helpful. Later, I developed another partnership with Partners in Hope in Lilongwe, which was under the leadership of Dr Perry Jensen, then a fellow church member of Capital City Baptist Church (CCBC). Another partnership that was to prove to be the strongest was between BTSM and Lydia Project, led by Rachel NyaGondwe Fiedler, which was committed to participating in the fight against HIV&AIDS in several ways. Not only did Lydia Project offer moral support, but also financial support that covered medical and transportation bills mainly for students.

The Seminary Concern for the Community

BTSM was not there for the BTSM family only. The seminary had concern for the community, too. Through a student, BTSM attended to a woman in Area 24 who was infected and needed help. I was able to encourage her to receive medical attention at the Light House when at that time it was at the old "Bottom" (later Bwaila) Hospital. Though she did not at first accept that she was infected, she agreed to be taken to hospital. She did not live long, but the family felt loved and cared for throughout her days of infection. To date, the family members view me as a brother and friend in need as a result of BTSM's involvement.

Another example of BTSM's concern for people living with and those affected by HIV/AIDS was when BTSM was introduced to my friend's

---

[6] From Baptist Theological Seminary, "Ministry of Hope to Persons Infected and Affected with HIV & AIDS" module, 2005.

extended family member in Area 36 who for some time refused to receive medical help, and the wife felt hopeless and was looking to the day she and her young child who was a couple of years old would die. She felt that she had been infected through sexual intercourse with her husband of which she had no proof, and the child through mother to child transmission of which she had no proof either. It was very difficult to convince both to get professional help and proof for the infection. When they finally did, it was only the husband who had been infected and not the wife and the child. After a number of visits to the hospital, the man was able to work and support his family. Joy and happiness returned in this family.

One involvement that made me more determined to be involved in the fight against HIV/AIDS was the death of one of my close relatives. Earlier, he had come to the seminary and took me aside where he told me that he was infected. I did not say anything apart from saying, "I see." I tried by all means not to show that I was shocked. The goodness is that he did not blame himself or others for having contracted the infection or for having infected others. Since he had admitted that he was infected, I needed to bring hope to him. The following day, I took him to the Light House at the Central Hospital. It was a time when people infected were put on antiretroviral drugs (ARV only when the health care personnel had verified that the person's CD4 cell count had reached the recommended (low) level to start treatment at the same time when the drugs were hard to come by, and if they were available, one had to buy.

My close relative was told to wait, and in a couple of months his situation deteriorated and my wife and I took him to the hospital early one morning. He was admitted and before lunch time, he died. After burial, I talked to his wife who seemed to have known that she too was infected as a result of having sexual intercourse with her husband. I took her to the African Bible College (ABC) clinic where they diagnosed her positive and that it was full blown AIDS. She received her first treatment there and then and I paid for it. She lived in our home for a few months during which time I regularly took her to the clinic for checkups. For every visit I had to pay for consultations and medication. Once she was ready to resume work, she went to live with her children in their family home. She has been able to work and not only provide financial support for her children, but also leadership.

Two other cases of interest involved two service providers to BTSM who were young professionals. The first one showed signs of infection, and I challenged the artisan to seek help from the hospital and I was prepared to pay for the cost incurred therein. The more I talked to the artisan about HIV/AIDS, the more he denied and remained stubborn, until he could not stand the challenge. The last thing I heard was that he had been admitted at the central hospital. I visited and encouraged him in hospital several times. His health deteriorated very fast and within two weeks, he died.

The other service provider had a sore on one foot. I noticed that the artisan did not wear closed shoes even when it was cold that one needed to wear closed shoes to keep oneself warm. I asked about the wound, and the artisan said it could not be healed. He had been to several healthcare providers, and none could solve the problem. I offered to take the artisan to a hospital that I trusted would heal the sore, and I was also going to clear the medical bills until that wound disappeared. Thank God, the artisan agreed and we went to Partners in Hope. The hospital found out that the artisan was HIV positive, but the HIV had not developed into AIDS yet. I paid for the treatment as promised until the wound had disappeared. The artisan continued to give professional services to the seminary, of which the seminary was very grateful. A close relationship was fostered as a result such that sometimes the work was done for free especially when there were no material costs involved.

Seminary Concern for its Students

In 2010, a seminary student was ill and was on medication at home outside of Lilongwe and, was expected to resume classes from September 2011 if the student's health improved. The student did not however turn up in 2011. Instead, I heard that the student's health was deteriorating drastically. I drove to the student's home. The mother welcomed me with tears on her cheeks. She was convinced that our student was going to die. I encouraged her to look to God the giver of life, and to the human efforts of dealing with the pandemic. The student had swollen stomach and feet and could not stand up and walk without extra help. The student had been instructed not to eat *nsima* (hard porridge from maize flower) which is Malawi's most popular staple food. I immediately asked the mother for permission to take the student to Lilongwe, and it was granted.

I took the student straight to Partners in Hope where the doctors instructed the student to stop taking any drugs the student had been receiving from the district AIDS programme, and to eat *nsima* and a lot of vegetables and fruits. The doctors gave the student antibiotics instead, and a date for the next appointment. I drove the student back. For the following weeks I kept in touch with the student through the phone. In the meantime, I arranged with a friend at the district hospital to transfer the student's medical records to Partners in Hope, and that was done. When the appointed date was close, the student told me that there was no need for me to go and pick the student, for the student was well enough to travel by the local bus. I agreed and the student arrived at the seminary walking slowly. Only the feet were still swollen. We went back to Partners in Hope for a review. The doctors were very happy with the progress, and were able to prescribe different retroviral drugs plus TB drugs which were to be deposited at a nearest hospital from where the student's TB would be monitored on behalf of Partners in Hope. Within three months, the student was able to walk and eat well such that the student managed to attend the remaining class terms and later graduated. By 2015, the virus was under control and the student could enjoy every aspect of a normal life.

One student had shingles and I challenged him to have his immune system checked, but he refused. I told him point blank that from what I had learnt it was a sign of HIV. He accused me of condemning him of having been unfaithful to his wife. Instead, I assured him that it was because of my love for him as I loved myself. I did not want to see both him and his family suffer. Nevertheless, he did not heed my counsel. A few months after he had left the seminary, he sent me a message that he was in hospital suffering from TB and that his heart was swelling. I drove immediately to see him. A few days later he asked me to provide a vehicle to take him to a specialist hospital. Instead of going alone to pick him, I drove with another pastor friend from Lilongwe, and we took him and his wife to the hospital.

When we arrived at the reception centre, the nurse on duty requested that she be left alone with our former student and his wife. The reception area was surrounded by clear glass panels. My pastor friend could read lip-language since he had some experience in sign language. Where we sat, we could see the three. She asked our former student and my friend told me that she had asked whether he had been tested for HIV, and he answered, no. She told him that that was the first thing to do. After about 15 or so minutes, she told him and his wife that he was HIV positive, and she advised the wife to be tested also after helping the husband. Then she called us to wheel him into a side ward close to the reception, and we did. Whilst in the room, without us asking him or the wife, he revealed what had transpired and that he was discovered to be HIV positive.

We encouraged the wife to go to the reception and have her blood tested. For almost ten minutes she refused saying she was all right. Anyway, she went and came back saying she was also HIV positive, but her immune system was still in good shape. She was told to look after herself but continue to report to the hospital in her area for regular tests so as to keep track of her health status. We were very happy and told her that that was the way to go, to know and make informed decisions. The two lived for several years, but he succumbed to the pandemic. The wife lived on with HIV.

In 2012, another student confided in me that he and his wife were both HIV positive, and I made sure that he received the support he needed while at the seminary. During the course of his studies, he looked pale and continued to miss some classes. Before coming to the seminary, his sister had taken him to a number of hospitals and well-known doctors in his home district, but to no avail. Several hospitals tested him for TB but the results were negative. I offered to take him to where I knew results would be good. He immediately agreed. He said he agreed because he had seen my concern and love for the students' welfare. I took him to Partners in Hope, and immediately the doctor told us that he suspected that the student had TB and he gave him medication to start taking immediately. After three weeks he felt a big change in his health. After six months of taking TB drugs, his health had been restored. They stopped him from taking the ARVs until further notice. In a few days, his health had improved.

We went back to the hospital according to the appointment. The doctor told the student that he was happy with the improvement in his health, and that he wanted him to go back on to the ARVs as he continued taking TB drugs. As we walked towards the seminary vehicle, the student with a broad smile on his face looked at me and said, "*Kusadziwa nkufa komwe.*" I asked what he meant and he said one could die when help was around just because one did not have the right information to act upon. He asked me to look at how long it had taken him to know that he had TB and his health continued to deteriorate in spite of visiting many hospitals. Then he said the truth was that he was now free to continue with his studies and life since he knew the truth and had hope to live for many more years serving God. He would not want anyone to die because of ignorance. I assured him that he was going to live. The other thing to note, I said, was that people were still learning and researching about HIV/AIDS and no one was really an expert, only God was. But, thank God that he had put knowledge in some and that people were beginning to enjoy positive lives and long life.

If that was not enough, he came back sometime later in the year and told me that he wanted to remarry. His first wife had died some years back. He told me that the woman he wanted to marry was also positive. Calmly, I told him I was behind him. I asked him if she knew he was also positive. "Yes," he said. I arranged that we sought some health advice from the Light House. We went and we had good and fruitful discussions. When his fiancée visited the seminary, I asked her of the marriage and she looked forward to it. She understood what she was entering into. She had enough information and she believed in the success of their relation, and when God would give them a baby, it was her prayer that the baby would be HIV free. The marriage took place; later they had a baby free of HIV. The family continued to serve in their local and surrounding churches. I have been in touch with them, especially the man, on a regular basis. They knew the truth and the truth saved them.

Conclusion

The responsibility for bringing people to know Jesus Christ as Lord and Saviour, and serving human needs are inseparable. Evangelism and service to humanity linked together, give a strong witness in which the love of Jesus Christ is made evident. The Baptist Theological Seminary not only preached but lived the Word and brought hope to those in desperate struggles for life.

It is the Church's responsibility to be a healing community. As a result, the government is there to compliment the Church's efforts. God challenged the Church, and not the government on our response to HIV&AIDS. The real evidence of our faith and belief is the way we act. According to Ezekiel 34:1-10; God criticized the leaders for taking care of themselves rather than taking care of their people. Everyone must be careful not to pursue self-development at the expense of PLWA and their loved ones. No family in Malawi could claim to be unaffected by HIV&AIDS. One can safely say the Church in Malawi is sick. As a result, no Christian can look aside and say it is their business and not mine. No single Malawian should die when help is available.

Chapter 7

Achewa Providence Industrial Mission: African Independent Church or Baptist?

One Baptist strand that contributed to the development of the Baptist - Convention of Malawi (BACOMA) can be traced back to John Chilembwe through the Achewa Providence Industrial Mission (APIM) and Peter Kalemba, probably one outstanding follower apart from Daniel Sharpe Malikebu, who passed on Chilembwe's legacy. Kalemba and Malikebu worked together for some time, but later went their separate ways. Both men were Baptists as were the churches they led. In partnership with Southern Baptist Convention (SBC missionaries, Achewa PIM became the backbone of the founding and development of BACOMA congregations first in Lilongwe District, and second, in other parts of the Central and Southern Regions of the country, although eventually the two bodies continued separately.[1]

Peter Kalemba and Achewa PIM

Pete Kalemba was the first PIM convert from Mangoni. He attended PIM School under Chilembwe at almost the same time as Daniel Malikebu. After finishing school, he was employed in one of the shops in Chiradzulu and he attended church at the Mission. During that period, he became a prominent and trusted member of the Church. Kalemba was aware of Chilembwe's opposition to foreign rule and of the preparations for the 1915 Rising.

Sometime before the Rising, Chilembwe ordered Kalemba, and Anderson Nyangu, the second convert from Mangoni, to leave Mbombwe and escape to Mangoni so that Kalemba would be the head of the church. By preserving one of his own trusted products, Chilembwe believed that the future of PIM was secured no matter what was to become of him and the

---

[1] Hany Longwe, *Christians by Grace – Baptists by Choice*, p. 31.

Mission. Sometime in October 1914 Kalemba and Nyangu arrived at Kalumbu south east outside Lilongwe City.[2]

One of the major results of Chilembwe's opposition to colonialism and the 1915 Rising was the establishment of PIM, a Baptist church, in Mangoni.[3] As a result of the 1915 Rising, Kalemba was imprisoned and harassed and later released. He was identified with PIM which was labeled as "the warring church" because of the Chilembwe Rising. Those who were interested in the teaching of PIM met with Kalemba in their homes at night. Those who attended the meetings became *uthenga* (the communication) to others in the neighbourhood. The human communication spread into several villages across Diamphwe River into Dedza.[4] *Mpingo wa Mpatuko* (Church of deviation) as it was nicknamed, the PIM in Mangoni grew when it was free to meet and worship openly during the day. Through Kalemba, Chilembwe was successful in spreading his nets for both educated and uneducated converts outside the Yao and Lomwe tribes. In spite of the lifting of the ban on church meetings by the government in 1924, both black and white people were still suspicious of African-led and other small churches. Until very recently, Chilembwe's church in Mangoni was called Mpingo wa Mpatuko.[5]

In 1926, Malikebu visited Mangoni and baptized many of the Mangoni PIM members. No young person was baptized during this first baptism by PIM in Mangoni. Immediately Malikebu was recognized as the head of the church both in Chiradzulu and Mangoni. In 1927 another group of converts were baptized, followed by another in 1928 where Malikebu baptized three hundred candidates in a dug-out *chitsime* (pool) in one day at Kalumbu. That was as a result of the introduction of a Bible School in which men systematically learnt the word of God through those who had had some training under Malikebu. Later baptisms saw young adults coming in. There was no question of baptizing young children. People were serious about

---

[2] Hany Longwe, *Identity by Dissociation – a History of the Achewa Providence Industrial Mission*, Mzuzu: Mzuni Press, 2013, pp. 11-12.

[3] Hany Longwe, *Identity by Dissociation*, p. 13.

[4] Ibid, p. 15.

[5] Ibid, p. 22.

conversion. Baptism was only for those who had made a decision to divert from the ordinary and join this strange church. Most children followed their parents. Baptism was by immersion and for regenerate church membership. Children were brought to Malikebu and he blessed them.[6]

Among the many things that happened in the five or so years of good working relationship that passed, was leadership training. The majority of men studied *ulaliki* (preaching), while several studied ministerial and teaching offices of the church. Not many, though, qualified and that had an impact on the church in Mangoni that was surrounded by other churches which provided training not only for all members, but also for leadership teams. As a result, the Mangoni church had to put its hopes in Chiradzulu. For efficient management and operation of PIM churches, Malikebu grouped them into sections, which were directly under the central church, New Jerusalem Baptist Church, the Mission. Congregations in Lilongwe/Dedza were designated as one section under Kalemba, but the mission did not support him financially.

Baptist Practice

This extreme centralization is a feature of PIM, but it contradicts worldwide Baptist principles.[7] It is also a feature of National Baptist Convention (NBC) Inc., with its history of strong presidents. The president serves as the chief executive officer, and over the years this office has acquired enormous power. The president almost singlehandedly controls the convention. Usually the presidents serve for life or until poor health sidelines them.[8] NBC is more centralized than SBC who are shaped and identified by their commitment to the autonomy of the local church.[9] SBC does realize, however, that as with all biblical principles, there is the potential for distortion and misapplication. The principle understood

---

[6] Hany Longwe, *Identity by Dissociation*, p. 26.

[7] H. Leon McBeth, *The Baptist Heritage: Four Centuries of Baptist Witness*, Nashville: Broadman, 1987, pp. 121-122.

[8] H. Leon Mcbeth, *Baptist Heritage*, pp. 786-787.

[9] Robert A. Baker, *A Baptist Source Book with Particular Reference to Southern Baptists*, Nashville: Broadman, 1966, p. 214.

correctly gives no justification for church teaching or practice that is unorthodox and destructive. Baptists have for long not found theological and/or historical support for ecclesiastical hierarchy. They contend that passages of Scripture suggest that God's design and intent for the local church was that it functions under the direct authority of God and without any outside authoritative ecclesiastical body. That is to say, the whole congregation: under the Lordship of Jesus Christ: has the final say over its life and affairs, including the appointment of its leaders. While the Bible depicts the local church as independent of outside human authority, it also presents evidence that God designed his church to function as part of a larger fellowship. Therefore, all churches are joined in the bond of Jesus Christ. Churches have the opportunity and obligation to relate to each other as partners on various levels. The core of Baptist heritage is the recognition of the Lord's authority over each autonomous local church. Baptist churches are ready to cooperate with other churches in broad ventures and to be accountable for biblical fidelity.[10] The churches in Mangoni had to come to terms with the centralized PIM practice though it was different from the general Baptist practice.

Mpingo wa Mpatuko Breaks Ties with Chiradzulu

Peter Kalemba saw his accomplishments in Mangoni as PIM achievements. He understood himself as a member of PIM, and therefore, a Baptist.[11] Throughout the years of his relationship with Mbombwe, Kalemba followed PIM church polity. He led the church in Mangoni under the leadership of Malikebu such that Kalemba had no final authority on certain issues such as church offerings and tithes. These had to go to Mbombwe without fail. This was not new to Kalemba, since he had learnt it from the Chilembwe era.

---

[10] Morris H. Chapman, president and chief executive officer of the Executive Committee, SBC, "Local Church Autonomy," *SBC Life*, December 1997, pp. 4-5.
[11] Int. Foulger Kafulatira, PIM Mangoni leader, Majondo, 21.5.1999.

Separation of APIM from PIM

In 1934, an opportunity came for APIM to challenge PIM church government. In 1935, Kalemba and his leadership team had a series of discussions with chiefs Mazengera and Kalumbu at which the issue of separation from PIM in Chiradzulu was discussed. Both parties later met with the District Commissioner (DC) of Lilongwe. Mpingo wa Mpatuko initially chose "Achewa" as its name but that was not accepted; they had to add PIM at the end of the name. This was deliberate on the part of the DC who wanted to remind Mpingo wa Mpatuko of their roots. On 19 October 1937 the Achewa (APIM) was registered by the Lilongwe DC who represented the government. Kalemba chose Nyanje as the site for APIM's central office.

Church Polity of Achewa PIM

The way Kalemba related to different ministries, the way they all functioned under APIM, and when they started, is not easy to understand. In general, it is agreed that the church polity was a result of experience, rather than of special study. Most of the time Kalemba made choices on the basis of what he thought Jesus or Chilembwe would have done in the same situation and in the light of what he thought the Bible taught. As *mtsogoleri* (the leader), Kalemba was looked to for leadership and guidance. He made the final decisions on matters pertaining to doctrine and practice. During that period, Aaron Kamkalamba emerged as *mtsogoleri wa chiwiri* (the second leader, or the second in command) because he proved himself a leader in his own right.

Baptist church polity in general supports servant leadership rather than authoritarian roles. It recognizes the importance of oversight of the community of believers, *episkope (utsogoleri)*, as a gift of Christ to his church for the care and discipline of the people of God. The community has both the responsibility and freedom under God to commission certain persons to fulfill particular aspects of *episkope*, especially the ministry of preaching, pastoral care and teaching. By calling Kalemba *mtsogoleri* and Kamkalamba, *mtsogoleri wa chiwiri*, APIM did not distinguish between the function of the two leaders. Both men were leaders, invested with *episkope*, which they fulfilled as servant leaders: a biblical challenge that is facing Christian leadership today.[12] Generally Baptists cannot justify in the light of Scripture the development of monarchical, metropolitan bishops, and archbishops or patriarchs, or any other forms of the episcopate, although some Baptist leaders, especially Black, have chosen to use "bishop" in place of "pastor."

Local Churches

Local churches began as home churches in which the members learnt worship of God, the importance and content of the Bible, and church membership. They were also taught some church history beginning with that of Chilembwe. Everyone needed to know that and tell others even if they were not members of APIM or PIM. People presented themselves for membership of APIM in a local church. Local churches were centres of fellowship and mutual support. They were viewed as *mpingo*, which meant a group of people with a common cause or calling. Although children were seen as part of the home and then the local church, Kalemba did not baptize them into membership: membership in APIM was officially open to adults only.[13] Baptists only baptize when an individual has made a personal confession of faith. It was risk taking for anyone to declare that they were a member of APIM (including PIM). In the local churches members met for worship, proclamation, evangelism and education.

The idea of total independence from other local churches never existed and was never taught and thought in APIM. All the churches needed each other and had to share together their joys and sorrows as one church. Since all the churches were facing similar problems, they looked to area leaders who in turn reported the matters to Kalemba, who was *mtsogoleri* of APIM. Issues that were affecting any part of APIM were discussed by all the leaders present from the local churches, and they agreed on the best possible solution available to them.

---

[12] Gottfried Osei-Mensah, *Wanted Servant Leaders: The Challenge of Christian Leadership in Africa Today*, Achimoto: African Christian Press, 1990, pp. 9-21.
[13] Int. Yosofati Ndege, Bishop of Achewa PIM, Kakwere, 5.7.1999.

7: Achewa Providence Industrial Mission 133

Monthly Fellowship Meetings

Apart from the usual Sunday meetings, Kalemba introduced monthly fellowship meetings at which all the congregations met as one church. These began late in the afternoon on Saturday and ended in the afternoon on Sunday. It was a time of fellowship during which members met at meals and worship. The meetings were like large family reunions because they were attended by many people from all APIM congregations. It was the only time when baptism and the Lord's Supper were administered. That attracted members and members-to-be to attend these meetings.

Church Leadership at the Central Church at Nyanje

Even though Kalemba chose Nyanje as the central church for APIM, he did not move from Kalumbu to settle at Nyanje. It was the opposite of PIM where the leader, Malikebu, ministered from the central church at Mbombwe. Kalemba served from Kalumbu while *mtsogoleri wa chiwiri*, Kamkalamba, was at Nyanje. Early in 1945 Kalemba ordained Kamkalamba as pastor. Fenias (Peter) Kalonga, a brother-in-law to Kamkalamba, was ordained *mlaliki* (preacher).

Financial Support for Church Leaders (Pastors)

Generally, Baptists have been known to have aggressive programmes on giving including tithes and offerings which are basically used to support ministry. That includes payment of the pastor, the shepherd of the members at a local church. Only those elected into the denominational offices of the conventions or unions receive payment for their services to the churches that are members of those organizations. School teachers and other workers are paid through appropriate boards or committees responsible for the institutions under the conventions or unions. On the other hand, the founding and the re-opening of PIM was done by Chilembwe and Malikebu who were paid as missionaries to Malawi by the Foreign Mission Board (FMB) of NBC, Inc. After their departure the FMB continued to pay stipends of PIM ministers and other church workers including school teachers, as well as funding certain mission projects.[14]

Kalemba did not receive any financial support from the FMB because, firstly, Mpingo wa Mpatuko was started without FMB's knowledge; and secondly: Malikebu did not recognize Kalemba for mission support since he had not received any official training from PIM. In light of this, Kalemba did not consciously take time to teach his followers to give generously to the church. He did not ask APIM churches to give a monthly financial support. The opposite has been the church imposing on the pastors the "keep them humble; keep them poor" syndrome. In part it is linked with the pressure of image. The pastor is expected to be and has to be seen to be a saint. He is supposed to set an example of holy poverty.[15] Kalemba left it to his followers to decide when to assist him, he could not be sure of getting help when he needed it. That became the standard for future leaders and their support.

Social Organization and the Structure of Achewa PIM

Though Achewa PIM calls itself "Baptist," it tends to function like most Chewa social institutions, that is to say, under paternalistic control of a leader. Its form of church government fits the local social structure so closely that it does not allow for new creative leadership from within or outside itself. Since APIM placed broad control in the hands of the "elders," the bishop, pastors, *alaliki*, and *alangizi*, it almost overlooks young pastors' and other leaders' contributions.

As an indigenous church, it has grown with very little foreign leadership and guidance. Although APIM is one generation removed from the missionary cause in the sense that its founding leadership was led to the

---

[14] John Parratt, "Mbombwe Revisited: Dr. Daniel Malikebu and the Second Era of the Providence Industrial Mission," a history seminar paper, University of Malawi, 29 January 1985, p. 3. See also Patrick Makondesa, *Moyo ndi Utumiki wa Mbusa ndi Mai Muocha wa Providence Industrial Mission*, Blantyre: CLAIM-Kachere, 2000, p. 20.

[15] William H. Brackney, with Ruby J. Burke, *Faith, Life, and Witness: The Papers of the Study and Research Division of the Baptist World Alliance - 1986-1990*, Birmingham, AL: Sanford University, 1990, p. 377.

Lord by Chilembwe who was converted through missionary enterprise, it is for that reason entirely indigenous. The leadership is very close to the people. The church structure, therefore, has a good deal of local authority and considerable vagueness about statistics. The leaders cannot provide adequate information about the very organization they head because the leadership is dependent far more on their personalities than upon the organization of the local congregations, and of cause, Achewa PIM itself.

One would ask why APIM is so highly centralized if it is a Baptist church. The highly centralized form of government was fitting during Chilembwe's era, but it should have changed after more people had been trained to take up responsibility in the church. At the beginning of PIM, Chilembwe's role was that of a father to the new and young church. He died before the church had reached maturity in which case he would have worked side by side with the church as co-labourers or partners, with the church assuming more responsibility. National Baptist Convention, Inc., on the other hand, remained extremely centralized, first, because some of the boards to the Convention antedate the Convention, and the boards have sought to act independently of the convention or assert control over their own property. Second, NBC Inc has a history of strong presidents who have consolidated their power during their tenure of office. Nevertheless, Achewa PIM would have by now reached a stage where the leadership and membership were partners according to the generally accepted Baptist church polity. In the congregational form of church government, the denominational leaders really depend on the people for their power. In times of emergency, dependence on the people for their power may be a weakening because nothing can be done in time to save the situation. The leader has to have time to consult the churches before acting. That is not so with Achewa PIM. The bishop or his representative acts on behalf of the church with or without the consent of the church or *Chififitini*.[16] The church does not

---

[16] *Chififtini* was a monthly meeting for the leaders of the local congregations. The Bungwe (committee) met at the central church at Nyanje and it was open to all in positions of leadership from all congregations. They met on the 15 of every month or thereabouts, and thus the branding, Chififitini. It was during these meetings that the leaders discussed developments in their local congregations. Issues were tabled and

question his power to act on behalf of the church. The strong relationship to the chiefs and to Chewa culture may also have strengthened these conservative tendencies

Relationship to other Churches

Achewa PIM does not have close links with either PIM or BACOMA churches in the area though they claim to be one with PIM through Chilembwe, and with BACOMA through the American Baptists. Achewa PIM does not want to be lumped together with AICs, especially African Abraham and Zion churches. Surprisingly enough, the African Abraham, African Emanuel and Independent Baptist congregations in the area have on occasions attended APIM's monthly fellowship meetings. Sometimes local Churches of Christ and Seventh-day Adventist church leaders have made their presence known at such meetings. Since monthly meetings are festive in nature, people in the local areas want to be part of such gatherings even if they have nothing to do with their churches. In spite of their presence, one would hear Achewa PIM leaders presiding over the meeting saying that they are not an African Abraham church, but Baptist.

Gender issue

Though APIM is a male dominated church that accommodates women folk strictly on its terms, there is agreement among male members that the church needs not only look to men for leadership, but to women as well. The prominence of women in APIM is a sure challenge to the gender issue most Malawians are struggling with. If a Westerner came and experienced the relationship that existed between men and women in Achewa PIM, they would wonder why Malawians are looking to the West on gender issues. The Achewa PIM is a typical answer to the issue. Despite that women are not looked upon as pastors (an issue that is still challenging the modern Church including the Baptist Convention of Malawi), they play a major role as advisors or counsellors, not only to women and girls, but also to the church and its male dominated leadership. Nowhere does APIM gather

---

decisions made. No local church leader made resolutions on issues that would later affect the entire Achewa PIM without the matter being discussed at Chififitini.

without the presence of its women folk. It does not matter who sits where and on what in any gathering. If there are not enough seats, it is not strange to see a woman sitting on a chair and a man sitting on a mat. Women have a different role from that of men, but that does not make them in any way inferior to their counterparts.

A woman is as responsible for herself and others as is the man. They look at each other as partners in advancing the kingdom of God. I have never been to a church were African women were so proud of being who they were before men and God. While our schools are plagued with the gender issue, the Achewa PIM created an environment in which girls and women experience the unity of purpose with men and boys. Instead of Malawians looking to other nations for examples and answers to the gender issue, Achewa PIM is an able contributor to the search for an ideal relationship between men and women. The Achewa PIM members are conscious of how they differ on the gender issue with other churches. They are very proud of their relationship which they view as biblical from the standpoint of brotherly love.

The gospel of Jesus Christ revolutionized the place of women in Jewish society. For sure something like that would take some time to work through particularly against the backgrounds of deep prejudice. Jesus did not treat women like chattels, but as equals of men. The *imago dei* lay in the harmonious interrelationship between man and woman in God's creation, and not in domination of one by the other. Women had a role in the church of the first century. The value of this is immense especially in a culture which requires a high degree of segregation between men and women.[17] In Achewa PIM women are engaged in the ministry of teaching. In addition, women hold the office of deacons.

It has not been difficult for Achewa PIM to accept women as equals because women traditionally play a major role in the society, from the selection of a chief to choosing where to make a home for the family.

---

[17] For further treatment on women and ministry see Michael Green, *Freed to Serve: Training and Equipping for Ministry*, London: Hodder and Stoughton, 1988, pp. 82ff. See also Willard M. Swartley, *Slavery, Sabbath, War and Women: Case Issues in Biblical Interpretation*, Scottdale: Herald, 1983, pp. 152ff.

Women are present in the chiefs' courts and at all discussions that affect the community of which they are part. Sitting and discussing, working and sharing with men is not strange in the Chewa culture, therefore, the teaching of the gospel of Jesus Christ finds fertile ground on which women also have a lot to contribute in the life of the society and the church. It is also clear that in the family it is the task of the man, not the woman, to lead. It is differentiation of function and there is nothing derogatory about that. The harmonious interrelationships between men and women did not come about because of the presence of missionaries among the Achewa PIM. The Achewa PIM makes one think again that some of the sections of the Christian church which was in the forefront of women's liberation in the first century do remain some of the last organizations in the world today to respect women as equal to men, and allow them a significant place in leadership.

Achewa PIM: AIC or Baptist?

AICs are generally regarded as social groups that are apparently not progressive. The term depicts a society whose lifestyle is non-literate and primitive yet in their variety of facets and practices; they depict "the church of God," be it in Corinth, London, Philadelphia, Johannesburg, or South of Lilongwe. The term AICs has been applied to a very large extent by white Africans and Europeans who have had some interest in the churches in Africa. The writers came to the subject with preconceived conclusions which were mostly negative to anything African including the church.[18] They have used the word "church" as an ornament for the groups they did not accept as identical to churches in the West. Just as churches in the West have their own history and culture, so too the churches in Africa. The term AIC is foreign, Western, and not theological but sociological. It is not theological because wherever the church meets, it was and it is called the church of God. One would like to know which are European Indigenous Churches (EICs), American Independent Churches (AICs), or Asian Instituted Church (AICs). African churches are so called probably because

---

[18] See B.G.M. Sundkler, *Bantu Prophets in South Africa*, 2nd ed., London: Oxford, 1961, p. 302.

of the absence of *azungu* (white people) in these churches. The so called AICs are Christian churches in Africa although they are different in their organization from the so-called mainline or mission churches.

AICs are often called breakaways. Barrett suggested that a number of factors combined to produce the tribal "*zeitgeist* (spirit of the times), with its tendencies toward independence. Independence is the more likely the more these factors are present in the tribal unit. That suggestion has no reference to the Anglican, Presbyterian, Baptist and Methodist churches, to mention a few which broke away from the Roman Catholic Church which also broke away from the Catholic Church. Why should a break-away church in Africa be described as and be called African when no break-away church in Europe or America is called European Independent or American Initiated? I contend to call churches in Africa as either Christian or non-Christian or pagan.

If they are Christian churches, one would find theological weaknesses just as one would experience in churches in Europe, America and elsewhere. They may be different in type and depth and so on, but there would be some weaknesses that need to be addressed in either church. The churches in the West have brought the message of Jesus Christ in Western packages, and found it difficult to accept the same message in African packaging. While churches in Africa are being accused of not openly condemning the practice of Traditional Religions in their congregations, some of the Western churches are watching individual freedom and human rights steer them to condone homosexuality to the extent of allowing them to be pastors and to marry in church.

Achewa PIM are independent or autonomous not because they are African, but because they have chosen to follow the Baptist form of church government (with some modifications). It is important to note that throughout the history of the Church, new groups have been forming and will continue to do so as the spirit of renewal is manifested.

If a church is a Christian gathering, it must be called Christian. Christian churches which were started by Africans for Africans are not just movements, but churches in their own right. Achewa PIM is a church in its own right. Barrett also suggested that the root cause common to the entire AICs is the missions' failure to demonstrate considerably the biblical concept of love in the African context. One may ask: has that changed? If so, are there no more churches breaking away? If not, then one would expect to see more and more churches breaking away. Achewa PIM is not a breakaway from the "mission," that is, mainline church, and therefore, its existence is not as a result of a failure on the part of white missionaries to demonstrate love towards APIM. PIM is a church started by a Malawian for Africans. Therefore, Achewa PIM and of course, PIM, are lumped together with churches that broke away from white mission churches for lack of a better term.

Be reminded that there are no African Church Fathers, but Church Fathers. Missions are as much the result and undertaking of Christians from the world over. Again describing some churches as "missionary" and others as African does not do justice to the teaching and command of Christ to go. Westerners have deliberately divided the Christian church in Africa into the one brought by Westerners and the other that was started by Africans themselves.[19] Calling other churches "AICs" is a way of perpetuating segregation in the church of God.

Some attribute the rise and development of AICs to the need for fellowship and security.[20] That is not so with Achewa PIM. They started as a church and not as a "fellowship" group.[21] People gather for fellowship in their churches, but the type of fellowship depends on the group needs. Every Christian and every person looks for fellowship and security and that cannot be only for AICs.

---

[19] See Hilary Mijoga, *Separate but Same Message*, Blantyre: CLAIM-Kachere, 2000, p. 1.

[20] Hilary Mijoga, *Separate but Same Message*, p. 34.

[21] The term "fellowship," came to mean those Christian groups that were formed specifically around the 1970s and 1980s by Christians who were not happy with their churches such as CCAP and Assemblies of God which did not involve their laity more in the ministry of the churches. In recent years BACOMA members are more and more getting involved in fellowship groups, especially in the towns and cities, for several reasons: one is of association, and the other is of piety and recognition as spiritual by the outside world.

Here in Malawi the Christian Council of Malawi (CCM) have looked upon the so-called AICs as schismatic and syncretistic. AICs stimuli have been misinterpreted. CCM has considered division and segregation as a denial of the unity of the body of Christ.[22] AICs cannot be admitted into the CCM as they are not considered truly Christian churches. For them to be admitted into the national organization it seems the AICs have to justify their existence to the gatekeepers and meet their criteria before they can have the right of admission. AICs are thought of as having no idea whatsoever about what theology is all about because they are led by unschooled pastors. As a result, the mainline clergy refuse to be in the same meeting where AICs are in the majority. Such churches as Achewa PIM are viewed by mission church ministers as being inferior. They don't see themselves as equal before the God they both serve.[23]

Achewa PIM has maintained the centrality of Jesus Christ as Lord and Saviour. They do praise John Chilembwe as an earthly leader who founded the church, but he is not regarded as Lord and Saviour of their lives. Just like in other mainline churches, the knowledge of the Christian faith of some of the members is limited. As a result, some discrepancy exists between the doctrine accepted by the church and the practice of some of its believers. Despite that, Achewa PIM affirms faith in Jesus Christ in African traditional forms just as it is in many BACOMA congregations. The celebration of the Lord's Supper and believer's baptism are seen as symbolic of the death, burial and resurrection of Jesus, and each believer's identification, by faith, with Jesus, in both dying to sin and rising to new life with him. This Christocentric gospel is preached from Achewa PIM pulpits Sunday after Sunday, for its proclamation retains the central place in Baptist worship.

Achewa PIM is conscious of its obligation toward BACOMA and BMIM and is willing to re-establish fraternal relations with them. Its leadership team accepts that there is need to engage BACOMA's Bible teachers to

---

[22] Peter Falk, *The Growth of the Church in Africa*, Grand Rapids: Zondervan, 1979, p. 460.
[23] James Tengatenga, "Religious Pluralism in Malawi: A Challenge to the Church," *Religion in Malawi*, no. 8, April 1998.

instruct pastors and other church leaders if the church is to survive as a Christian church in the 21st century. APIM has not been like Baptist churches in the area of evangelism. Baptists take pride in evangelism because they are committed to sharing their faith, to the extension of the kingdom of God, both at home and afar. Despite that, Achewa PIM's radiant joy and assurance of conviction that testifies to their relationship with Jesus Christ is convincing evidence of their Christian faith.

One other area that Achewa PIM has not matched other Baptists is prayer. The demands for Christian witness and discipleship necessitate prayer. Baptists encourage corporate prayer and a pattern of individual spirituality that requires each member to engage in regular prayer and Bible study. Nevertheless, Achewa PIM are very much aware of the freedom of opinion and religious practice, not only for themselves, but for all people, including non-believers. Each individual needs to be free to make choices about faith and commitment undisturbed by outside agency. Such freedom has led Baptists to be diverse people with no overarching rule demanding common thought or practice among all Baptists.

Achewa PIM is definitely different from mainline churches. It is also different from individual BACOMA congregations especially those that are in the towns and cities and have been led by a pastor or church leader who has had theological education from a seminary or college. If one visited some BACOMA churches in the rural areas and later visited Achewa PIM congregations, one would probably find it hard to differentiate between the two. The only difference noticed easily is the women with their uniforms. Some of the Achewa PIM churches that have had close contact with BMIM in the 1970s are much more organized than some BACOMA churches in terms of worship services. The preaching may not be very different from most BACOMA churches either in towns or in the rural area. The interesting thing is that Achewa PIM is part of the whole God-fearing Christian family.

A Religious Island

The periods Achewa PIM stayed without meaningful interaction with other Christian groups, were times of retardation. The use of "Achewa" in the title of the church meant that it was a local church which became an umbrella for religious individualism and separation. The people of Mangoni felt that they were just as good, if not better, than the people across the Shire River, and were capable of living in isolation from PIM with its headquarters at Mbombwe. PIM grew considerably from about 1924 until 1934, but even more so for just over ten years when the "Chewa" people worshipped in isolation from PIM, despite being labelled "Mpingo wa Mpatuko." The Christianization of many Achewa people was more evident because of a strong group identity and good communication channels. Face-to-face relationship and homogeneity were the underlying factors to the conversion of many households to APIM. This linguistic and cultural group became a religious island though most of its leadership at the time had had some influence from PIM and DRCM in terms of secular and religious education. The decision taken by Malikebu to excommunicate Kalemba also contributed to Achewa's development in isolation from the world of their day. Instead of thinking of the world at large, or to be more practical, to think of all ethnic groups in Malawi, as their goal for evangelism, APIM limited themselves to their own cultural group, Achewa.

It was not long that some of the stalwarts of APIM began to question the viability of APIM in the face of increased culture contact. Already Mangoni, and not to mention the whole country, was becoming a small village with the arrival and ministry or work of people from within and from outside the country. Trading Centres were being flooded with people from other tribes who were looking for work or education. Missionaries from Europe and South Africa were increasing their activities in both rural and urban areas. There was increased culture contact within that ten-year period, and it was going to increase even further. A few of those who had had some contact with PIM and DRCM took a rather serious look at their responsibility and their ministry as a church in the light of rapidly increasing culture contact. That was not questioning the validity of the indigenous church philosophy, because they knew very well that in every cultural environment those who feared God were acceptable to him since God is no respecter of language or culture. They quickly realized that culture contact and integration of Achewa PIM into the larger PIM group was inevitable and desirable. In that case, some of the men attempted to serve as mediators between APIM and PIM, a child and parent so to speak, respectively. In 1945 a good number of families moved back to PIM.

Between 1945 and 1962 Achewa PIM slowly ran out of steam. They were isolated from the information that had stimulated growth during the period before 1945. People cannot survive on the good old days. Since no newer information was being infused into the life of the church, Achewa PIM soon lost power to win more converts, and power to develop as a whole. From the time of PIM through the formation of Achewa PIM to the time when others went back to PIM, the training of church leadership insured the introduction and diffusion of new information which was needed for the survival of the church. The re-establishment of ties with PIM brought hope and momentum to PIM in Mangoni under Kalemba. PIM (Mbombwe) introduced training programmes for church leaders, especially in the pastoral ministry, and secular education with schools in and around Chiradzulu district. Several individuals and groups from the Mangoni section of PIM had some training there. They, in turn, introduced what they had learnt to the rest in Mangoni. That in itself acted as fuel for PIM congregations. Those who had received some education in PIM schools brought new ideas and impetus to the church that kept rekindling their fires to do more for the church. The church had a vision, to reach the people with the Word. It was not limited to the people of Mangoni. They wanted to apply what they had learnt to the communities they came into contact with. Lack of continued renewal of information through education blurred that vision, and was then restricted to "Achewa" as the target people.

The little bit of information they had soon became so familiar that it did not challenge Achewa PIM members enough to do more for the church. No more members were receiving education anywhere apart from what I would term 'in service training' provided by Kalemba and later by Kamkalamba. That remained so until the period of partnership with BMIM. After Achewa PIM was separated from BMIM in 1976 the situation returned to an 'in service training' period in which the church just dragged its feet and sort of folded in. Even if they had wanted to receive training from outside, it was not going to be easy for them. Limitations of both finances and personnel restricted their educational possibilities. As village people their financial resources were too meager to pay for the education. When they were part of PIM and later of BMIM, Achewa PIM overcame the limitation because the mission met the cost, in part or in full, of the training some of their members received. Since most of those who had received some education from PIM had separated themselves from Achewa PIM and had since returned to PIM, APIM was left without enough personnel of that ability.

Even if they had been found, they needed to be sent outside the Achewa environment to acquire the needed education. Unfortunately, Achewa PIM has not produced eligible candidates for further training amongst its membership. Generally, education has not been one of the major thrusts of Achewa PIM such that very few families have children who have finished secondary school education, and only one family had produced at least one college graduate. Supposing a person of ability had been found who had gone through school and had finally acquired theological education, he would not be able to find a meaningful niche in his society. It would be very difficult for that individual to come back into the tribal setting of Achewa PIM or any other church in a constructive way. School leavers and college graduates leave Achewa PIM and, either join churches of other denominations, or stop going to church altogether. Lack of people of ability greatly retarded the speed at which Achewa PIM could minister to the modern world and thereby slowed down its own development as a church.

There was a realization amongst some of the members that they were missing out by keeping the church "Achewa." Christianization by means of a group movement was by no means the perfect answer to the evangelization of the people. It reinforced existing tribal ethnocentrism. The "Achewa" did not only separate themselves from PIM, they also separated from people who were different from them. To be part of Achewa PIM became something to be proud of: "*Ife ndife Achewa*" (We are Achewa). As a result of isolation from people who are different, Achewa PIM became limited in their conception of the gospel.

Although Achewa PIM has been ill equipped to evaluate adequately new information that comes in, no havoc has been caused by sects and self-appointed prophets because none have come APIM's way. Another reason might be that up to now Achewa PIM's church polity has not created room for outsiders to come in and impose themselves or misguide them. Achewa PIM has remained very much close to the Chewa culture such that it has copied almost nothing from other churches such as BACOMA and other evangelicals. In using the popular Christian cliché's such as "Amen, brother or sister," "hallelujah," "praise God, amen," singing of choruses accompanied by clapping of hands and dancing, mass prayer, and theological debates on such issues as speaking in tongues that have opened doors to world-wide brotherhoods of believers. On account of not participating in interdenominational meetings and the so called "fellowship" meetings of Evangelical and Protestant Christians, Achewa PIM has remained virtually unaffected by controversies in these churches, and its members being swept into the fold of some highly evangelistic sects or churches that are deviating from the normal.

The missionaries traced the origin of the Malawi Convention to the arrival of two SBC missionaries from Zimbabwe in 1959. No credit was given to other groups such as the Achewa PIM and individuals like Kachaso Gama and Galatiya for the beginning of BACOMA. The majority of BACOMA members knew very little or nothing about Joseph Booth and his contribution toward Baptist work in Malawi. The little they knew was probably the negative attitude the BMIM had against Booth. Very few BACOMA members, like most people in the country, knew or know PIM as Baptist, let alone the founder, John Chilembwe. The BMIM again downplayed the contribution of Chilembwe and PIM to the beginning of the Malawi Convention. Some members, especially in Lilongwe, did not want to hear about Achewa PIM and their influence of the beginning of the Convention. These and other non-Baptist missions such as the Churches of Christ and some AICs formed the cradle in which the Baptist Convention of Malawi was begun. Their contribution coupled with that of SBC made the Baptist Convention of Malawi's beginning to be polygenetic because local priesthoods are on the same general mission.

Achewa PIM and PIM (Mbombwe) were heavily involved in the evangelistic outreach that resulted in the beginning and multiplication of Convention churches mainly in the Central Region. They probably preached to more people in the rural areas of Lilongwe East than BACOMA leaders and missionaries combined. That may have been because the Achewa PIM were more familiar with the area since they had many of their congregations in this area. They also spoke to their own people in the language and culture they understood very well. BACOMA leadership was new to the people and the area, and they were still working as individuals and not as a team, as was the case with Achewa PIM.[24]

Change of Name from APIM to Achewa Baptist Association (ABA)

For a while the APIM was known as Achewa Baptist Association (ABA). This began in October 1964 because LeRoy Albright, an SBC missionary, did not want to be seen as working with a group that was associated with John Chilembwe and Joseph Booth who were both Baptists but with differing histories. Probably he did not want other white people and missionaries to regard him as preserving the activities of APIM and PIM's founder. Albright understood Baptist Mission in Malawi (BMIM) as a faith mission. Although ABA was the agreed name, in practice people continued to use "Providence" in the title and called themselves Achewa Providence Baptist Mission. It should be noted that the cooperation was a local affair. Though Albright spoke as representing BMIM, he did not make the decisions made between him and Achewa PIM binding. There was no formal agreement between the two organizations. It is likely that Albright began to work with Achewa PIM because they were the first to respond to him. He started to work with them as friends. Albright was trying to start a people's movement using an African Instituted Church. Achewa PIM was happy to work with a Baptist expatriate without losing their autonomy in reaching people for Christ. According to Achewa PIM and Albright, APIM was a Baptist church, and they would not necessarily interfere with each other's church government.

Conclusion

Achewa PIM is a Baptist-type church. It has all it takes to be called "Baptist" like other Baptist churches that have chosen to have a centralized

---

[24] See Hany Longwe, *Identity by Dissociation*, pp. 65-111.

government, and focusing on particular people groups, for them, the Chewa.

Chapter 8

The Church, the Laity, and the Priesthood[1]

Through the examination of the historical development of the role of the laity in the light of order, priesthood and authority, this chapter aims at reflecting upon the tension between the ordained clergy and the laity and their concerns. It examines the role of the laity and the ordained ministers in the light of the priesthood of all believers, and also gives examples of how the two can complement each other considering that the Christian God is a God of diversity and not of conformity.

Introduction

The distinction of "royal priesthood, holy nation" mentioned in Revelation 5:9-10 and in 1 Peter points out a particular problem for Christian churches that have an ordained priesthood in their structures because much of Protestantism ceased to designate Christian ministry as priesthood.[2] Formerly, it was the unquestioned premise that the ministry of the church belonged to the ordained clergy who were conceived as the ministers, and the rest of the Christian community as the laity. That meant that in the life of the church the clergy were the ones doing something on the laity. This view of ministry came under sharp attack in both theory and practice.[3]

Sometimes the ministry of the laity has been interpreted to mean that there is no privileged class, and that all services by both clergy and non-clergy are of equal importance before God and in the life of the church. From time to time, it has been conceived as the complete mobility of functions within the church, each person being empowered to perform any function. Further

---

[1] First published as chapter 1 in Volker Glissmann, *Towards a Malawian Theology of Laity*, Mzuzu: Luviri Press, 2020, pp. 15-34.

[2] Raymond E. Brown, *The Churches the Apostles Left Behind*, Ramsey: Paulist Press, 1984, p. 80.

[3] Gabriel Fackre, *The Christian Story: A Narrative Interpretation of Basic Christian Doctrine*, Grand Rapids: Eerdmans, 1984, p. 175.

still, the ministry of the laity has been understood to mean that the real ministry of the church is in the world, and thus the laity constituted the fundamental ministry of the church, with the clergy serving as resources to, and enablers of, the laity in their *secular* mission. At times it is seen to be the only ministry, with baptism as the act of ordination, and the necessity of a clergy in any sense of the word is put radically in question. As a result, it is the laypeople who assume the functions normally associated with the clergy in the inner life of the church as well as the ministry to the world.[4]

Such views of ministry have contributed to the loss of a sense of identity among the clergy who have attempted to honour the enlarged perception of ministry. In response, some have recognized the need for an official, ordained clergy who fulfill authoritarian ministerial functions within the community of faith. Nonetheless, balancing the authority of laity and clergy has proven to be a delicate exercise. That has also seen a rising generation of women not only seeking ordination and equal participation in the church as pastors or clergy, but also their rightful place in theology.[5] This challenge assumes there is a unique and important meaning to worship and the proclamation of the Word.[6]

Historical Developments

The word lay derives from the Anglo-French *lai*. This is from Late Latin *laicus*, and Greek *laikos* meaning of the people, and from *laos* meaning the people at large. At first there was a sense of unified ministry for the whole people of God, but later, in the patristic era, there was a growing distinction between clergy and laity. In the Middle Ages there was a rise of clerical authority and status, which was followed by a monastic and sectarian reassertion of lay ministry in the church. It was the Church Reformation that emphasized the vocation and the priesthood of the believers. The Free Church Tradition produced democratic polity, and voluntary church membership. Although there has been a growing trend toward ministerial

---

[4] Gabriel Fackre, *The Christian Story*, p. 175.
[5] Erhard S. Gerstenberger, *Yahweh the Patriarch: Ancient Images of God and Feminist Theology*, Minneapolis: Fortress Press, 1996, pp. 111-128.
[6] Gabriel Fackre, *The Christian Story*, p. 176.

professionalism, there also has been a reassertion of the role of the laity through lay renewal, and the growth of clerical authoritarianism among evangelical Protestants.[7]

The Entire Church as the People of God - Laos

A history of the laity or a theology of the laity is a history and theology of the whole church because the entire church was and is *laos*, people of God, sharing a priestly function as members respond to each other and to the world (1Pet 2:9).[8] 1 Peter 1:13 – 2:10 applies to the Gentile converts the whole Exodus experience of Israel. They have left their former servitude, and have been redeemed by the blood of a lamb, while going through a period of wandering toward a promised inheritance. The Levitical priesthood has been replaced by Christ, and now Christians constitute a royal priesthood.[9]

Yet the distinction between clergy and laity is a real one in Christian history and must not be underestimated. Its earliest roots were evident in the struggle over questions of authority, order, and leadership in the New Testament churches. It would be a mistake to interpret the priesthood of all believers to mean "an unstructured, democratic fellowship."[10] The priesthood of all believers, like other metaphors of the church, speaks of order and design. The church can be described as "structural," or "spiritual," or a "gathered" community. Although some churches embarked on a lifelong relationship with the doctrine of the priesthood of all believers, they have had a difficult time agreeing on the precise language for describing this most important belief to which they hold fast.[11]

---

[7] Bill J. Leonard, "Southern Baptists and the Laity," in the *Review and Expositor*, vol. LXXXIV, no. 4, 1987, p. 633.

[8] Bill J. Leonard, "Southern Baptists and the Laity," p. 634.

[9] Raymond E. Brown, The Churches the Apostles Left Behind, p. 26.

[10] Bill J. Leonard, "Southern Baptists and the Laity," p. 634.

[11] Hany Longwe, *Christians by Grace, Baptists by Choice*, Zomba: Kachere; Mzuzu: Mzuni Press, 2011, p. 19.

The Vision of Equality

The picture of the first Christian church made plain a revolutionary vision of equality. When Habakkuk complained to God about the violence and injustice God's people had experienced, God told him to write the vision and spell it out on tablets (2:2-5). Joel made plain the vision of the Spirit's empowerment of all that would result in the demolition of barriers erected on the basis of gender, age, race and class (Joel 2:28-29). On the day of Pentecost, Peter declared the vision (Acts 2:17-18). Not everything mentioned by Joel happened that morning, but the Spirit empowered believers to live out the discipleship of equals initiated by Jesus.

The Development of Divisions between the Ordained Clergy and the Laity

Around A.D. 96 the term *layman* (*ha laikos anthropos*) first appeared in probably the earliest of the sub-apostolic writings, the Epistle of Clement of Rome to the church at Corinth, in which he stated that "the layman is bound by the lay ordinances." [12] It appears that the Corinthian church had deposed some presbyters, and Clement urges the church to reinstate these presbyters to the office and comments at length on the evils of jealousy and faction.[13] The letter is an indication that already certain divisions had developed between the ordained clergy (presbyters and deacons) and the rest of the congregation, yet, Clement acknowledged that all Christians had a priestly function in the church's worship. Every believer received this "ordination" to a royal priesthood by virtue of baptism symbolized by laying on of hands as a sign of the coming of the Holy Spirit.[14]

As early as the beginning of the second century, the Christian leaders began to make a distinction between the clergy the laity. The very names they adopted showed the official attitude of superiority; for the clergy means,

---

[12] A.M. Renwick, *The Story of the Church*, Guilford: Billing & Sons, 1958, p. 25.

[13] Robert A. Baker, *A Summary of Christian History*, Nashville: Broadman, 1959, p. 26. See also, Cyril C. Richardson (ed), *Early Christian Fathers*, New York: Touchstone, 1996, p. 64.

[14] Wayne Grudem, *Systematic Theology: An Introduction to Biblical Doctrine*, Leicester: InterVarsity, 1994, p. 961.

8: The Church, the Laity and the Priesthood

"those who have been called of God', while laity means, "the people."[15] By the fifth and sixth centuries, the distinction was becoming more pronounced partly due to controversies over heresy, authority and order in the rapidly growing congregations. Efforts to develop order, fight heresy and maintain orthodoxy influenced the rise of an elaborate clerical hierarchy.[16] The church regarded the clergy as having special grace and being indispensable in the Christian's approach to God.[17] The priesthood of all believers was practically forgotten.[18]

Reassertion of the Role of the Laity

The Church Reformation of the sixteenth century produced a reassertion of the role of the laity. Martin Luther rediscovered the claims of Scripture, with its gift of justification by grace through faith and restored the idea of the church as a spiritual communion of believers, all of whom were priests to God.

Primacy of the Word and the Priesthood of All Believers

Luther held that ordination was an invention of the church, nonetheless, he admitted that as a rite that had been practiced for many ages it was not to be condemned, but all Christians were priests. That resulted in a distinction between calling and office. All followers of Christ were called to the gospel, and no vocation was less Christian than any other. All Christians had equal access to God, but not equal ability to interpret the Word correctly. Those that were called priests were ministers selected from among the Christians to act in their behalf, and their priesthood was the community's ministry.[19] Luther and other Protestants stressed the primacy of the Word of God as

---

[15] Robert A. Baker, *A Summary of Christian History*, p. 37. See also, Kenneth Scott Latourette, *A History of Christianity* Vol. II, New York: Harper & Row, 1975, pp. 133, 183.

[16] Bill J. Leonard, "Southern Baptists and the Laity," p. 634.

[17] A.M. Renwick, *The Story of the Church*, p. 72. See also Cyril C. Richardson (ed), *Early Christian Fathers*, p. 47.

[18] A.M. Renwick, *The Story of the Church*, pp. 72,73.

[19] Bill J. Leonard, "Southern Baptists and the Laity," p. 635.

contained in the Scriptures and, holding to the priesthood of all believers, insisted not only that all Christians read the Bible, but also on their competence, guided by the Holy Spirit, to understand it appropriately.[20]

Unity, Equality and Spirituality

Among the Radical Reformers were the Anabaptists, who went beyond Luther and reemphasized the equality of all believers. They sought to restore the New Testament church as a community of adult believers bound by covenant in faith, witness and discipline, and called to minister to the people of God. To them the distinction between clergy and laity undermined the nature of the church itself for it created a church organized around religious professionals. They suggested the laity should become again what they were in the early church: the carriers of the faith. Immediate individual experience of the grace of God became central.[21] That encouraged the unity and equality of all believers; clergy and laity were co-labourers in ministry.

Some of the descendants of the Radical Reformers looked to the New Testament church equality which originated in the common experience of baptism. They emphasized the evangelical identity and spiritual unity of all believers as witnesses to and as followers of Christ. The various groups promoted the equality of believers and denounced the ecclesiastical elitism inherent in the knowledge and work of the priest. They also insisted upon a spiritual, often political, egalitarianism in the face of clerical and aristocratic hierarchy. To be a Christian was to be a minister.[22] These egalitarian notions led to results quite different than those intended by the Reformers themselves. Nevertheless, the priesthood of all believers and the obligation of private judgment conserved the root of individuality.[23] The individual was and could be moved and guided only by their own personal

---

[20] Kenneth Scott Latourette, *A History of Christianity*, vol. II, p. 719.

[21] Bruce Milne, *Know the Truth: A handbook of Christian Belief*, Nottingham: Inter-Varsity Press, 2006, p. 302.

[22] Bill J. Leonard, "Southern Baptists and the Laity," p. 636.

[23] George F. Thomas, (ed), *The Vitality of the Christian Tradition*, New York: Harper & Brothers, 1945, p. 140.

8: The Church, the Laity and the Priesthood

experience of such grace, and herein lay their autonomy – their independence in Christ.[24]

Congregational Form of Church Government

Various groups continued to insist that all believers were called to minister to the church and the world. They believed all persons could preach and teach without regard to ministerial training. They made it possible for laity to perform all ecclesiastical functions when authorized by the congregation. The laity had final authority under Christ in the endeavours of the church.

Voluntarism

This congregational spirit became even more powerful when united with the ideals of democracy and religious freedom which was based on the non-coerced consent of the individual. The church became a voluntary association. The voluntary principle in religion had a powerful influence on the role of the laity. Voluntarism meant church leaders were dependent as never before on the laity for spiritual and temporal support. It was more evident in the basic ecclesiastical organization, the denomination. Voluntarism shaped the understanding of the nature of the church as "operating through democratic process under the Lordship of Jesus Christ."[25]

Evangelical Conversion

Perhaps evangelical conversion – warm, personal, and individual – was the greatest equalizer. Conversion transcended race, education, or class. In turn, the converted were called to convert others; that was the universal Christian ministry. In common spiritual experience, congregational polity, and communal responsibility the 19th century cultivated a "people's church," which accentuated the call to ministry as given to all Christians. Final authority for church government came from Christ through the congregation. The clergy derived their authority to preach and administer

---

[24] Bill J. Leonard, "Southern Baptists and the Laity," p. 637.
[25] Bill J. Leonard, "Southern Baptists and the Laity," p. 637.

the ordinances from Christ through his churches. That does not suggest, though, that churches refused to distinguish between clergy and laity. Free Church traditions recognized that some individuals were called to particular ministerial functions within the churches. The congregational form of church government has maintained a tension between the universal calling of all believers and the "strange" calling of ordained ministers.[26]

In the congregational form of government everything must come to the congregational meeting, and as the church grows, decision-making reaches a point of near paralysis. While this structure does attempt to do justice to the scriptures regarding the need for final governing authority to rest within the congregation as a whole, it is unfaithful to the New Testament pattern of recognized and designated elders who have actual authority to rule the church.[27]

Training Programmes for the Laity

On one hand, Congregationalists have developed one of the most far reaching programmes for equipping and motivating lay ministry. The Sunday school represents the most important source of lay education and activity in the life of a local church. Church programmes for lay witness place emphasis on the need for every Christian to be a soul-winner, properly trained in witnessing, that was to be an integral part of every Christian's life. Nonetheless, history reveals an increasing theological and practical segregation between clergy and laity in the churches.[28]

The Laity – A Prominent Feature of Protestantism

Laymen and laywomen gradually came to the fore partly through their financial gifts to the churches and various religious organizations and institutions. Laymen's organizations sprang up, first in connection with local churches, and then as denominational fellowships. Some of the

---

[26] Bill J. Leonard, "Southern Baptists and the Laity," p. 639.
[27] Wayne Grudem, *Systematic Theology*, p. 935-936.
[28] Bill J. Leonard, "Southern Baptists and the Laity," p. 639.

outstanding evangelists were not ordained.[29] This made for a kind of lay Christianity that for the most part had little patience with what it regarded as theological details. Lay Christianity respected, studied and taught the Bible, sought to win individuals to a personal Christian commitment, was activist, and was generous in giving time and money.[30]

The lay component and the emphasis upon evangelism and revivalism with the consequent mass conversion were phases of a kind of popular Christianity. Among other expressions were hymns which had about them the quality of folk songs. Here was a singing faith which voiced and helped to shape the aspirations, prayers and actions of multitudes. Undoubtedly nothing of this kind of similar dimensions had previously appeared in the history of Christianity or of any religion.[31]

Women as Laity

In his time on earth, Jesus was very attentive to women as human beings on par with men which was radical in the Jewish culture. Jesus did not proclaim a part of the gospel to women and most of it to men. At the beginning of his movement, Christianity seemed to follow Jesus' lead in his treatment of women, many of whom were among the organizers and leaders of the early church. The early history of the church reflects an active participation of women in the spread of Christianity, not only as listeners and followers, but also as leaders.[32] "Biblically and in Christian teaching, women have a right to nothing less,"[33] because in the high dignity and

---

[29] Examples are Dwight Lyman Moody of Chicago, and Charles Huddon Spurgeon, the most famous preacher of his age. His son Thomas, the pastor of New Zealand Tabernacle in Auckland, the congregation to which Joseph Booth belonged for five years, was not ordained either (Klaus Fiedler, *The Making of a Maverick Missionary. Joseph Booth in Australasia*, Zomba: Kachere, 2008, p. 19, nor was Joseph Booth, who was instrumental in founding six major Evangelical denominations in Malawi.

[30] Kenneth Scott Latourette, *A History of Christianity*, vol. II, p. 1265.

[31] Kenneth Scott Latourette, *A History of Christianity*, vol. II, p. 1265.

[32] Patricia Wilson-Kastener, *Faith, Feminism, and the Christ*, Philadelphia: Fortress Press, 1983, pp. 72-73.

[33] Erhard S. Gerstenberger, *Yahweh the Patriarch*, p. 115.

respect Jesus accorded to them there is a remarkable affirmation of equal access to all the blessings of salvation for both women and men.[34]

Jesus had more than twelve disciples; once he sent out 70 among whom were women (Lk 8:1-2) as *apostles*. He also chose to meet his female disciples first after his resurrection (Mt 28:10). Jesus perceived men and women as his disciples. They all joined together constantly in prayers (Acts 1:14). Women were also there when the promised Holy Spirit came upon the disciples. God gave the gift of Pentecost to both women and men (Acts 2:17-18).[35]

The apostle Paul has been accused and viewed as being anti-women, and yet the New Testament evidence is against this assessment as is evident in Romans 16. Paul introduces Phoebe and greets 25 individuals, nine of whom are women,[36] prominent in the advancement of Paul's mission to the Gentiles particularly on Macedonian and Roman soil. While this reflects the greater freedom enjoyed by women in such areas, it also testifies to Paul's flexibility of practice where that would not lead to offence. His approach resulted in the elevation of women to a place of religious work of which there is little contemporary parallel.[37] From the first days of the church and the grand proclamation of Paul in Galatians[38] a change can be traced, that in Christ there is neither male nor female, but all are one in Christ, to the much more restrictive legislation of the Pastoral Epistles. As the church

---

[34] Wayne Grudem, *Systematic Theology*, p. 937.

[35] Klaus Fiedler, *Baptists and the Ordination of Women*, Zomba: Lydia Print. No. 5, 2010, pp. 8, 9.

[36] Klaus Fiedler, *Baptists and the Ordination of Women*, p. 11; Janet Kholowa and Klaus Fiedler, *Mtumwi Paulo ndi Udindo wa Amayi mu Mpingo*, Blantyre: CLAIM-Kachere, 2001, pp. 7-14.

[37] Robert Banks, *Paul's Idea of Community: The Early House Churches in their Historical Setting*, Exeter: Paternoster, 1980, p. 160. See also: Janet Kholowa and Klaus Fiedler, *Mtumwe Paulo ndi Udindo wa Amayi mu Mpingo*, Zomba: Kachere, 2000 (Mzuzu: Luviri Press, 2020)..

[38] For a detailed discussion see: Lazarus Chilenje, *Paul's Gender Theology and the Ordained Women's Ministry in the CCAP in Zambia*, Mzuzu: Mzuni Press, 2021.

8: The Church, the Laity and the Priesthood

became more organized and hierarchical, the place of women was being moved toward the periphery.[39]

Women in Ministry

In the Free Church movement there was openness to women in ministry. Women were encouraged to evangelistic work especially in the foreign countries, but men had serious reservations about it.[40] The continued influence and energy of women's missionary organizations served as the center pieces for the "women's sphere" of activities in the churches and denominations. On the British Isles, Congregationalists admitted women to their ministry. One of these, Agnes Maude Royden, who became an assistant pastor in 1917, was the first woman to hold that post. From the 1920s to the 1940s, she made several worldwide preaching tours.[41] In 1931 Royden was the first woman to become Doctor of Divinity and was well known on both sides of the Atlantic.[42] Although there were at the time a few gifted speakers, these lay preachers were crucial in the early development of the Free Church movement.[43]

Women and Ordination

Questions regarding the role of lay women increasingly involve ordination for both clergy and laity.[44] As a vocation, ordination was reserved for men.[45] The argument is the ordained priest represents Christ who is the husband

---

[39] Patricia Wilson-Kastener, *Faith, Feminism, and the Christ*, p. 73.

[40] Ruth A Tucker and Walter Liefeld, *Daughters of the Church: Women and Ministry from New Testament Times to the Present*, Grand Rapids: Academie Books, 1987, pp. 379, 380.

[41] Ruth A Tucker and Walter Liefeld, *Daughters of the Church*, p. 379.

[42] Kenneth Scott Latourette, *A History of Christianity*, vol. II, p. 1387.

[43] Ruth A Tucker and Walter Liefeld, *Daughters of the Church*, p. 390.

[44] See Klaus Fiedler, *Baptists and the Ordination of Women*.

[45] Klaus Fiedler, *The Story of Faith Missions*, Oxford: Regnum; Sutherland: Albatross, 1994, p. 308.

of his bride, the church. Limiting ordination to men was also based on patriarchal culture.[46]

In some churches, ordination is given to two types of ministers, clergy and deacons, the latter being lay officers of a local church. Through the office of deacon, the churches created a class of ordained lay leaders. Recent developments have stressed the servant role of the deacon with less distinction between temporal and spiritual functions. This trend suggests that the deacon – male and female in a growing number of churches – represents the ministry of the laity. Deacon family ministry and leadership in worship and teaching activities of the church have tended to foster a ministry centered approach to the diaconate.[47] "Throughout the history of modern missions, women have been more strongly attracted than men to the challenge of sharing the gospel worldwide, especially with other women."[48]

The Laity and Missions

God expected and demanded Abraham and his successors to be missionaries. God brought Abraham's descendants to himself, which means they were to encounter the living God and enter into a new covenant relationship with him. Abraham's descendants' entry into the covenant had to be of their own free choice. But, if they chose to enter the covenant, it had to be in accord with conditions laid down by God. They had to be willing to obey his voice and keep his covenant. If they were obedient and kept the covenant, they would enter into a unique relationship with God. The uniqueness indicates three ministries for Abraham's descendants:

---

[46] See Isabel Apawo Phiri, *Women, Presbyterianism and Patriarchy: Religious Experience of Chewa Women in Central Malawi*, Blantyre: CLAIM, 1997. See also, Rachel NyaGondwe Banda, *Women of the Bible and Culture: Baptist Convention Women in Southern Malawi*, Zomba: Kachere, 2005.

[47] Bill J. Leonard, "Southern Baptists and the Laity," p. 643.

[48] Ruth A. Tucker, "Women in Missions" in Joel A. Carpenter and Wilbert R Shenk (eds), *Earthen Vessels: American Evangelicals and Foreign Mission, 1880-1980*, Grand Rapids: William B. Eerdmans, 1990, p. 279. See also, Klaus Fiedler, *The Story of Faith Missions*, pp. 292-309.

1. They were to be God's own possession or special treasure emphasizing on the portability of the message and the fact that God has placed such high value in people.

2. They were to be a kingdom of priests. Here Israel's mission became explicit; the whole nation was to function on behalf of the kingdom of God in an intermediary role in relation to the nations. This became the basis for the New Testament doctrine of the priesthood of all believers. Unfortunately for Abraham's descendants, they rejected this priesthood of all believers and urged Moses to go up to the mountain of Sinai on their behalf and as their representative. Even though God's original plan was for a moment frustrated and delayed until New Testament times, it was not defeated, substituted or scrapped; it remained God's plan for believers. In addition, Abraham's descendants were to be a holy nation, "wholly" the Lord's.

3. They were to be set apart not only in their lives, but also in their service.[49]

Israel and the Church – "People of God"

One would argue that Israel is not the same as the church. The fact is what separated the two and demanded death for any Gentile that transgressed and passed its boundaries in the temple complex has now been knocked down by Christ's death. Maleness, femaleness, Jewishness, Gentile-ness, slave status or whatever no longer matter. All who believe are one "people of God." Peter calls the Gentile believers of his day "a chosen race, a royal priesthood, a holy nation, God's own people" (1Pet 2:9). The use of Exodus 19 is very obvious and transparent. The point is to recognize the continuity in the purpose and plan of God. The reason why Israel and now Gentile believers have been named a royal priesthood, a holy nation, the people of God, a chosen race, his special, moveable possession, is that we might announce and declare the wonderful deeds of him who called them out of darkness into his marvelous light and be his missionaries and witnesses.

---

[49] Walter C. Kaiser, Jr., "Israel's Missionary Call," pp. 29-30.

Peter is trying to show that the people of God in all ages have been one. The unity of all believers and the continuity of that plan between the Old and New Testaments is a certainty.[50] The primary emphasis of this passage is missionary outreach as a response to this privileged status.

The Laity as Effective Communicators

Multiplication of congregations must become a part of the joyful obedience of every Christian, clergy and denomination. If trained in evangelism, the laity are the most effective communicators for they reach their fellow workers, faculty members, fellow employers and employees.[51] Effective evangelism is carried on by a joint effort of the clergy and the laity. In it the clergy perform a small and very important percentage while the laity does larger part of the total work. If any denomination or congregation wishes to become effective in its proclamation of the gospel, it must inspire and organize a substantial number of its laity to become ardent and well trained lay evangelists.[52] The training of committed Christians to find and nurture unsaved relatives, friends and neighbours is the key to growth needed by every ordained clergy.

If the entire life of the church is missionary, then there is need for a theology of the laity. It does not mean that the laity should be trained to become little pastors. Instead, their ministry or service is everywhere. The contingent form of this ministry must be recognized as the contingent shape of the clergy ministry, and it will not be the same for every age, context and culture. Where the church's efforts may be more than those of the government, and where the church is left as almost the only voice of the voiceless, in most cases, it will be a combined ministry of the clergy and the laity so that it becomes impossible to distinguish who is doing what.[53]

---

[50] Walter C. Kaiser, Jr., "Israel's Missionary Call," pp. 30, 31.

[51] Donald A. McGavran, *Effective Evangelism: A Theological Mandate*, Phillipsburg: Presbyterian and Reformed Publishing company, 1988, p. 6.

[52] Donald A. McGavran, *Effective Evangelism*, p. 131.

[53] David J. Bosch, *Transforming Mission: paradigm Shifts in Theology of Mission*, Maryknoll: Orbis Books, 1996, p. 472, 473.

8: The Church, the Laity and the Priesthood

Ecclesiology of the Laity

Some form of ordained ministry is indeed essential and constitutive as guardian, to help keep the community faithful to the teaching and practice of apostolic Christianity. The clergy do not do this alone, but together with the laity. The priesthood of the ordained ministry is to enable and not to remove the priesthood of all believers. The clergy are not prior to or independent of or over against the church; rather, with the rest of the laity, they are the church sent into the world. As a result, there is need for a more organic, less sacral ecclesiology of the laity.[54]

Creeping Clericalism

"Clericalism," that is, the increasing dominance of ordained professionals in the churches was developing which would influence the understanding of the role of the laity. This trend may be attributed to several developments.

Tension between Clergy and Laity

The historic distinction between congregational polity and ministerial leadership continues to create tension. In some Protestant churches the congregation is the final authority. Pastors have long known frustration of congregational divisions and lay inflexibility. Power struggles between clergy and laity have often characterized these churches. These conflicts have sometimes led ministers to claim greater authority for the ministerial office, less by virtue of congregational approval than by divine mandate. These churches increasingly view the ministerial call as a divine imperative which is confirmed, though not necessarily verified, by the congregation through ordination. The call is seen as unique in and of itself apart from the confirmation of the community.

Professionalization and Multiple Ministers

The increasing professionalization of multiple ministers has had a significant effect on the theology of the laity. Once the pastor was the only

---

[54] David J. Bosch, *Transforming Mission*, p. 474.

ordained cleric in the congregation, but now, in increasing numbers, churches are hiring and ordaining ministers to serve specialized functions. These ministers provide valuable services for the church and the denomination. Their presence, however, implies that ministry or at least ministerial leadership may best be done by specially trained, preferably seminary educated professionals who are paid to direct various facets of church life. While this may be a reality of modern ecclesiastical life, it has significant implications for attitudes toward the priesthood of all believers. This approach may foster a view of the laity as clients who hire a professional to perform certain special services for a particular community. There is no real need to motivate the believers to be involved in ministry.[55]

Denominationalism added another dimension to the issue of ministerial professionalism by creating the office of "denominational worker," lay or clergy, an employee of the denomination who produces and administers programmes but is not related directly to the traditional ministerial functions evident in local congregations. In contrast, denominational workers serve as religious professionals, not "pure" laity, but neither are they preachers or ministers in the traditional sense. Denominational professionals have had limited authority in shaping and even addressing controversies and policies.[56]

Autocratic Model of Ministry

Most significantly, some Protestant denominations have been confronted with one particular model for ministry which emphasizes the ultimate authority of the pastoral office. This view suggests that there is only one biblical model for ministry and congregational authority, the pastor. As "under-shepherd" he (women are not considered) represents Christ in the congregation and is responsible only to God. Spiritual, financial, and practical ministries are directed by the pastor who articulates the Word of God to the people. Church growth studies frequently confirm that this

---

[55] Bill J. Leonard, "Southern Baptists and the Laity," pp. 644, 645.
[56] Bill J. Leonard, "Southern Baptists and the Laity," p. 645. See also, Klaus Fiedler, "The 'Smaller' Churches and Big Government," in Matembo S Nzunda & Kenneth Ross, (eds), *Church, Law and Political Transition in Malawi 1992-94*, pp. 164, 165.

autocratic model for ministry produces significant numerical advancements for many congregations. Practically speaking, this style of ministry reflects the business model of the chief executive or chairman of the board whose powerful direction leads the corporation to ever expanding statistical and financial success. Therefore, the laity are considered constituents to be guided by a caring chief executive who by virtue of divine enlightenment and spiritual responsibility is called to lead and direct the church authoritatively.[57]

"Creeping clericalism" among the clergy plus spiritual inferiority complex among the laity have continued to minimize believers' perception and fulfillment of their priestly call. However, that call remains God's call and commission for all God's people to accomplish.[58]

Conclusion

The presence of an ordained priesthood can have the unfortunate side-effect of minimizing an appreciation of the priesthood of all believers. There is need to recover for the Church membership 1 Peter's sense of priestly dignity and spiritual sacrifices precisely as a way of understanding the status conferred on all Christians – the priesthood of all believers. The ultimate aim of the priesthood of all believers is the joint service of all believers, men and women, who are theologically competent in a unified mission to the world. Incidentally, this is an encouragement to theological training institutions to develop programmes for training the laity in specialized ministry rather than requiring all who provide such ministries to acquire a professional, clerical identity.

The priesthood of all believers gives each Christian, male or female, the responsibility to be a witness for the faith as an individual and as a part of the local church or denomination. Although churches are growing so quickly that coping with the ever-increasing numbers is a major problem,

---

[57] Bill J. Leonard, "Southern Baptists and the Laity," p. 645. This is a development that shows in many of the Charismatic churches.

[58] *What Presbyterians Believe*, www.pcusa.org/believe/past/mar04/priesthood.htm, [10.12.2007].

they lack missionary vision. There is much energy for missions available on the level below that of the clergy, and that is the laity. All Christians are priests, and all priests are Christians. The greatest power is not in the pulpit, but in the lives of those in the pews.

Chapter 9

The Ordination of Women in the Baptist Convention of Malawi

Whether as deaconesses or preachers, women have been involved in ministry in the Baptist denomination from its inception in England and continuing throughout its growth in the United States. Although Baptists ordained women in the U.S. as early as the 1880s, the practice has not been shared by all congregations. Throughout the history of Baptists, the role of women in ministry has been a divisive theme.

Both sides of the debate regarding women's role in Baptist ministry rely on Scripture to support their positions. Those advocating a male-only ministry point to Genesis and state that the woman was created to help the man; they also refer to a distinction between the roles of males and females recognized by Jesus and by Paul's call for women to be silent. Baptists in favour of an uncensored outlook also cite Scripture, noting that Acts 18:26 speaks of a woman named Priscilla, who alongside her husband Aquila, taught a man. Paul also made a favourable mention of another female believer, Phoebe, whom he described in Romans 16:1 as a deacon from the church at Cenchreae. Supporters of gender equality in ministry cite Paul's declaration that there is no longer a distinction to be made between Jew and Gentile, master and servant or male and female (Galatians 3:27-28).

In the late 1980s and early 2000s, Southern Baptists announced a harder line toward women in ministry, stating it was no longer encouraging the ordination of women. However, outright prohibition of such ordinations has not been possible due to the autonomous nature of local Baptist congregations.[1]

---

[1] Trudie Longren, Baptist Beliefs on Women in the Ministry. https://classroom.synonym.com/baptist-beliefs-on-women-in-the-ministry-12087385.html [12.11.2019].

Southern Baptist Convention (SBC history and their rural background forged strong ties of loyalty to traditional cultural values that also influenced Baptist Convention of Malawi (BACOMA)'s theology and women.[2] SBC theology had not much room for women. Only ordained men were recognized as missionaries, and not their wives.[3] They were there to support their husbands. Unmarried women were accepted as missionaries though not of equal ranking with men. Women were not allowed to stand before men, that is, to preach or teach. Although Southern Baptists and Malawian Baptists believe in the priesthood of all believers, they have not freely accepted women to be ordained as pastors of local churches.

The issue of women pastors came to the fore and continued to remain a bone of contention amongst pastors, pastors' wives and the members as more women received higher theological education alongside men, and in some cases higher than men. The issue became more heated with the arrival of Molly Longwe as a lecturer at the Seminary in Lilongwe. Although the BTSM was not there just to train pastors, many members of the Convention, including its leadership, believed that it was there for the training of men only to be pastors. The question was, who had the right to stop her from teaching men who were "pastors to be," and others who were already serving as pastors, and some had been ordained many years back? The only way was to react to her office of teaching.

Klaus Fiedler wrote and published his plea for the ordination of women in his little book, *Baptists and the Ordination of Women*. In it he states that Baptists want to be and to build their church "according to the New Testament,"[4] and if that is the case, men and women are one in Christ. Therefore, no one should hinder women from becoming what God intended for them. I, instead, discuss the reality on the ground in the Baptist Convention of Malawi.

---

[2] John Lee Eighmy, *Churches in Cultural Captivity: A History of the Social Attitudes of Southern Baptists*, Knoxville: University of Tennessee, 1987, p. 55.

[3] See also Klaus Fiedler, *Story of Faith Missions*, p. 292f.

[4] Klaus Fiedler, *Baptists and the Ordination of Women*, p. 1.

Position of Women in BACOMA

In 1984, the SBC adopted a lengthy resolution that opposed the ordination of women,[5] and part of the last paragraph reads:

> That we not decide concerns of Christians doctrine and practice by modern cultural, sociological, and ecclesiastical trends or by emotional factors; that we remind ourselves of the dearly bought Baptist principle of the final authority of Scripture in matters of faith and conduct; and that we encourage the service of women in all aspects of church life and work other than pastoral functions and leadership roles entailing ordination.[6]

BACOMA, on the other hand, though they have not produced a written resolution, has had difficulties to accept women as pastors because the position involves ordination.

As a result, SBC missionary wives taught homemaking to local women that included other methods of cooking and skills in sewing and knitting. It gave women opportunities to break away from the monotony of their homes and be able to socialize with other women who were being drawn to the church. In the process both women groups were able to witness as the Lord led them, consequently the numbers of women in the churches grew larger than those of men because men were custodians of traditions, customs and religion and laws, while women found liberty, and human solidarity in Christianity.

BACOMA women also engaged themselves in support roles that included singing, praying, giving and works of service. They were involved in all social functions such as weddings and funerals, initiation rites and counselling of mainly girls and young married women members of the local churches. They brought life not only to the church, but to the community in which they ministered. Although men lead, women put the final touches to all family and church activities. That ministry soon was to develop into

---

[5] H. Leon McBeth, *The Baptist Heritage*, p. 693.
[6] Southern Baptist Convention, "Resolution on Ordination and the Role of Women in Ministry," Kansas City, Missouri – 1984.

women's organizations at local, regional and national levels.[7] Local women and missionary wives worked together much of the time in the background, but BACOMA women did come out though from the background, and they proved to be effective evangelists and preachers of the gospel, and that greatly helped the spread of the good news of Jesus Christ. It was not their culture alone that barred African women from standing before men and teach in public places, it was also the SBC missionary culture.

Though *Umodzi wa Amayi aBaptist ku Malaŵi* multiplied through their witnessing efforts and fellowship, and had the tremendous potential to do meaningful evangelism and church planting, they were still excluded from taking office in the Associations and BACOMA EC not by the policies of BACOMA, but probably by what BACOMA had learnt from BMIM's understanding of the woman's role, both in the home and in the church. It was not necessarily cultural, because many Malawian tribes have women in positions of leadership and authority alongside men. Some *Umodzi wa Amayi* members were beginning to query the practice. Their local and national assemblies were accepted by men as women's meetings, and men were not to interfere. Many pastors were not directly involved in the women's ministries in their local churches because they saw it as one of those occasions where women met and discussed women issues, though in the name of the church. They were only a church when they met on Sunday where generally male leadership presided and preached. At no time did the male dominated BACOMA regard the women assemblies with suspicion. Generally, at local church level there was a good relationship between *Umodzi wa Amayi* and the rest of the church membership. They contributed both in cash and labour towards church development projects. Men were men, and women were women. However, women meetings under *Umodzi wa Amayi* grew in attendance and membership and activities. Because women were able to use their gifting to edify each other under *Umodzi wa Amayi* that provided the scope for leadership talent development that was soon to surface. Despite the fact that there were a lot of difficulties, women began to climb in church leadership through *Umodzi wa Amayi*.

---

[7] See also Rachel NyaGondwe Banda, *Women of Bible and Culture*, p. 47.

Yet, *Umodzi wa Amayi* failed to speak to BACOMA and the nation on issues that oppressed women in the churches and in society. Though some pastors' wives were uncomfortable about the oppression that included segregation of women from church leadership, chances of challenging their husbands on the issues were minimal. They had been taught to respect the 'pastor'. According to some oppressive cultural teachings, women were forbidden to go against their husbands. In some Christian teachings they were supposed to 'submit' to their husbands. It was on the husbands' tickets that the wives were able to receive some theological education and other benefits from the church. They could not challenge their husbands for a while until several pastors' wives later received (and continue to receive) higher theological education, and there was increased participation of educated women church members and leaders as well in the *Umodzi wa Amayi*.

An increasing number of committed Christian women feeling called of God went out to serve within the churches. They encounter masculine determination that is wrapped in both scriptural and cultural references to stifle or subordinate their womanhood. This is a manifestation of fallen human nature or relationships rather than redemption and fellowship of the children of God. Since we are all called to be ambassadors of Christ, it should be the responsibility of men to insist upon the freedom of women to serve in whatever capacity in the churches than for women to be put in the position of having to defend their priesthood.

An understanding of segregation on the basis of gender led others to respond to the situation in BACOMA calling for a move towards full recognition of all people as redeemed of God with equality to serve according to the gifts of the Holy Spirit. Evangelism can be fulfilled as women and youth are affirmed as full partners in this calling. With full engagement of all the redeemed, BACOMA will grow both in quantity and in quality.

The numbers of women involved in decision making increase although at a small scale as compared to their population in BACOMA, which remains a man's world. There was a deliberate effort, though, by some men and women to engage women more in all ministries of the church, which included pastoral work, which was and has been designated as men only ministry. The issue that there were certain ministries which were for men only has no biblical basis. It was more of a cultural construction than a teaching from God's Word. In spite of that false teaching, pressure continued to mount against the wall that separates men and women in ministry. The number of women in theology continued to grow. It was just a matter of time before it fell, in part or entirely.

Soon women in BACOMA began to speak openly against the subordination of women in the roles they played in church and society. The visibility of the rights of a girl child and human rights, and the increasing numbers of women qualifying from theological seminaries and colleges, took the form of politeness of not just ordaining women to the ministry, but also accepting them as equals in the BACOMA setting. They saw no passage in the Bible that states that the roles of women in church are different from those of men. Although women were already assuming more leadership roles and representation in many positions of church government, ordination remained a sticking point.[8].

BACOMA did not issue any solid resolution on the role of women in churches, especially that of pastor, whether ordained or not. It seems some people thought the issue was going to die a natural death. It was hard for the Convention to come up with a resolution that barred women from holding the office of pastor because it violates the autonomy of the local church. The final authority of whether to call or not to call a woman to pastor a church is the local church. If a local BACOMA church decided to call a woman as its pastor, it would be difficult to have no fellowship with them, and it would also equally be difficult for a while for many BACOMA members to accept the situation. It was just a matter of time.

The discrimination of any person or group of people according to gender and/or age points to yet most often neglected responsibilities implied in the

---

[8] There are women pastors (in the sense of the word though not one ever baptized), preachers and evangelists in many local churches especially in urban and semi-urban areas of the Lower Shire, Blantyre, Zomba, Lilongwe and Mzuzu Districts. Another office not open to women was that of elders, promoting the priesthood of male believers, though there were women elders in Blantyre Baptist Church in 1994.

concept of the priesthood of all the believers, Baptist hold to, which is the duty of each Christian to serve as a priest in relation to others. Believers have a responsibility to each other as parts of the same Body that belongs to Christ.

Probably recognition by the congregations of spiritual gifting in the pastors through ordination made the pastors feel accepted in their relationships. Many Baptist Convention of Malawi pastors took ordination as a means of recognition by other ministers, and that called for respect from the members and the public at large. Ordained pastors have been seen as a class on its own. It is a step higher than those who are not ordained even though they have served for many years. Some pastors made their churches to ordain them without the idea coming from the congregation itself. Once they were ordained, they considered themselves truly pastors. Some pastors wanted ordination to be the criteria for the pastors' fraternal, while others felt that the best was education, whilst another group felt that both, ordination and education were the best requirements for ordination. That had nothing to do with ministry, but self-acclamation. To allow women ordination, it would mean that women could be truly pastors and in a class with male pastors.

National Discussions on the Ordination of Women

The issue of having women pastors in BACOMA was brought up during the pastors' meeting that was running concurrent with the annual general meeting of BACOMA in Lilongwe in 2002. The president, Emmanuel Chinkwita Phiri, and the secretary, Fletcher Kaiya, tabled the motion to allow women's ordination at an annual BACOMA meeting, but the motion was rejected. The President gave an example of the Baptist Convention of South Africa that had ordained women pastors. A committee of three pastors was chosen to study the issue and to bring their findings to the 2003 pastors' meeting, but they never did. During the 2003 conference pastors and their wives unanimously voted against women pastors in BACOMA. It was not a theological conviction, but a cultural stand in which men are men, and women follow behind. Other women questioned how they could stand in a baptistery and baptize men. They could not imagine that. Chinkwita

Phiri told the women that they had lost an opportunity. No Malawian Convention women would be eligible for the post of chair of BWUA because it was agreed that only Baptist women pastors would contest for it.

The issue came up again during the 2008 Annual General Meeting this time to deliberate the issue of Sigerege Baptist Church that had called Grace Kachere to be their pastor. The issue was discussed and in no way decided. Because he could not attend the meeting, Klaus Fiedler published, *Baptists and the Ordination of Women*, as his plea for the ordination of women.[9] If it had been agreed upon, she would have been the first woman to be ordained. That would have led to more women being ordained since there were several who had been serving as pastors, who started churches and the members affirmed their work and ascribed the title of pastor to them.

In 2006, Sigerege Church called Grace Kachere to be their pastor after she had completed studies with the Localized Bible School as well as BTCP studies. When the church wrote a letter to the Blantyre Baptist Association informing them about the call, the Association did not accept the call citing that the Convention had not yet given a go-ahead to churches to call women as pastors. The Blantyre Association advised Sigerege Baptist to bring its matter to a South-South Regional Meeting. It is the Regional meeting that referred the matter to the BACOMA Annual General Meeting.

In January 2009, Sigerege Church wrote a letter to Blantyre Baptist Pastors Fraternal, reiterating that they were not changing their decision of calling Grace Kachere their pastor. Part of the letter read, "*Ife a Sigerege Baptist Church tati tikuuzenibe kuti maganizo athu okhudzana ndi abusa athu mayi Grace Kachere sitikusintha ayi.*" (We, members of Sigerege Baptist Church, want to reiterate that we are not changing our decision on our pastor, Mrs. Grace Kachere). Nonetheless, instead of addressing the matter of the letter, the pastors perverted the issue, saying that the tone of the letter was disrespectful. The fraternal chose Revs Alex Govati, Joseph Mpombwe, Bizwick Nikoroma and Rustin Kalenga to go to Sigerege Baptist and express the fraternity's concern on the tone of the letter. Eventually, only

---

[9] Rachel NyaGondwe Fiedler, *A History of the Circle of Concerned African Women Theologians (1989-2007)*, Mzuzu: Mzuni Press, 2017, p.110, footnote 284.

Joseph Mpombwe and Rustin Kalenga went to meet the Sigerege leadership. During the discussion, the Sigerege leadership apologized and promised to follow the right procedure, while upholding the decision that Grace Kachere was their pastor. The church put its foot down on the decision failing which it was ready to renounce its link with BACOMA.[10]

The way Blantyre pastors handled this matter shows that indeed Baptist churches are autonomous. In all conscience, the pastors could not address the real matter of Sigerege Baptist; it was not the tone of the letter, but the calling of Grace Kachere, a woman, as pastor. The pastors knew that every Baptist church had the freedom to decide on a pastor of their choice. It does not hold water when the Convention kept on postponing the conclusion on the issue of women pastors and ordination. Grace Kachere had been leading the church for more than three years. The Convention was trying to prevent the germination of something that had already grown and was then bearing fruit.

Definitely, it would be awkward to stop Grace Kachere from leading this church. In 2003, there were three people, and in 2011 there were 230 members. In addition, in 2008, Sigerege Baptist Church started a preaching point at Chitakale, about 4 km away from Sigerege. The priesthood of all believers has more to do with the believer's service than with the individual's position or status; the ultimate goal being the joint service of all believers in unified mission to the lost. Sigerege church under the leadership of Grace Kachere discerned God's will for their corporate mission.[11]

Throughout 2009, the issue of women's ordination was discussed at each of the six Regional Annual Conventions with a speaker for and another against, but no conclusions were reached. For example, at a South East meeting, the pastor of Zomba Baptist Church, Funwayo Mafuleka spoke in support of women's ordination, whilst the pastor of Liwonde church, Graham Chipande, spoke against it. Rachel NyaGondwe Fiedler was given

---

[10] Int. Grace Kachere, pastor, Sigerege Baptist Church, Blantyre, 18.10.2010.

[11] Rustin Kalenga, "Compromising the Baptist Heritage: The Re-defining the Qualifications of and the Place of Ministry for a Pastor in the Baptist Convention of Malawi (BACOMA)," BA, Baptist Theological Seminary of Malawi, 2012, p. 23.

the opportunity to speak from a woman's perspective.[12] In 2011, the women's association invited Hany Longwe and Klaus Fiedler to present the case for women's ordination at their annual meeting in Mzuzu. Hany Longwe presented the practical side, Klaus Fiedler the biblical side. The President of the *Umodzi wa Amayi a Baptist ku Malawi*, Bridget Mwenefumbo asked those women who wanted to be ordained pastors to stand in front, nine women did so, including Bridget Mwenefumbo! These were mature women with years in church life and work.[13] When the issue and the wish of some women to be ordained as pastors was brought to the Pastors' Fraternal Annual Meeting, the members, all male, requested that the issue be laid to rest as it had the potential to divide BACOMA.

The contradiction here is that the decision was taken at a time when many of them had gone through training by women lecturers, for example at Gweru, where there was "sister Harris," as people called her because she was single, and Molly Longwe at the Baptist Theological Seminary, who were not "pastors" and were not ordained. They played an important role in the formation of the same pastors who were rejecting the ordination of women. In the case of Molly Longwe, she met some resistance. At first, some male students, many of who were "pastors," did not accept to be taught by a woman. If the Seminary made someone to be a pastor, she was qualified to be one. She had more qualifications than the students she was teaching. The issue was not of seminary qualifications, but of gender. She was a woman and not a man; therefore, she could not be accepted as a pastor. In general, many men and women including pastors and their wives in BACOMA did not approve of women pastors. The attitude soon changed and with time she earned support as a lecturer, not only by such students, but also by many pastors,[14] inside and outside of the Convention.

---

[12] Rachel NyaGondwe Fiedler, *A History of the Circle of Concerned African Women Theologians*, p. 110.

[13] Rachel NyaGondwe Fiedler, *A History of the Circle of Concerned African Women Theologians*, p. 110, footnote, 285.

[14] Hany Longwe, *Christians by Grace – Baptists by Choice*, 2011, p. 287.

Women Pastors not a New Thing in BACOMA

Consistent with Baptist beliefs and practice, it is not the job of the Convention or any of its organs to make someone a pastor, it is the job and responsibility of the local church. When someone, male or female, hears God's call, they inform the church, and the church has to test the call and hopefully will be able to confirm it. That is how a pastor is made. Although theological training is highly recommended, it is not a precondition for the decision of the local church to make someone a pastor.

Women pastors have not been a new phenomenon among the Baptists in Malawi. Before Pastor Grace Kachere, there have been several women who have served in that capacity shepherding a congregation or more than one congregation at a time.

One of the earliest recorded woman pastors is Mellia Makina. In 1988, she became pastor of Mwanafumu Baptist Church after the founder, who was her uncle, fell out of fellowship with the church when he became polygamous. She was one of the founding members of the church. Although she was a young widow, church members voted her in as the pastor because of her abilities. As a pastor, she preached all Sundays except when Rev Davidson Lichapa from Makolija, which was a supervising church, visited. Mellia Makina was pastor of Mwanafumu for two years until she remarried to an evangelist, Makina. As a result, the supervising church appointed her husband as pastor. The change did not reduce respect the Mwanafumu church members and the region had for her. They still referred to her as pastor. Mellia still remained the pastor of the church in her own right, exercising her pastoral role even though her husband was nominated pastor.[15]

At Liwonde, Sellina Nasimango abandoned the Catholic Church and became a Baptist in 1970 after hearing a message of salvation from a Baptist deacon. Unfortunately, where she lived at that time, in Chinyung'unya, there

---

[15] Rachel NyaGondwe Banda, *Women of Bible and Culture: Baptist Convention Women in Southern Malawi*, Zomba: Kachere, 2005, pp. 132, 133. This wide respect became obvious at her funeral, Rachel and Klaus Fiedler reported that they had not seen a Baptist funeral so highly attended by Umodzi women and pastors in their uniforms.

was no Baptist church; as a result, she started holding worship meetings with her family. Her husband left Islam and followed her. Others joined this house church; she led the worship services and preached. Until 1996, Sellina Nasimango was the pastor of this church that took the name Chinyung'unya Baptist. Nevertheless, she continued to be referred to as pastor of the church although a male pastor had taken over. She felt that God called her to start the church, and that she welcomed anyone God wanted to use as pastor at any given time.[16]

In Lilongwe, Liddah Kalako was an evangelist, church planter and a pastor. She was probably one of the female stalwarts of BACOMA. She was a faithful evangelist, disciple and teacher, instrumental in founding a number of Convention churches. She fought her way to end up as a great woman of God.

She was one of the founder members of Lilongwe and Area 23 Baptist churches. From 1987 Kalako began to think through why in the world most churches did not permit women to be pastors or even equivalent. Her prayer since then was that women also take up the responsibility of shepherding God's flock.[17]

Kalako went to Haggai Institute on 4 October 1988. Upon her return that very year she observed that no member in particular of Lilongwe church was directly responsible for the work at Area 23. She also thought of the need for the congregation to have its own building and a pastor's house since the work was growing as well as the number of people moving into the area. Kalako considered herself as the right person to lead Area 23 congregation. She asked for her membership to be transferred to Area 23 church, and that was granted. She began by visiting people in their homes during the week, and taught Bible to members on Sundays. However, she had special classes with those who requested studies in the Word, whether they were Christians or not.[18]

---

[16] Rachel NyaGondwe Banda, *Women of Bible and Culture*, pp. 134-135.

[17] Hany Longwe, *Christians by Grace – Baptists by Choice*, p. 268.

[18] Int. Liddah Kalako, member, Lilongwe, 15.11.1997.

As Area 23 location grew with the arrival of more people and construction of new houses, so did the congregation. In 1989 the congregation asked Tsabango Primary School authorities for permission for the church to meet in one of the classrooms every Sunday morning for worship. Permission was granted and the church began meeting at the school. They extended the net over Area 23 such that more people joined the church, and the result was that the classroom became too small to accommodate all who attended the Sunday worship service. The congregation decided to move to Muloza Local Education Authority (LEA) School that had larger classrooms, and they did.[19]

When the Baptist Seminary created space for women to do theology, she entered the seminary as a widow in September 1996.[20] She was the only female student in a class of 13. Not only did other students ask, but also church members, whether she was going to be a pastor or not. She had all the qualifications of and had been serving Area 23 as the pastor, so why not call her pastor. Women who were inclined to the traditional roles of women did not appreciate Kalako being at the Seminary. That in a way fueled her desire to be a pastor. Unfortunately she died soon after her graduation in 2000,[21] at a time when another woman pastor, Nellie Phiri was already in her second year at BTSM.

Nellie Phiri believed it was her right and a call from God to learn his Word and later to serve him in whatever capacity. She did not shun away from the fact that she could be a *mbusa* if God called her to that ministry. She was ready to take the challenge.[22] Nellie Phiri graduated from the seminary and she was a member of Ufulu Baptist Church where she continued to teach other women and young people, not men. She opened a nursery school at her home. She was also a member of the Mandarin to Malawi Mission Taskforce, an arm of First Baptist Church of Mandarin, USA, which was trying to assist local churches in outreach. After seminary studies, Nellie

---

[19] Int. Liddah Kalako, member, Lilongwe, 15.11.1997.
[20] Hany Longwe, *Christians by Grace – Baptists by Choice*, p. 269.
[21] Hany Longwe, *Christians by Grace – Baptists by Choice*, pp. 269, 270.
[22] Hany Longwe, *Christians by Grace – Baptists by Choice*, p. 270.

Phiri had some training in teaching adults and children to read and write, and in HIV&AIDS prevention. She ministered and continued to do so amongst the youth of Lilongwe and Yao speaking communities in the country.

Lydia Chinkwita Phiri, a pastor's wife, did not find it wrong to accept the call to be a pastor. When she told her husband, Emmanuel Chinkwita Phiri, of her call to pastoral ministry, he was so excited. He did not find it difficult to accept her as another pastor in the home and church. He supported his wife's ministry both as a husband and a fellow minister.[23] Lydia exercised her gifts through preaching in the church and also during outdoor meetings arranged by the church. She did not hesitate to go to seminary to prepare herself for the work God had planned for her.

Outside of Lilongwe there was another woman theologian, Rachel NyaGondwe Fiedler [Banda] who sensed that God called her to be a pastor. She was instrumental in the beginning of Ndangopuma Baptist Church at her home, and later of Naisi Baptist Church.. Rachel Banda did not wait long to know how God wanted her to reach women. What started as a sewing evangelism project through the help of Hughes Baptist Church, Canberra in Australia, was to develop into Lydia Project which was committed to participating in the fight against HIV&AIDS in several ways. The project networks with BACOMA congregations.[24] The project served orphans, widows and elderly people in different areas.

Another woman who has been serving as a pastor within BACOMA is Mary Kagwa. Her husband, Milward Kagwa was a BACOMA Home Missionary in Mangochi from 2001 to 2008. When they moved to Mangochi in 2001 Milward began studies at the Baptist Theological Seminary in Lilongwe. As a result, it was an opportunity for Mary Kagwa to carry out the missionary task. She started a church in her house. Together with her children and grandchild, they met every Sunday morning for worship. During the weekdays, she went out witnessing to neighbouring homes. Within six

---

[23] Emmanuel Chinkwita Phiri, Lilongwe, 22.11.2011, email to Rustin Kalenga. Rustin Kalenga, "Compromising the Baptist Heritage," p. 24.
[24] Int. Rachel Fiedler, Zomba, 5.4.2004.

months, a few people had been converted. They rented a classroom at a Roman Catholic School where the church met for worship services. In 2007, the school authorities discontinued the use of the classrooms by other denominations. The Maldeco Baptist Church, a name they took later, went back to the Kagwa's home. They erected a temporary church building next to their home. In 2008, Milward died when Mary Kagwa was in her last year of study at the Lilongwe Seminary, and immediately the church accepted her as their pastor. She was mature and an experienced shepherd and they affirmed God's call for her to minister as a pastor. At that time, she took charge of three churches: Maldeco, Njerezu and Matawi.

For almost nine years, Mary shepherded the three churches until some members, for fear of falling out of fellowship with the Convention, instead of confirming her call to pastor, let alone ordination, the church reversed the decision and appointed a male person to take over as pastor of the church. Immediately, the church was moved to another location and the named changed to Chisomo. The man had been working in a bar of one of the nearby holiday resorts. In 2018, the man was working in another tourist resort in Mponela, leaving his wife, the pastor' wife, who had no clue about the ministry, to lead the church. As a result, she had no choice but to call on Mary to lead. Although Chisomo church had a male pastor, Mary continued to shepherd Chisomo as members continued to call upon her to lead.[25]

Conclusion

Because of the examples of women leadership in the Bible such as Deborah and Anna, women felt mobilized. They recognized they were able to take and preach the Gospel and act as prophets, bishops, and priests among others. The centralized church structures tended to oppress women in local churches by denying them freedom to engage themselves in spiritual ministries they felt called to. Although some women felt called to be pastors, they had to wait until men who, though fewer in church

---

[25] Int. Mary Kagwa, Mangochi, 2.4.2018.

membership than women, formed the church leadership, approved that women could be ordained.[26]

In most Christian churches ordination differentiates between clergy and laity, and only the clergy is allowed to administer the sacraments. In most Baptist communities there is ordination, but not to set apart the clergy from the laity, but to set people apart for ministry. Baptists also have insisted that ordination is the matter of the local church, not of any higher authority like Association, Convention or Union. For Baptists, ordination does not convey a higher position, but a special commitment.[27] The Baptist Convention of Malawi failed to live by what they believed by denying women ordination when they qualified to be set apart for ministry. The work of God can be done equally by all, bringing salvation to all.

Women pastors were not ordained, but were either chosen to be pastors of congregations, or became pastors because they started the churches, and by members affirming them as their shepherds, they ascribed the title of "pastor" to these women, ignoring the cultural construction. That is the reason why, while the local congregations' membership of both men and women, and young people accepted them as pastors, many male pastors did not recognize them, thereby denying the women shepherds the ordination that male pastors felt was necessary for ministry, but exclusively for them. Baptist doctrine and polity were thus sacrificed due to a number of factors that included missionary influence, biblical interpretation and the Malawian culture that was in bondage.

---

[26] Rachel NyaGondwe Banda, *Women of the Bible and Culture*, p. 134.
[27] Klaus Fiedler, notes on women pastors, n.d.

Chapter 10

Baptist Churches in Africa[1]

Baptists prefer to speak of themselves as convention, union, fellowship, assembly, association or churches, for example: Baptist Convention of Angola, Baptist Union of Gambia, Baptist Fellowship of Zambia, African Baptist Assembly, Association of Baptist Churches in Ruanda and Free Baptist Churches of Burundi. This is in reference to local Baptist churches that are characterized mainly by their emphasis upon voluntary association, congregational form of local churches or congregational form of church government and religious liberty. Because of that Baptists do not speak of themselves as "The Baptist Church," but "Baptist churches" and as members of a local congregation or convention, and so on.[2] Baptists are a denomination where the local church is paramount.[3]

History of Baptists in Africa

In 1792 Baptist black British ex-soldiers from Nova Scotia in Canada established the oldest Baptist congregation in Africa, the Regent Road Baptist Church, in Freetown, Sierra Leone. In 1822 Lott Carey with six other freed slaves from the USA planted a second congregation in West Africa, Providence Baptist Church in Monrovia, Liberia. In spite of their early beginnings, Baptist work, not only in West Africa but also on the continent as a whole, was slow.

The other country Baptists established missionary work in West Africa before the First War is Nigeria. In 1850 Thomas Bowen, a Southern Baptist Convention (USA) missionary, arrived at Badagry from where he proceeded

---

[1] First published in Isabel Apawo Phiri and Dietrich Werner, Chammah Kaunda and Kennedy Owino (eds), *Anthology of African Christianity*, Oxford: Regnum, 2016.
[2] Hany Longwe, *Christians by Grace – Baptists by Choice*, p. 7.
[3] Hany Longwe, *Christians by Grace – Baptists by Choice*, p. 24.

inland to Abeokuta with the aim of reaching Igboho.[4] Two years later he was able to establish work there among the Yoruba. The team that took over from him went down with malaria that rendered the work of Baptists slow during the early years.[5] It was only during the 1930s that Baptists began to grow significantly.[6] The Yoruba spread the gospel of Jesus Christ to other parts of Nigeria and West Africa. The Nigerian Baptist Convention boasts of comprising 10,000 churches across the country, while the Mambilla Baptist Convention has 261. This makes Nigeria the most productive Baptist field in Africa.[7] Baptists are found in every country in West Africa except Mauritania.

In 1843 the first Baptists in Equatorial Africa were from the West Indies Baptist Mission. Many of their missionaries were freed Jamaican slaves who wanted to take the gospel of Jesus Christ to their homeland of Africa. They began work on the island of Fernando Po,[8] but the Spanish terminated the work in 1845. The work was taken over by the English Baptists (Alfred Saker). The first Baptist church in Cameroon was formed in 1849, and in 1891 the German Baptist Mission came in. German colonial rule affected the working relationship between missionaries and the Germans that led some local Baptists to work independently of any missionary group.[9] By 2012 there were over 1,532 Baptist congregations in Cameroon.

In 1878 the Baptist Missionary Society (UK) started at the mouth of the Congo River, reaching Kinshasa and extending its work along the Congo River. At the decision of the interdenominational Livingstone Inland Mission the American Baptists took over all the mission stations on the

---

[4] For his life see: Alversonde Souza, "A Black Heart: The Life and Work of Thomas Jefferson Bowen among Blacks in Africa and in Brazil between 1840 and 1875," MA, University of Natal, 1998.

[5] Jonathan Hildebrandt, *History of the Church in Africa: A Survey*, rev., Achimota: African Christian Press, 1990, p. 104.

[6] Baptist World Alliance Heritage and Identity Commission, "Who are the Baptists? – Africa," www.bwa-baptist-heritage.org/hst-afr.htm.

[7] Baptist World Alliance – Statistics, www.bwanet.org/about-us2/statistics.

[8] Jonathan Hildebrandt, *History of the Church*, p. 132.

[9] Jonathan Hildebrandt, *History of the Church*, p. 163.

10: Baptist Churches in Africa 185

Congo River in 1884 and then began to develop new stations of their own.[10] In 1918 the Norwegian Baptists entered northern Congo and were followed by others.[11]. There are over 5,300 Baptist churches in the Democratic Republic of Congo according to Baptist World Alliance statistics.

In 1921 an independent Baptist mission from the USA entered the Central African Republic and it was followed by another from Sweden. In 1925 the American mission extended their work northward into Chad. Central African Republic is the home of over 750 Baptist churches.

Although they were one of the first Protestant denominations to begin work in West Africa and in the Democratic Republic of Congo, Baptists had a weak start in South Africa and a late entry in East Africa. In 1823 English Baptists established the first Baptist congregation in the Republic of South Africa among English settlers. In 1858, German settlers also formed their own churches.[12] In 1887 the mainly white churches formed the Baptist Union of South Africa. The Union also included the early African Baptist churches established by the work of the German Baptists and the National Black American Baptists. They were later incorporated into the Union as separate associations called the Banthu Baptist Church. Around 1888 work began among the people of mixed race, and in 1903 among the people of Asian origin. The Union later included the Afrikaanse Baptist Kerk, the Indian Baptist Mission and the National Indian Baptist Association. In 1987 the black Baptist Convention withdrew its associational status from the Baptist Union to form an independent group called the Baptist Convention of South Africa.[13] In 2004 there were five bodies of Baptists in the Republic of South Africa: Baptist Convention, Baptist Union, Baptist Mission,

---

[10] Livingstonia Inland Mission is the oldest interdenominational Faith Missions (1873). For the handover see Klaus Fiedler, *Interdenominational Faith Missions in Africa. History and Ecclesiology*, Mzuzu: Mzuni Press, 2018, p. 46.

[11] For all the Protestant missions in Congo see: Cecilia Irvine, *The Church of Christ in Zaïre. A Handbook of Protestant Churches, Missions and Communities, 1878-1978*, Indianapolis: Christian Church (Disciples of Christ), 1978.

[12] Fritz Haus, *Carl Hugo and Mary Gutsche and the "German" Baptists of the Eastern Cape*, Mzuzu: Luviri Press, 2019.

[13] Louise Kretzschmar, *Privatization of the Christian Faith: Mission, Social Ethics and the South African Baptists*, Legon: Legon Theological Studies Series, 1998, p. 28.

Baptist Association and Afrikaanse Baptiste Kerk. There are over 820 Baptist churches throughout the country.

In 1818, in an attempt to enter the Congo, Baptists from England arrived in Angola. The comparative weakness of the Roman Catholic Mission and Portuguese colonial rule in the interior provided opportunity for the Baptists to be the first Protestant denomination to open many stations in the northern part of Angola from 1878.[14] Today, Angola has nearly 600 Baptist congregations.

Baptist work in Malawi had beginnings with an English Baptist, Joseph Booth. In 1893 Booth was instrumental in the organization of Nyasa Industrial Mission as an Australian and largely Baptist component of the interdenominational Zambezi Industrial Mission which he had founded a year earlier. Booth was also instrumental in establishing three Baptist missions in Malawi: the Baptist Industrial Mission in 1895, the Providence Industrial Mission in 1900, and the Seventh Day Plainfield Mission in 1901.[15] Southern Baptists of America influenced the establishment and registration with the Government of the Baptist Convention of Malawi in 1970.[16] There are approximately 2,700 Baptist churches in Malawi.

Although it was in 1921 when Baptists entered Mozambique, it was only in 1968 that the United Baptist Church emerged in the country, and they are the largest Protestant body in the nation. Baptists are also present in Zambia with nearly 3,000 churches[17] and Zimbabwe with just over 480 churches. There is a sizeable community of over 55 Baptist churches on the island of Madagascar.

In East Africa, Baptists were first in Burundi in 1928 and Rwanda in 1939. They were in Kenya and Tanzania in 1956 from where they established work in other neighbouring countries. In 1950 Baptist work began in Ethiopia. There are approximately 2,500 churches in Uganda, in Kenya

---

[14] Steven Paas, *The Faith Moves South: A History of the Church in Africa*, Zomba: Kachere, 2006, p. 83.

[15] Longwe, *Christians by Grace – Baptists by Choice*, p. 30.

[16] Hany Longwe, *Christians by Grace – Baptists by Choice*, p. 68.

[17] Reinhard Frey, *A History of the Zambia Baptist Association*, Mzuzu: Luviri Press, 2020.

approximately 3,000 churches, in Tanzania over 3,300, and in Ethiopia over 50 churches.

There is a small presence of Baptists in Egypt. An Egyptian, Seddick W. Girgis, was instrumental in establishing a community of Baptists which numbered 500 by the end of 2010.[18] It is only of late that Baptists have increased their presence in South Sudan mainly through Baptists and assistance from Uganda, Kenya and the USA. Despite the political situation, the Baptist Convention of South Sudan has a membership of approximately 1,000. Nevertheless, Baptist presence and activities are still very weak in the rest of North Africa where Islam dominates where in ancient times Christianity had flourished. Despite the strong efforts of good will from many religions, denominations and other institutions over many decades, the denial of freedom to practice religion is prevalent in this part of Africa as it is many other parts of the world.[19] This has affected not only Baptists, but all religious witness whether Christian or otherwise.

In many African countries Baptists are in the minority, and in a few, they do not exist as congregations, but possibly as individuals. The saying "to be a Baptist is to be a missionary" has been demonstrated in many ways and illustrated by the fact that Baptist witness in many areas in Africa was started by laypeople who had moved out on their own to settle, trade or work in other areas. Baptist are zealous for evangelistic outreach. To a great extent, the growth of Baptist work in Africa can be attributed to this passion.[20] Like other Baptists, African Baptists have certain common features that stem from their historical background and theological heritage.

Baptist Distinctiveness

Baptists in Africa express some evidence of Anabaptist influence in spirit and thought blended with a moderate Calvinism. The Anabaptist

---

[18] "Who are the Baptists? – Africa," www.bwa-baptist-heritage.org/hst-afr.htm
[19] Tony Cupit, "Religious Freedom and the Baptist Perspective," www.bwanet.org/Ministries/Human%20Rights/rfreedom.htm
[20] B. Uche Enyioha, "Baptist Presence in Africa," in *All Africa Baptist Theological Educators' Conference*, Ibadan: All Africa Baptist Fellowship, 2000, 69. See also Longwe, *Christians by Grace – Baptists by Choice*, pp. 73-238.

movement may have been nothing more than an episode in the history of the 16th century Germany society, no other reformation movement symbolized so much the break between the medieval and the modern worlds. Their influence outweighed the number of adherents. Their rejection of the Constantinian state and church relationship, their emphasis on believer's baptism, their belief in religious and civic liberty, and their stress on mission and social ethics more significantly influenced the Baptist tradition than did the Separatists in which African Baptists are rooted.[21]

If properly understood, the Anabaptist concept of church and all its ramifications provides a clue to the essence of Anabaptism. The implementation of the believers' church is what separated Anabaptists from the Magisterial Reformers. Since then, several developments have occurred among Baptist churches. Baptists find guidelines for the church and Christian life in the New Testament alone. They do not see any justification of state churches even in the Old Testament. They acknowledge the legitimacy of the state as God-given, but deny its jurisdiction in matters of religion. People should not be coerced to join the church. Baptists insist that the state must recognize both its limitations and responsibilities. Although there are variations of interpretations, Baptists believe that the demand for religious liberty is nothing less than a biblical principle inherent in the gospel.[22]

The foundation of Baptist ecclesiology is congregational polity. The local church is fully the church, the body of Christ, and not a branch of a national association. They are competent to determine a strategy of missions in their locality, and to appoint their ministers and other officers. Nevertheless, the meeting of the whole local church remains the first authority for all decision making. Nonetheless, the congregational government has been marred and distorted by an individualism that insists on the independence of the local congregation rather than practicing its interdependence. In interdependence, co-operation and the combination of talents and gifts is stressed. This is seen in the New Testament and the 17th century English

---

[21] Louise Kretzschmar, *Privatization of the Christian Faith*, p. 333.
[22] Earl E. Cairns, *Christianity through the Centuries*, Grand Rapids: Zondervan, 1996, p. 299.

Baptist churches where constant movements of apostles, preachers, messages of encouragement and letters between the churches testify to their interdependence. The positive aspects of congregational government are that it prevents the misuse of power by the church leaders, propagates the growth of maturity and responsibility on the part of the members, and affirms the principle of freedom in Christ. However, when congregational government is misunderstood, it can retard progress and promote the exploitation and oppression of the leadership. This happens when the congregations choose to disregard the position and responsibility placed on the leadership.[23]

Beyond the local church, Baptists organize themselves into voluntary associations. Early Baptists met for fellowship, evangelistic cooperation, and clarification of their belief and practice. These later developed into national organizations. Each local church or congregation is free, and indeed duty-bound by the concerns of the gospel, to enter into covenant relationship with other Christians, both locally, nationally and internationally to support mission work.

Being church also means a coming together of people who have personally confessed their sins and personally acknowledged Jesus as Saviour and Lord of their life, being baptized, and living a continued life of discipleship of being learners of God's Word. Baptism is a commitment to follow Christ. Baptists also believe that a call to repentance and a born again experience is at the heart of Christ's call to discipleship. The church is composed of believers who are priestly, meaning relating to and acting for God.

According to the doctrine of the priesthood of all believers that Baptists cherish, no minister is mediator between God and people. Baptists have always believed that the vertical relationship also implies a horizontal expression of all believers being priests and servants to one another. As a result, there is no distinction in terms of function between clergy and laity. This means that the individual ultimately must answer only to God and not to human authority without overlooking the corporate nature of the

---

[23] Louise Kretzschmar, "Authentic Baptist Leadership in Africa," in *All Africa Baptist Theological Educators' Conference*, Ibadan: All Africa Baptist Fellowship, 2000, pp. 43-44.

Christian priesthood. The priesthood of all believers has as much to do with the individual believer as it has with the church with Christ as the great high priest. Like all other Baptists worldwide, Baptists in Africa, being marked with such diversities of cultures, racial identities, and ways of expressing theological convictions, have difficulties in agreeing on the precise language for describing the doctrine of the priesthood of all believers.

Since the individual ultimately must answer only to God, Baptists also believe in the freedom of conscience in defence of religious freedom, that is, no authority or religion can force anyone to believe. Soul liberty is at the center of their understanding of human nature before God, at the same time it affirms the principles of Christ alone, faith alone, grace alone and Scripture alone. The liberty is not only for Baptists, but for each individual to make choices about faith and commitment unfettered by outside agency. Baptists are a diverse people with no overarching rule demanding common thought or practice of such freedom. Yet, there is unity among them because freedom from both outside and inside orders have meant freedom to develop in each situation a style of being church that they believe best serves the interest of the Kingdom of God.

Contribution to Social Witness

Baptist in Africa have generally been somewhat lukewarm on social and political issues mainly due to the Baptist tenet of separation of church and state that has been practiced in excess. They have not been fully active in matters of social, economic or political empowerment of people although these areas of concern cannot be totally divorced from Christianity. The indifference displayed by Baptist in some parts of Africa on the issues that impinge on the lives of the people cannot be part of authentic Baptist heritage. They have not been in the forefront of the fight against apartheid, and such issues as corruption, prostitution and women and child abuse. That has not left a good image of Baptists in Africa. They have failed to serve as effective agents of change.[24] Some reasons why Baptists have had a less spectacular role in social reform than other denominations include:

---

[24] Enyioha, "Baptist Presence in Africa," p. 71.

evangelism priority, separation of church and state, individualism and the theological liberalism of much of the social gospel.[25]

Self-understanding of Baptists in Africa is a result of the Christian mission which began in the colonial context of the 19th century that was followed by a disastrous and very painful decolonization process in some places. Consequently, north of the Zambezi River Sub-Saharan Africa's encounter with Christianity has been different from that of the south of the Zambezi and especially south of the Limpopo where apartheid imposed racial divisions. Baptists in these two regions of the sub-Sahara have at times responded by variously participating in social revolt, withdrawing from social involvement and being part of the nonconformist movements. At the same time, they have not been spared from constant temptations to abuse their faith to satisfy political and economic interests. Since many of their adherents are uncritical, uninformed and intellectually and theologically poor, Baptist churches experience at first hand these temptations of abuse of power within their own ranks. Drawing from their rich theological heritage, in some cases Baptists have been able to escape, although partially, from the limitations of their background or group interests and develop new religious perceptions and structures.[26] This is appropriate for the promotion and facilitation of social well-being of all peoples of Africa.[27]

One of the limitations to Baptists' meaningful contribution to social witness apart from their numbers in different countries is the congregational structures of church government. Though Baptists, while insisting on local autonomy, do have a national "convention," this is a comparatively weak structure, with very limited possibilities of the leadership speaking for the church. The Executive Committee can make statements as the Executive Committee, but the "resolutions or statements are not binding." In Baptist churches social involvement therefore is in most cases to take not corporate but individual forms with the local congregation's support if the initiative is

---

[25] Don A. Sanford, *A Choosing People: The History of Seventh Day Baptists*, Nashville" Broadman, 1992, pp. 33-34.

[26] Kretzschmar, *Privatization of the Christian Faith*, p. 60.

[27] All Africa Baptist Fellowship, Mission Statement, www.aabfellowship.org/-aabf/index.php/items/3-vision-mission.

viewed as corporate responsibility. Because of their very strong doctrine of separation of state and church, Baptist churches are usually not keen on publicly commenting on social and political issues.[28]

Religious freedom and freedom of conscience forces individuals or groups to personally challenge the social issues at hand. They have had to work through other organizations to achieve reform. Many join special interest groups to confront moral problems. This method appeals to Baptists because they can choose the areas in which to make their contribution. Yet they often have had problems in these groups because, in an organization composed of member denominations rather than individuals, the corporate body may take a stand contrary to the position of an individual.[29]

Some leaders have created spaces within their church buildings and homes in which those fighting for social changes could meet. They support groups that are fighting for an end to any form of oppression. Their homes can become nerve centres for the exchange of information and for counselling the oppressed The individual Baptists or groups help with prayer, advice and practical assistance, and bringing those suffering into touch with relevant bodies gives assistance to the suffering such as the Red Cross and legal aid institutions. In the case of Baptists, the individual attitude is a typical Baptist attitude. It is not the national leadership which is supposed to act, but individuals who are committed to their faith based on the whole biblical message, and are willing to take up a minority position. Many uncritical and uninformed Baptist members may be more willing to go along with the status quo. This does not make many Baptist adherents leaders for social change, nor willing supporters for social oppression.[30]

However, several Baptist national leaders have been leaders for social change, with or without the support of their local churches. They have done that as individuals, not under instructions from their conventions or unions.

---

[28] Klaus Fiedler, "The 'Smaller' Churches and the Big Government," in Matembo S. Nzunda and Kenneth Ross (eds), *Church, Law and Political Transition in Malawi 1992-94*, Gweru: Mambo-Kachere, 1997, pp. 158-159.

[29] Don A. Sanford, *A Choosing People*, p. 331.

[30] Klaus Fiedler, "The 'Smaller' Churches and the Big Government," p. 162-163.

Though some church members may question the individual's actions, and others may not be happy with the position taken, at the end the congregations have supported the leaders' actions. Because of the Baptist understanding of congregational church government, the congregation's support may be more relevant. The result is that either the Baptist leader accepts or refuses any position in the social movement.[31]

In times of national and international disasters, Baptists in Africa have been involved in all kinds of relief work. They have distributed food items to people in need especially during droughts. They have been involved not only in providing relief items, but also in dissemination of practicable information needed during endemic outbreaks such as Ebola. Baptist churches in the area have had televised public service announcements nationwide on the outbreak, and local evangelists distributed pamphlets to outlying villages. Like other concerned Christians, they prayed, gathered and handed out food items and some financial support to some of the victims. With the help of overseas partners, Baptists have supported the government's efforts in the fight against such pandemics as Ebola.[32]

In an attempt to address the HIV&AIDS problem, many African Baptists have introduced True Love Waits programmes to bring people together and spread the message of biblical purity to school and college youths and communities. True Love Waits assists the youth to abstain from sexual intercourse until they marry. Through the efforts of trained leaders in churches and communities touched by the problem of sexual activity among the youth, True Love Waits can fight HIV&AIDS and other sexually transmitted diseases as well as unplanned pregnancies and a number of emotional, social, psychological and spiritual problems by helping the young people change their attitudes and behaviour. The programme uses a proven verbally based, culturally appropriate teaching approach to carry the message. In Uganda the programme is said to have contributed to the drop of the HIV&AIDS infection rate.

---

[31] Klaus Fiedler, "The 'Smaller' Churches and the Big Government," p. 164.
[32] Baptist Press, "Ebola Kills 6 in Baptist Woman's Family," www.bpnews.net-/bpnews?id=43477.

Development and Diakonia in African Contexts

Baptists believe and teach that God owns everything including a person's right to existence. Therefore, human beings are just stewards or mangers of God's property. One day they will have to report on how they have used that which was entrusted to them. For one reason or another, people have not managed the resources well, as a result there are many poor and marginalized people throughout the world, many of whom are in Africa. Every Baptist is called to serve the poor and marginalized. Since God is concerned, every individual should be concerned about life wholistically.

Nevertheless, in terms of Christian service, Baptist women in Africa follow the paths that have been laid down for them. Although some seek out broader forms of witness and Christian service, Baptist women in Africa hold meetings and Bible studies and do evangelistic work. They hold sewing and cooking classes through which they seek out new members as well. Women are also engaged in welfare work and in visiting the sick and troubled. The social witness is not fostered by the church leadership, and often it is not even noticed.[33]

Women's services enforced in part by culture and skills taught by the church agencies were frequently of use only in a subordinate and domestic role. The training concentrated on subjects like cooking, sewing, nursing and homemaking. Female elders play an active role as congregational advisers, settling disputes and supervising morals among women and girls. Even before the church era, women played the leadership roles like midwives, village elders, clan chiefs, religious leaders and mediators in family, village and clan disputes. The subordination of women to men in the home, in church, school and society in general has been interpreted as the will of God.

Baptist churches in Africa heavily depend on women members to provide services. Many Baptists are female. Though they live on the margin of life, they minister to others, male and female. Women are proud to be instruments of service, inside and outside the community of faith.

---

[33] Louise Kretzschmar, *Privatization of the Christian Faith*, pp. 250-251.

All Africa Baptist Fellowship

Many Baptist churches in Africa are members of the All Africa Baptist Fellowship (AABF), one of the six regions of the Baptist World Alliance (BWA), existing as an expression of the cohesion of Baptists in the Lord Jesus Christ. AABF has more than 50 member bodies that include conventions, unions, associations, fellowships, assemblies, churches and institutions. It has five sub-regions: North Africa, West Africa, Central Africa, East Africa and South Africa. Each of these has fellowships for youth, women and men. Like many Baptist bodies worldwide, women's role in the AABF is limited.

Chapter 11

The Contribution of "Fellowships" in the Evangelization Process in Malawi[1]

Borrowing words from one language by another has been a practice since the beginning of time. Some words have been transliterated and kept their original meanings, while others have lost their original meanings, and furthermore, some have had different meanings attached to them when used in another language. In Malawi, the word "fellowship" has two major meanings; one that portrays what is good and acceptable and the other that represents what is hopeless and offensive. Though the nationalist struggle was often couched in Christian terms, the revival was also part of the worldwide reaction against the "liberal" spirit of the 1960s.[2]

At a funeral ceremony I attended of a non-church going brother to a member of the Baptist Convention of Malawi (BACOMA), a leader of the Village Evangelistic Ministries (VEM) said the "fellowship," meaning VEM,[3] was not a church, therefore, there was not going to be the laying of wreaths on the grave of the deceased. They were not a church, he said, because only a church is authorized to baptize, perform wedding ceremonies or celebrate the Lord's Supper. VEM was there to preach the Gospel to the rural people and not to replace established local churches. He assured the audience that VEM was not there to bury the dead only, but to complement the "church" in preaching the good news of Jesus Christ.

---

[1] First published in *The South African Baptist Journal of Theology*, vol. 19, 2010, pp. 141-149.

[2] Klaus Fiedler, "The Charismatic and Pentecostal Movements in Malawi in Cultural Perspective," *Religion in Malawi*, vol. 9, Balaka: Montfort, 1999, p. 33.

[3] Village Evangelistic Ministries (VEM) was started by the then Bunda College of Agriculture of the University of Malawi now Lilongwe University Agriculture and Natural Resources (LUANAR) students to reach all the villages in Malawi with the Gospel of Jesus Christ. They have managed to set up village groups in almost all the districts of Malawi. Members of VEM belong to different denominations and churches. They usually meet at neutral venues like government primary and secondary schools. VEM does not operate in towns or cities.

When he said they were just a "fellowship," it proved that he was in agreement with the general derogatory designation of such Christian endeavours by some members of established churches.

Because the BACOMA member and his parents were Christians and distinguished not only in the village, but also in the country and beyond, people from all walks of life attended the funeral. Apart from representatives of the government and some international organizations and "churches," there were those from para church organizations, such as the Student Christian Organization of Malawi (SCOM) and the Evangelical Association of Malawi (EAM), which are also called "fellowships." Klaus Fiedler defines a para-church organization as a specialized Christian agency, which has no intention to start a new denomination(s) or to become one, but which nevertheless has a tendency to claim the primary spiritual allegiance of its members. He also states that in the last aspect they differ from the Bible Society.[4]

Another type of "fellowship" can also be a church nicknamed *ampatuko* (those who have deviated from the norm), for example Achewa Providence Industrial Mission (APIM),[5] and therefore, a fellowship in the Malawian sense of the word. From what is known of the genesis and development of African reflections of God, we cannot understand the fortunes of Christianity in Malawi if we ignore the impact of the country's culture coming into contact with the Western culture.

American Black Baptists viewed the return of John Chilembwe to Malawi as that of John the Baptist making a path for them in the wilderness of Central Africa. They saw such a missionary venture as evidence to the white that black people could succeed as well as the white in any sphere of existence. They believed the gospel of Jesus Christ ruling in every heart, black or white, would bring the change. Jesus will not come to this earth until black and white people who preach the doctrine of the brotherhood

---

[4] Klaus Fiedler, "The Charismatic and Pentecostal Movements in Malawi in Cultural Perspective," p. 3.
[5] Hany Longwe, *Identity by Dissociation*, p. 16.

of people and the fatherhood of God believe so supremely in that gospel that one shall not deny the other inalienable and sacred rights.[6]

That was the spirit in which the first Malawian Baptist, John Chilembwe, began his missionary work among his people.[7] During his missionary period that ended with his death in what is called the Nyasaland Rising of 1915, he envisaged a primarily African state in which the African inhabitants would run their own industries and enterprises. He seemed to realize that such a state would need not only ideological, but also spiritual sources which would be achieved by a union of all the independent African churches. However, Chilembwe's Providence Industrial Mission (PIM) stood in fairly good relationship with white controlled and African-led churches.[8]

Like PIM and APIM, for many years BACOMA did not find it easy to start local congregations in certain areas of the country where mission churches existed because one reason was, where people of the area were tight knit, the members did not want to step out of line or make decisions outside the group and be called *wampatuko* (one who has or those who have deviated from the norm).[9] In some parts of the country some mission churches accused members of BACOMA as *a mpatuko* (rebels) against the Church that had been the only church for many years since the arrival of missionaries in that part of Africa.[10] In that sense, BACOMA, APIM and PIM, were not "churches" but examples of "fellowships." But that has since changed. From 1926 Chilembwe's vision to empower the people was later carried on by his successor, Dr. Daniel Sharpe Malikebu and by Peter Kalemba.[11]

---

[6] George Shepperson and Thomas Price, *Independent African: John Chilembwe and the Origins, Setting and Significance of the Nyasaland Native Rising of 1915*, Blantyre: CLAIM-Kachere, 2000.

[7] George Shepperson and Thomas Price, *Independent African*, p. 123.

[8] D. Phiri, *"Let Us Die for Africa"*: *An African perspective on the Life and Death of John Chilembwe of Nyasaland/Malawi*, Blantyre: Central Africana Limited, 1999, p. 24.

[9] Hany Longwe, *Christians by Grace – Baptists by Choice: A History of the Baptist Convention of Malawi*, Mzuzu: Mzuni; Zomba: Kachere Series, 2011, p. 76.

[10] Hany Longwe, *Christians by Grace – Baptists by Choice*, p. 209.

[11] Hany Longwe, *Identity by Dissociation*, pp. 9, 10.

Kalemba's APIM, though it was a Baptist-type church, was never recognized as a Christian church but as a "fellowship." It was only in 1961 that a Southern Baptist Convention (SBC) missionary couple, Leroy and Jean Albright, invited the APIM leadership to their house in Lilongwe that a gentleman's agreement to work together as "Baptists" was reached.[12] The results of the partnership between a white missionary couple and an African Instituted Church was the beginning of many churches mainly in Central and Northern Malawi that became part of what is now BACOMA. APIM was very evangelistic unlike Chilembwe, whose relationships with white missionaries were coloured more by political than doctrinal sentiments.[13]

The terminology which has been very useful in describing human relationships has been and is still facing new problems of acceptance by some Christians and non-Christians in the country. People have not accepted both types of fellowships, each as important as the other in its own right. In this article that shows the two sides of the same coin, as it were, I want to briefly attempt to prove their credibility and show how they have contributed to change the face and landscape of Christianity in Malawi.

Fulfilling the Need

Traditionally, Europeans see Africans as being on the receiving end, and themselves on the giving end, of a relationship which is often equated with black-white relations. European missionaries once believed in their divine task of evangelizing what they called the Dark Continent. David Livingstone explored Central Africa between 1853 and 1873 during and after which came the beginnings of older missions: the Anglican and largely English and Welsh missionaries of the Universities Mission of Central Africa at the centre of Lake Malawi; the predominantly Scottish missionaries of the Livingstonia Mission of the Free Church of Scotland up in the Ngoni lands, and the Church of Scotland Mission on the Shire Highlands.[14]

---

[12] Hany Longwe, *Identity by Dissociation*, p. 66.
[13] D. Phiri, "Let Us Die for Africa," p. 23.
[14] George Shepperson and Thomas Price, *Independent African*, p. 13.

The progressive paternalism of a closed society of predominantly Scottish missions was breaking up rapidly after 1892.

By the early 1960s, approximately a third of Malawi's population was Christian, about half of them Protestants and about half Roman Catholics.[15] Missionary and indigenous churches existed throughout the country. The rapid growth of Christianity was the result of the African zeal to share the Gospel with others.[16] The massive embracing of Christianity and its fast spread in Africa was due to the religiosity of the Africans, which acted as preparation for the Gospel message. It was among such people with a rich religious heritage that the churches started their work. Bediako argues that the gospel was, therefore, the fulfillment of that which the African had been waiting for.[17]

To show the development of that fulfillment during the 1970s and beyond, I used the steps Klaus Fiedler called interdenominational, fellowship and ministry.[18]

Interdenominational Phase

During this period, an alliance of para-church organizations and local churches organized revival meetings which championed the message of a personal relationship with Jesus by being "born again" as opposed to "cold" religion.[19] This began in Blantyre. Malawians have responded to the Gospel from where they were, not from where the missionaries were; they responded to the Christian message as they heard it, not to the missionaries' experience of the message. The first hearing and the first response is not the whole, nor necessarily the climax, of the story. The impact of the gospel

---

[15] Hany Longwe, *Christians by Grace – Baptists by Choice*, p. 28.

[16] Adrian Hastings, *The Church in Africa, 1450-1950*, Oxford: Clarendon, 1994, p. 306.

[17] Kwame Bediako, *Christianity in Africa: The Renewal of a Non-Western Religion*, Edinburgh: University Press, 1995, pp. 123, 175.

[18] Klaus Fiedler, "The Charismatic and Pentecostal Movements in Malawi in Cultural Perspective," p. 34.

[19] Felix Nyika, 'Apostleship amongst Malawian Neocharismatics,' PhD module, University of Mzuzu, 2010, p. 2.

message upon the people created a new set of questions and a yearning to be able to make assured choices with good conscience.

A small group of evangelical missionaries and denominational leaders of Protestant churches, including Southern Baptist missionaries and BACOMA leadership, which spearheaded the fight against liberal theology which they felt was being sponsored by the World Council of Churches (WCC) through overseas theology scholarships which they offered to Malawians during the 1950s. It was felt by the group that the solution to liberal theology was aggressive evangelism in which the Holy Spirit would bring transformation in people's lives.[20] The group met frequently for prayer and consultation, as a result the Evangelical Association of Malawi was instituted which played the role of organizing the week-long annual evangelistic meetings that became known as Keswick Conventions.[21] During the 1960s some of the speakers at such meetings included the Nigerian Baptist theologian, Byang H. Kato.[22]

By 1967 the conventions took on a national character. Participants who were in most cases, leaders, came from many parts of Malawi and they represented many denominations and churches and that made it the biggest interdenominational fellowship. In the main convention church leaders, youth women, men and children met in different group seminars throughout the day, and then the main speaker preached during the evenings. In addition, the main speaker presented a 15 minutes' sermonette during the Sunday morning worship service on Malawi Broadcasting Corporation (MBC), the national radio station from 5:45 in the morning.

In 1969 the fellowship also developed a programme called New Life for All (NLFA) whose philosophy was to mobilize every church member for evangelism. Local church leaders prayed, and the congregations were sensitized on the evangelistic programme. The fellowship also carried out

---

[20] Jack Selfridge, *Jack of all Trades Mastered by One*, Fearn: Christian Focus, 1996, p. 186.
[21] For the spiritual and historical background of Keswick (and the resultant movements) see: Klaus Fiedler, *The Story of Faith Missions*, Oxford: Regnum; Sutherland: Albatross, 1994, pp. 213-229.
[22] Felix Nyika, "Apostleship amongst Malawian Neocharismatics," p. 2.

weekly Bible studies and encouraged Scripture memorization to ensure that the members were "born-again" (BA), and they had enough armory for evangelism, and that they were filled with power from the Holy Spirit for effective witnessing. They went from house to house, distributed tracts, and did follow-ups for those who had shown interest to know Christ and those who had been born again. Local churches of different denominational affiliation cooperated in evangelistic crusades that sparked revival first in Blantyre, which later spread to rest of the country.[23] The revival did not exclude prisons and hospitals.[24]

This evangelistic mobilization revolved around the intense competition of old and new churches to win adherents who were born-again. The converts were Christians by faith, and Baptist or Presbyterian, for example, by choice. The new way of evangelization made its mark as a skill to present the truths of God as it was a means to bring people to Christ through the power of the Holy Spirit. This ushered in what I call the democratization of the Christian faith.[25]

The country was on fire for Christ. Many churches recorded growth as a result of the evangelistic efforts of the fellowship. Churches that adopted the evangelistic methods and ideas purported by the fellowship registered much more growth both quantitatively and qualitatively. BACOMA was one of the beneficiaries of the fellowship's evangelistic ministry. For BACOMA, though the crusades were described as national, the spirit of revival was prominent in Southern Malawi from the late 1960s.

The revivals were the origins of a new fellowship order. They were an innovative and highly effective organizing process. Religious recruitment was intensely local, designed to draw people into local congregations. But recruitment into a local Baptist or other church, also inducted people into a national organization and affiliation network that they could participate in wherever they felt was their area of ministry. Moreover, adherence to a

---

[23] For the history of the revival see: Brighton Kawamba, *The Blantyre Spiritual Awakening and its Music*, Mzuzu: Luviri Press, 2018.
[24] Felix Nyika, "Apostleship amongst Malawian Neocharismatics," p. 3.
[25] Hany Longwe, *Christians by Grace – Baptists by Choice*, p. 504.

particular evangelical denomination also inducted them into the broader evangelical fellowship campaign. Not only did the conversion bring the converts into a new relationship with God, it also brought them into a new but powerful institutional organization that provided them with personal discipline and a sense of fellowship. Aggressively exploiting a wide variety of media, evangelicals launched radio programmes through MEMA studios in Lilongwe onto the national radio, MBC, and distributed millions of devotional and reform tracts.

For example, BACOMA printed nearly 120,000 tracts, adult, youth and children Sunday school materials. Individual witnessing remained central. They shared with diligence and compassion the Good News of Jesus Christ with people they met. They went from town to town and village to village preaching revivals, organizing new Bible study fellowship groups and churches, and distributing Bibles and other religious materials.

Though Baptist men like many from male dominated fellowships applied what they understood to be Paul's admonition for women to be silent, and applied cultural segregation in the realm of evangelism, I contend that without the participation of women, no matter how little or insignificant it might have seemed to be, not only BACOMA, but also the Church in Malawi, would not have been what it is today.[26]

Fellowship Phase

As a result of city-wide outreaches came fellowships that were preaching in groups at agreed or designated points in various parts of towns starting in Blantyre. They further developed lunch-hour fellowships and prayer groups in the residential areas of the towns. Lunch-hour fellowships usually met in any kind of public hall or special halls like the Red Cross at Chichiri, Agricultural Development and Marketing Corporation (ADMARC) at Kanjedza and Malawi Railways in Limbe. Kawamba cites Emmanuel Chinkwita Phiri who grew up as a Seventh-day Adventist turned Baptist, who was later to play an important role in the development of BACOMA,

---

[26] Hany Longwe, *Christians by Grace – Baptists by Choice*, p. 75.

was one of the leaders of such a fellowship that was meeting at ADMARC.[27] NLFA encouraged Christians, who lived near each other, or worked together to spend some time each day to pray for a number of people they knew were not Christians, then they had to look out for opportunities to witness to the ones they had been praying for.[28] Many of these prayer meetings were held not only in villages and towns, but also in homes and offices. Since many who worked in offices, factories and shops did not use all their lunch break time, they decided to organize lunch-hour prayer meetings. It all started with two people, but soon numbers grew until they could not meet in one place. As a result, they divided into groups meeting in different places, both offices and public places. Eventually, approximately 450 people were meeting for prayer in Blantyre city alone for lunch-hour prayer meetings in 1974. That later spread to other parts of the country.[29]

These further developed into house meetings, cell groups, evangelistic teams, names vary, that usually met on a weekday evening in order not to clash with other church functions. The fellowships were interdenominational though in some cases a large majority may have come from one denomination or even from one congregation. In his study Klaus Fiedler notes that members of fellowships were often the most active members of their congregations,[30] but I would want to add that they were those who felt underutilized in their congregations and felt that the "born-again" message was not being advanced fully by their congregations.

These were the groups that were nicknamed "fellowships" because they were seen to be no more than just getting together Christians from different denominations or churches who did not meet the criteria of a church and were not expected to organize themselves into local churches. They were designated "born-agains" in short, BA's, groups of Christians who thought of themselves as "real Christians." Since then one can hear people trying to

---

[27] Felix Nyika, "Apostleship amongst Malawian Neocharismatics," p. 3.

[28] Jack Selfridge, *Jack of all Trades Mastered by One*, p. 192.

[29] Jack Selfridge, *Jack of all Trades Mastered by One*, p. 194.

[30] Klaus Fiedler, "The Charismatic and Pentecostal Movements in Malawi in Cultural Perspective," p. 34.

differentiate, if there is such a thing, between a Christian and a born-again Christian. Nevertheless, the major aim of the fellowships was to evangelize the community and, in that process, they would also attempt to meet the spiritual and social needs of the individual. Like in the New Testament, people whom they evangelized were encouraged to gather together and be discipled.

Fellowships need to be understood as a spiritual movement. As such, it was an integral part of a broader church revival that has transformed the Malawian society. For the most part, the early mission church Christians lived their lives believing that what the church taught was enough. They were oriented primarily to the denomination, and they valued order and stability in their churches and communities. However, as Malawians were increasingly looking for more of God's intervention, they became a people in motion, constantly moving across denominational lines. Under the force of this fluidity, churches and denominations lost much of their traditional capacity to regulate individual and spiritual life. Instead, Malawians formed different kinds of Christian fellowships to give needed structure and direction to their lives. They felt that they were "unfulfilled," for lack of a better word, as a result they needed to experience more than what their local churches were able to give.

Ministries Phase

By the end of the 1970s and the beginning of the 1980s, from these devices, in conjunction with the aggressive evangelistic revivals that were the hallmark of the new evangelical fellowship emerged ministries. These associations began as converts rallied around charismatic leaders with a personalized or specialized ministry call. Members of the ministries together with the leaders attended to the people though not on Sunday mornings to ensure that everyone could go to their local churches where their church membership was.[31]

---

[31] Klaus Fiedler, "The Charismatic and Pentecostal Movements in Malawi in Cultural Perspective," p. 34.

The messages were the same: "Be born-again." Apart from preaching about regeneration, they also prayed for the sick. Individual converts were great shoppers for preachers, ever ready to abandon a "cold" and "formal" preacher for someone from a different denomination whose "fulfilling" preaching was more to their liking. Some preached messages of empowerment with the Holy Spirit.

The fellowships took centre stage when Malawi was going through a social and cultural revolution. Many people, especially aspiring individuals, were beginning to move to the bustling industrial centres like Blantyre from the rural areas in search of a better life. Malawians were beginning to embrace this new society as unprecedentedly democratic, a land of vast opportunity in which male individuals in particular were free to rise to whatever position their talent and effort took them. For evangelical converts, self-esteem came not from secular social status but from spiritual standing, measured by intensity of feeling and dedication to evangelical disciplines. The respect of their brothers and sisters in the faith was more important to them than external social standing. They counted themselves in no way inferior to any person who possessed mere wealth and secular prominence.

While some attempted to address social issues, others ministered to specific people groups such as the youth and Muslims. A couple of youth bands were formed during this period.[32] Many youths joined the fellowships as a result of the music styles that were introduced at that time. The bands not only used accordions, guitars, both modern and traditional drums, but also made the churches to acquire the instruments for their choirs and youth groups.[33] That also was the beginning of changes in the music landscape in many churches and fellowships; a change that has transformed worship styles. The tie between democracy and evangelical fellowship was even stronger.

---

[32] Akim Chirwa, who is the Principal at the Baptist Theological Seminary of Malawi, was one such youth who was a member of one of the bands, Mustard Seed.

[33] Brighton Kawamba, *The Blantyre Spiritual Awakening and its Music*, pp. 77-141.

Conclusion

Not only had Christianity become more democratic, it was in itself a democratizing force. Evangelical fellowship reinforced the growing sense of the individual's independence: it made the individual's own religious experience the ultimate spiritual authority.

For many, fellowships provided a different atmosphere to the strict and firm grip of older churches. Evangelical fellowships held out a vision of independence and interdependence that came with the salvation promise. Out of evangelical fellowships came Christian activists imbued with a strong sense of the power of their own individual will. This evangelical activism can be seen not simply as a response to the new individualism but as an expression of it. Evangelical churches were essentially affectionate communities, gatherings of the like-minded and like-feeling that were organized around ideas of mutual concern, love, and obligation. Church membership was not simply a matter of going to church on Sunday; rather it involved participation in prayer meetings, other worship sessions all of which reinforced a sense of fellowship and obligation. Devotional forms were often highly communal. Sunday worship services deployed various forms of collective participation including the increased singing of choruses over hymns. In addition, enlistment in an evangelical church involved accepting rules for behaving towards each other that were designed to counter the conflict of the outside world. Church members, moreover, were charged to tend to the needs of the less fortunate among them and offer aid to others who had suffered misfortune. People often sought employers or employees, business partners, and marriage partners from the ranks of their Christian fellowships. And when they moved on, often one of the first things they did when they entered a new town or village was to seek a comforting church in which they could fellowship.

Chapter 12

Post-Classical Missions' Missionary Affair in Malawi

It is Klaus Fiedler who has suggested what some scholars have described as a "good" classification of Protestant mission societies, as "classical" and "post-classical." He proposed the term "classical"to mean mission societies that are (mostly) denominational organizations that originated in the Great Awakening.[1] They began with William Carey's Baptist Missionary Society in 1792; many consider this the true birth of modern missions and Carey as the "Father of Protestant Missions." On the other hand, "post-classical" missions refers to missions of the Brethren, including the so-called "free missionaries" and the Evangelical missions of which the Interdenominational Faith Missions were and are strong proponents, followed by the Pentecostal and Charismatic missions. Classical mission societies arose during the Great Awakening, while the Post-Classical faith missions began during the third Revival, the Evangelical or Holiness Revival.[2] The post-Classical missions comprise the major subdivisions of Evangelical missions and Pentecostal/ Charismatic missions, each of which can be further subdivided. The difference between the post-classical and classical churches can be seen not only in their different historical origins but also in their attitudes and relationships. Post-classical churches are minority churches in their homelands, while classical churches are usually the "national church." Besides, post-classical churches insist upon the separation of church and state, in contrast to the classical churches that gladly accept various forms of "establishment," if available. Lastly, post-classical churches perceive human society usually in a less positive light than the classical churches do.[3]

---

[1] For the details of his classification see Klaus Fiedler, *Interdenominational Faith Missions in Africa. History and Ecclesiology*, Mzuzu: Mzuni Press, 2018, pp, 9-30.

[2] Klaus Fiedler, *Interdenominational Faith Missions in Africa. History and Ecclesiology*, Mzuzu: Mzuni Press, 2018.

[3] Ibid, pp. 321ff.

Though classical churches and missions in the past tended to claim that the whole of the missionary spectrum rightly belonged to them, and they often saw no reason for the existence of 'all these new missions', now it is an established truth that there exist missions with a different identity sharing the missionary spectrum alongside the classical missions. Klaus Fiedler indicated that the fact that he was writing the preface of the English version of his book on faith missions while in Malawi where he was serving as a lecturer at Chancellor College of the University of Malawi was as good a proof as any that classical and post-classical missionary work in Africa, and in this country since 1875 and 1892 respectively, had not been in vain. In Malawi, post-classical missions began with the arrival of Joseph Booth, a Baptist, who broke the classical missions' domination in Malawi with the founding of Zambezi Industrial Mission (ZIM) at Blantyre. He started and influenced eight churches that still have impact today. In addition to the ZIM, post-classical missions in Malawi are represented by Nyasa Industrial Mission (1893), South Africa General Mission (1895), Seventh-day Adventists (1893/1902), Churches of Christ (1906), New Apostolic Church (1923), Nazarene Church, Salvation Army (1950s), Free Methodists, Living Waters, Agape Life Church, Assemblies of God (1930), Pentecostal Holiness Association (1932), Apostolic Faith Mission (1932), and many others.

Missions - The Foreigners' Affair

Malawi changed its religion and became a Christian country. The European and American missionaries initiated the enormous evangelistic effort that was required for this process of change, but it has been the Malawians who have done the biggest amount of work, whether through informal witness to their new found faith or through part-time or full-time service as teachers, evangelists or ministers. Although that was the case, the missionaries founded churches that did not consciously look beyond themselves. The Malawian churches lacked the missionary vision. The missions introduced a clear dichotomy. The mission was the foreigners' affair, while the local church was for the Malawians. The mission was the scaffolding on which the church had been established, and after which the scaffolding was to be dismantled and used elsewhere. However, the scaffolding has in many instances remained much longer than originally envisaged, and the missionary vision has not been imparted to the 'young' churches.

This process was enforced by the "indigenous church principle" that meant that 'white money' could not be used, neither for black missionaries nor for any activity the Malawian church wanted do that was not the missionary's idea. For example, a missionary minister of a city multi-racial Baptist congregation divided the church into two when he asked Malawians to support a Malawian "associate" minister, as he was "their" pastor. The congregation was largely supported by the tithes of the missionaries and by contributions of other white members of the church. The white minister even suggested that the Malawian associate minister opened and operated a bookstall in his home town. As if it was not enough, he suggested that the associate minister be a missionary to South Africa, his wife's home country. The associate minister decided to leave, and he did. One white missionary declared Malawians did not contribute to the missionaries' livelihood, and therefore no black person had any right to the money that was being sent from outside the country. The missionaries were willing to work with Malawians to whom the missionaries had come, but were not willing to share the money sent for the ministry in Malawi.

Another example is that of representatives of a Baptist mission who made several visits to an African Instituted Church (AIC of similar beliefs, and, during one such tour, inquired of ways they could help the church. In their recommendation the missionaries were to delay any discussion or action on the matter until the AIC had made a formal request. It was their desire that a request would never come since the "glory" of the AIC, they would say, was that it had accomplished so much through the years without any white person's assistance and it was going to be a step backward for the AIC to ask for help at that time. According to the missionaries the best they could do was to join the AIC in prayer that the AIC's work would continue and they would find personnel and money to meet the needs of the ministry. The issue of race played a major part in their decision making process. It seemed to the white missionaries that the AIC was a black man's enterprise and not God's. (They did not look at the AIC as being God's "glory," but a black man's glory). The missionaries were willing to play the role of advisers to the AIC and other Malawi churches with similar beliefs, but they were not willing to invest in their ministries the money that came from "some godly saints abroad" who gave as much as they could so that the financial needs of foreign missionaries were provided for equitably and adequately. The "indigenous church principle" enforced the missionaries' stand of removing financial and material support for the local missionary vision for mission was for the white missionaries who were self-financing and autonomous. The mission tended to be rather self-sufficient and self-contained.

Malawian Missionary Affair Agreeing with Klaus Fiedler's Sketch of the Missionary

Although there were these theological and structural inhibitions, there has been some spontaneous expansion of the church or cases that could be classified as missionary efforts. Today conscious missionary efforts are common. Klaus Fiedler contends that a missionary must not necessarily cross national boundaries; even crossing cultural boundaries is a missionary affair. In this case one could describe a missionary as someone doing primarily evangelistic or pastoral work in another country, or in an area of one's own country, which, in terms of culture and religion, is distinctly different from one's own background. Those who consider themselves as missionaries, or do such work, are also missionaries.

An example of one who did such work is John Chilembwe, a Baptist who was the first Malawian missionary to his own people, the Ayawo. He was followed by one of his outstanding students, Peter Kalemba from Mangoni, a second Baptist missionary to his own people, the Achewa. The challenge to use Chewa people in missions among their own people was a radical move in Baptist missions. One of the missionaries wanted the Chewa people to have Christ in an "at home atmosphere." Such a desired Christian experience of one's own faith could not be thought of indefinitely as foreign or imported. It had to be thought of as African to be really experienced and lived by the Chewa people. The challenge ultimately brought freedom for the continuation of a self-supporting, self-propagating, self-governing and self-theologizing Achewa Providence Industrial Mission.

Local Church Mission Strategy

The rapid growth of Christianity is attributed to the African zeal to share the Gospel with others. The growth of Christianity has been commendably an African rather than a missionary affair. Many post-classical missionary churches have consistently and organizationally been committed to and involved in missions and evangelism. Among the results have been the multiplication of churches and ministries of various sizes and concentrations.

Denominational Schools as Evangelistic Tools

After the first results of the church in Malawi, the question was how it was supposedly to be nurtured to maturity and expansion. Some denominations such as the Seventh-day Adventist Church used their schools as evangelistic tools through a programmed week of prayer meetings in all their schools every school term. The result was many students joining the church. The Malawi Adventist way of evangelism was a mixture of common missionary methods of responding to unanticipated opportunities, and the spontaneous sharing of religious persuasions in natural networks. Adventist education started early to touch the masses and laid the foundation of a comprehensive movement of religious influence and change.

Up until 1907, not all the teachers in Adventist schools were Adventists. Some of the teachers were members of such mission churches as Zambezi and Nyasa Industrial Missions. Then, the church had to baptize every teacher soon after employing them. Apart from teaching, the church expected each teacher to be an evangelist. Because of that, the church initiated more formal training in 1922 with the opening of Malamulo Teacher Evangelist Training. This development increased the number of out-schools in the region thereby increasing evangelistic work. By 1922 Adventists had fifteen out-schools in addition to the two central schools at Malamulo and Matandani with a combined 437 learners. The development accelerated especially until 1925, when 27 Malawian teachers served ten schools. Consequently, what had started as a foreign missionary affair and was technically under missionary control, soon became a predominantly African enterprise that involved some of the brightest minds. The impact of Adventist education on evangelistic work in Malawi was significant: in 1932, there were 228 baptized SDA members in Malawi out of 729 pupils in Adventist schools countrywide.

Evangelism Networking

During the early 1980s when Malawi had no towns and cities but only district headquarters with very low population density, the Adventist missionaries organized their evangelism campaigns in strategic places such as the district headquarters. The evangelistic campaigns operated from Malamulo Mission. Evangelism became the dominant note along these lines. Each year in August as soon as the schools closed, Adventists devoted two months to evangelism. The mission director, pastors, literature evangelists, school inspectors and teachers, all of them set aside their regular work and engaged in evangelistic campaign meetings.

They formed a network of small companies that they assigned to different districts. At these evangelistic campaign meetings, they emphasized Adventist beliefs such as the seventh day Sabbath, health reform and marriage and family. These meetings had a great impact on the life style and some of those who heard the message joined the church. In 1909, for example, from twenty-two meetings conducted, 73 people converted to Adventism. Those who showed interest to join the church were under instructions for one to three years before they could be baptized. This was considered not too long as it gave the converts the chance to learn more about Adventist beliefs and become Christians committed to the gospel work.[4]

Another evangelistic network was that of evangelistic outreach campaigns commonly known as "efforts." The Adventists conducted evangelistic meetings usually for six to eight weeks. At the end, one member from each

---

[4] The policy has changed. By now converts are baptized at the end of such evangelistic "efforts."

working force had to remain with the new company formed. They had to acquaint themselves with the new converts and also continue to guide them through Adventist beliefs and policies. They also divided the new converts into two groups for the baptism class. They brought together those with no Christian experience into one baptism class that was commonly known as "hearers." Converts from other churches formed another class of those who could be baptized earlier than the "hearers."

Indigenous Creativity

Schools remained the central element of the Adventist evangelistic strategy until Malawi became an independent state. However, a range of other tools of evangelism that often involved indigenous creativity increasingly supplemented education. The Seventh-day Adventist being a new church, the young people were naturally the agents in such evangelistic activities. Some formed a brass band that played the instruments as it went around the mission station, while other students went out in groups as the Branch Sabbath School that would, amongst other activities, sing songs of support for those grieving due to the death of family members, conduct Bible Studies in the surrounding areas, and dramatize Bible stories on issues such as the dangers of consuming intoxicating beverages.

During the 1930s and 1940s a group called *Asilikali a Yesu* (The Soldiers of Jesus) was in operation. It aimed at helping the youth channel their vigour into evangelism. The church required that every year each member led at least one person to become a Seventh-day Adventist. Every member had to concentrate on evangelizing at least two acquaintances. The Asilikali had to regularly visit and preach in nearby neighborhoods. Churches also followed in the footsteps of the Asilikali by evangelizing the areas surrounding the churches. These activities in conjunction with an increasing number of organized evangelistic campaigns and a Sabbath School that also functioned as a supplementary baptismal class, gave church members opportunities to apply their evangelistic abilities and share their faith with non-Adventists.

Evangelistic Zeal of Local Congregations and Individuals

As part of the Evangelical movement, Baptist churches are zealous and aggressive in evangelism. A local Baptist congregation perceives itself as being competent to determine a strategy for missions in its locality. It is free, and indeed duty-bound by the concerns of the gospel, to enter into covenant relationship with other Christians, both locally and nationally. Relationships have traditionally been associations, conventions or unions in support of missionary work, both at home and abroad, and internationally through regional associations or fellowships.

Baptist Convention of Malawi (BACOMA) has been engaged in evangelism that focuses on a personal relationship with Jesus. Baptists have been concerned with helping people follow Jesus and not just abide by a church's rather than with rules and regulations. A disciple or follower of Jesus is a learner. Baptists always believed the Holy Spirit was responsible for removing much of the filth on a person as they studied and believed in the Word of God. They underscored the fact that they were mere channels of God's grace and unmerited favour. Considering that, many people felt Baptists were welcoming, because they did not put rules as to who was eligible to witness, who was to give the permission, and where the person was to go to witness. Freedom to witness meant every follower of Christ was an evangelist.

That has encouraged a rise in personal involvement in evangelism. Another increase has been in voluntary work. Evangelism has not been for pastors only, but for all mainly outside the official church setting. God uses all and everything to make the world come to him. Several avenues to evangelize are open to believers. Throughout BACOMA individual members and teams have been committed to evangelism and discipleship that comes out of a sense of worship. They constantly seek the leadership of the Holy Spirit, study God's Word, and serve through local congregations. BACOMA has stood for evangelism that results in the establishment of more local churches of every ethnic group throughout the country.[5]

---

[5] Hany Longwe, *Christians by Grace: Baptists by Choice. A History of the Baptist Convention in Malawi*, Mzuzu: Mzuni Press, 2011, pp. 73-238.

Similarly, the origin and development of the Free Methodist Church (FMC) in Malawi from the 1960s is a result of the emphasis on the evangelistic zeal of both the laity and the clergy, thereby giving a sense of identity for the Free Methodist heritage of targeting the rural multitudes. Although that resulted in the establishment of churches throughout the country, its evangelistic focus has made it to continue being essentially a rural church just like BACOMA with little impact on the urban areas.[6] Since they perceived Christianity as not a private but a public affair, members of the Free Methodist Church embraced evangelism as the highest calling and challenge. Consequently, some have referred to the FMC membership as people who recognize evangelism as a privilege and receive it with admiration because the gospel message, Jesus Christ, is for all ethnic groups (John 3:16).

It was the natural impetus of early Adventists to share their faith with their families and friends. Even if this did not always result in conversions, the Christians' lives were often impressive testimonies. Some parents or relatives rejected their children or relatives after their conversion to Adventism, but once they observed that the converts had remained faithful people, they were reconciled. Such personal evangelistic work conducted on the level of individuals' daily lives did not always make extraordinary stories. But it has been a major force of evangelism. Once one family member converted, others followed more easily.

Bible Study Approach

Post-classical churches deliberately moved away from the "mission station" concept in which the chief intention was to attract the local people to a central place where they could be nurtured away from the "temptations" of their own societies. These churches shifted to one in which the mission acted primarily on the community level with only a small, though admittedly important, residential element. The new churches began by specifically teaching the Bible in the targeted areas, directing all efforts to evangelism and church development. The result was that those taught began sharing

---

[6] Henry Church, *Theological Education that Makes a Difference: Church Growth in the Free Methodist Church in Malawi and Zimbabwe*, Zomba: Kachere, 2002, pp. 72ff.

their faith with relatives, and if opportunities arose, with those outside of their family circles. Some disciples or learners went on to establish small Bible study groups. Those who were determined to start congregations shared the Gospel with their relatives and friends as they went about their daily work. Soon groups were gathered that met for Bible study and worship. The disciples would contact and ask church representatives for support. Certain individuals became instrumental in the organization of local congregations. Many groups began in or just outside homes and later moved into identified buildings, either school classrooms or other rented buildings. They chose venues that were centrally situated and easy to reach. Some of the earliest members later became official leaders of the new local churches.

Some churches have been started by members of families who moved to places either because of labour migration or just by choice where there were no churches they identified with. Most of these places would be distinctly different from one's own background; thus, by Klaus Fiedler's definition, the moving persons would qualify to be called missionaries. Probably, the first few nights they sang and prayed in their new homes before they went to bed. Normally, the worship would have been loud, and probably in high-density areas. Obviously, neighbours would hear and some interest was ignited. A few days or so later, some neighbours who identified themselves with Christianity would join for worship in their homes. Soon that turned into Bible study. Though they met mainly for Bible study, it was also a time for fellowship and for sharing personal experiences. During these meetings they would encourage each other to live the gospel. Their lives began to change towards maturity in faith in Jesus Christ. That saw the establishment of local churches in many cases. As local congregations, the membership took time to preach in their neighbourhood in order to win more people to Christ. The results of changed lives were the establishment of other Bible Study groups in different parts of the country. After several sessions of Bible study, the people would choose their leaders and would name their churches.

Church leaders spent some of their time witnessing and discipling and supporting new as well as old members. That contributed to both spiritual and numerical growth of the churches. In cases where some of the members walked long distances to and from church, they started new preaching points or mission churches. Those who had moved to new areas were happy to meet members of their churches also on transfer from other areas, and they would join hands and begin meeting for prayer and Bible study in their homes. Soon people would start to show interest and that would result in a mission church.

Bible study has been used as an evangelistic as well as a discipleship tool. The use of the Bible study approach to first develop the individual to be a useful instrument in God's hand, and second, to position the individual in such a way that people in the community would want to emulate him/her, set the ground for believers to be active in church planting and church growth. That is seen as being church on mission.

Women and Evangelism

With the organization of the women's groups, Malawian women were being led to use their energies and talents towards starting and developing women's groups marked the dawn of a new era in the expansion of the churches' evangelistic and missionary efforts. Although men have often not accepted them as co-preachers, many women have been engaged in missionary and evangelistic meetings countrywide. In the Baptist Convention of Malawi, women have been free to evangelize and independent in terms of decision making with regards to their call to minister within and outside the local congregations because of Baptist polity and doctrine.[7]

Others have opened their homes in which people have found salvation, and new congregations have begun. Through the good relationships and Christ-like character they portrayed to the neighbours, a good number of women have led other women and their families to profess faith in Christ. Some children from such families have later gone to be pastors. Some women

---

[7] For some aspects of the Baptist women's involvement see: Rachel NyaGondwe Banda [Fiedler], *Women of Bible and Culture. Baptist Convention Women in Southern Malawi*, Zomba: Kachere, 2006, esp. pp. 122-168.

have been pastors, though not in name but in function.[8] Without the participation of women, no matter how little or insignificant it might have seemed to be, the Malawi churches would not have been what they are today.

One-to-One and Door-to-Door Witnessing

When local churches began to look away from themselves, they carried out one-to-one and door-to-door witnessing as one way of reaching the world for Christ. Although the churches were relatively new, they experienced steady increases in the number of conversions. That was and has been largely influenced by one-to-one and door-to-door witnessing. Members go out and share the Good News of Jesus Christ with people they meet. They ask if the person has a few minutes to spare, and then they introduce themselves before sharing the Gospel. Malawi has been described as very responsive to the Gospel. That is proven by the number of people who are willing to listen to the Gospel message. Some members go and invite their relatives and friends and even entire villages to listen to the witness. Many members attribute their conversion to visits they had from other church members, pastors and foreign missionaries.

Although some witnessing strategies have brought many people to Christ during certain periods, nevertheless, individual witnessing has remained central. Through one-to-one witnessing many churches multiply their membership. In the process of evangelizing churches express the gospel they experience to those outside their churches. Since witnessing for Christ is supposed to be at the heart of every true believer, members move from village to village, house to house, street to street sharing their personal faith with people they meet. They achieve incredible success in the process.

Congregations have been able to carry out door-to-door witnessing and so to start several Bible study groups as a result. Many churches have been established in strategic areas, such as growing centres of trade and district

---

[8] Ibid, pp. 132-136. Women pastors at that time were Mellia Makina, Sellina Nasimango and Agnes Lufani.

administration. These churches are used as centres of missionary activities for the surrounding areas and those afar.

Sunday School

The Baptist Convention of Malawi (BACOMA) has used the Sunday school as an evangelistic tool. Sunday school is for all its member churches and the local congregations use Sunday school, which is for all ages, as a tool for evangelism. People who profess faith in Jesus are brought together and taught for some time before they are baptized. Members of Sunday school have the opportunity to verbalize their thoughts and learning experiences before their classmates and the congregations.

Lilongwe Baptist Church at one time decided to hold the Sunday school for adults in the community instead of holding it at the church. They also needed members of the congregation to volunteer to have their homes used for that purpose. A couple of families opened their homes for community Sunday school. The church bought some literature. Immediately the Sunday school began, church attendance rose to an average of 300 people meeting for worship every Sunday. Several weeks later the figure had moved from 300 to just over 400. Many people were baptized during that period. Community Sunday school went on for about 13 weeks before some of the members felt overwhelmed by the rate of church growth. They asked the church to go back to the old way of doing Sunday school. Immediately the congregation stopped the Community Sunday School, church attendance and membership also fell.

Mobile Clinic Evangelism

The Mobile Clinic began its work in 1970 in six primary areas that they perceived as strategic on the western shores of Lake Malawi, covering over a hundred miles north and south of Senga Bay. The teams began to develop strategies for outreach ministries. Before they ministered to the patients, they preached and prayed and then handed out tracts. They believed God wanted people not only to heal spiritually but also physically. For example, during 1993 the Baptist Medical Clinic staff of ten--two medical assistants, two nurses, one nutritional worker, four assistants, and an ambulance driver--treated approximately 63,647 patients with whom they also shared the gospel.

Each patient who was seen at these places that also served as Mobile Clinic centres was exposed to solid Bible teaching. The evaluation of the past ministry of the clinics indicated large numbers of professions of faith in Jesus Christ. However, the figures did not reflect a visible impact on the local BACOMA churches that was attributed to lack of follow up. To reverse the situation, the Clinic focused on local leadership training, discipleship and evangelism. The Clinic also encouraged local churches' participation at all Mobile Clinic centres where the churches would do follow-up and enlist new converts. People living around Mobile Clinic centres were led through a four-week study of the Bible, from Genesis to the Ascension of Jesus Christ. Steady growth in BACOMA churches at Mobile Clinic sites was noticeable. The mobile clinic later turned into a permanent clinic at Senga Bay. This did not change the mission to evangelize, but it did restrict it somewhat.

Theological Training

The founders of the FMC in Malawi aimed at developing spiritual, soul-winning churches with Free Methodism's touch. They wanted a theological programme that would be able to prepare full time workers to manage and care for an expanding work of evangelism. The programme required students to establish three churches as a partial requirement for graduation. This helped the FMC begin churches wherever the students came from or went to. Many of the churches the students established were along family lines. Several planted churches in their home villages or districts. Almost all the first churches in all districts started because of theologically trained pastors. Many theological school graduates planted more than three churches each. Some planted these in one district, while others planted churches in two or more districts. In addition, the programme gave freedom to the laity to start churches indiscriminately. Theologically trained leadership contributed substantially to the growth of the FMC in Malawi, especially before 1996.[9]

The participation of theological students in evangelism not only resulted in additional churches, but also strengthened the young churches that the FMC had established. Theological education programmes provided opportunities for the training of evangelists and lay leadership who guided the churches to spiritual maturity and further numerical growth. Some of them soon ministered as supply pastors during the school's vacation periods. Consequently, the FMC planted many churches through these programmes.

Those who felt God calling them to ministry left their work and moved back to their villages where they began churches. They planted more churches during and after receiving theological training. Others retired from formal employment, received theological training and then were sent by the FMC to begin churches in different places away from their homes and sometimes regions. Because of the training that the Bible School had given them, they were able to begin and minister to several churches. Others were not able to plant more than three churches. At the most, they planted a church that was able to plant a branch or two later.[10]

Bible School and Baptist Publications

While the FMC used a particular theological programme, BACOMA used the Bible School together with Baptist Publications as evangelism tools. The Bible School was used as a centre for recruiting human resources and training for personal witnessing and evangelism. It was the centre for gathering and disseminating information. Many Malawians knew it as "the Mission." The Bible School premises became the church's "headquarters" per se. That was also strengthened by the presence of the printing press on the adjacent plot. The Baptist Publications printed not only hymnbooks and Sunday school materials, but also tracts that were used in witnessing and

---

[9] Henry Church, *Theological Education that Makes a Difference: Church Growth in the Free Methodist Church in Malawi and Zimbabwe*, Zomba: Kachere, 2002, esp pp. 81ff.

[10] Ibid.

evangelism. BACOMA was not only involved in evangelizing Malawi; when opportunities arose, they spread into neighbouring countries as far as South Africa. Even those who were out of the country for theological training at seminaries were also involved in evangelism and church growth in those countries. Some of the churches and the work they started could be identified as evidence of their involvement in crosscurrent evangelism.[11]

Theological Education by Extension (TEE)

There were many opportunities for evangelism and discipleship in many parts of the country. Many classes were composed of both men and women. Some groups started mission churches. These began as the people were studying TEE; they went out on witnessing experiences two by two, and they targeted nearby areas. They started more Bible study groups, and a good number of people were saved. By the end of the year new doors of opportunity were opening around the areas. Churches that held TEE classes had the highest number of baptisms in the 1980s. That also helped to build church leadership and grounded many in the Word.[12]

In 1984 BACOMA organized and supervised TEE courses in several areas. It was felt that TEE was the direction to go because it involved more people and was less expensive than local leadership training. Local leadership training was very good for the new Christians because it dealt with subjects the people wanted to study on a very basic level. TEE, therefore, was for those who had been through local leadership training. Since TEE books were written in a format that the answer was given in the next text sentence, the students could study and check their answers immediately. The problem was that many would not try to remember the answer but look at the next sentence, thereby lessening their learning. Nonetheless, TEE books helped people to study daily. TEE required them to read the Bible daily and encouraged them to study it. The studies were organized around a given subject or a book in the Bible so there was some continuity to it. Seminars were held at designated areas that included local churches.

---

[11] Hany Longwe, *Christians by Grace – Baptists by Choice*, pp. 73, 74
[12] Hany Longwe, *Christians by Grace – Baptists by Choice*, p. 96..

Once a week, the teacher responsible met with students in one of the churches. By coming together one day a week to be tested on what they had studied and to have an in depth study on the same material, students were motivated to study and to use the material as lessons for Sunday school or as sermon material. In addition, they found fellowship and encouragement from other students. TEE classes kindled desires for fulltime ministry for some students. If one visited areas where pastors and lay people attended TEE courses, one would find them still dedicated to the Lord and serving him.

Evangelistic Crusades of the 1970s

The Baptist Convention of Malawi (BACOMA) like other observant churches noted that a spirit of revival was noticeable especially in Southern Malawi in the late 1960s. There was a great openness not only to Christ, but to the Christian faith and message.[13] As a result, in 1967 the Baptist Publications had produced banners that read, 1968 1969 1970 *Chidzaoneka nchiani* (What will be seen or happen?). The question kept everyone in anticipation. In early April 1970 BACOMA, with the assistance of Achewa PIM, and some Southern Baptist Convention missionaries conducted the opening ceremony of the first BACOMA national crusade in Blantyre that brought together local and international Baptist preachers. After the opening ceremony both clergy and laity went into the country in an attempt to make disciples of all ethnic groups. There were among them preachers, interpreters, "counsellors" and interested members who went to assigned locations to proclaim the good news of Jesus Christ for a week. In many places the crusade was successful. The revivals were as it were a new beginning for BACOMA.

The first unlimited crusade (1970) was described as national since the expectation was to reach as many areas as possible throughout the country. By April 1971 BACOMA laid the foundation for its work in the Northern Region. Two Bible study groups were established in Mzuzu and Nkhata Bay. Throughout the country members intentionally went out to the market

---

[13] For a full study of that revival see: Brighton Kawamba, *The Blantyre Spiritual Awakening and its Music*, Mzuzu: Luviri Press, 2018.

place and visited homes as they shared the gospel of Jesus Christ. They also distributed two tracts, "Muyenera Kubadwa Kachiwiri" (You need to be born again), and "Zikhulupiliro za Baptist" (What Baptists Believe). They invited people to a cinema that was usually at night at predetermined places. In between the films they would take 15 or so minutes to inform the audience who they were and again share the good news of Jesus Christ and tracts. They invited those who wanted to know more to stay behind after the film shows.

Although women did not preach in these crusades, they participated in large numbers. They were and are still the majority of BACOMA's membership. Women attracted a lot of attention wherever the meetings were being held. Because they were in the majority, the meetings were lively since Malawian women love to sing and dance. Some women participated as counsellors for women who professed faith in Jesus Christ. They also led in follow up meetings not only for women but also for men and youths. The revival provided and endorsed an alternative avenue for women to exercise and develop their gifts and talents as missionaries in areas of the country that, in terms of culture and religion, were distinctly different from their own backgrounds. When BACOMA talked of numerical gains, the majority were women. Some women participated in the Crusaders' meetings that saw the beginning of several BACOMA churches. They were directly involved in the establishment of certain congregations.

BACOMA owes its growth to the large numbers of women who responded to the preaching of the Word. The growth of women's missionary activities has reflected the development of BACOMA from Blantyre, Zomba and Lilongwe to all districts of the country. BACOMA women in Blantyre, like in the Jali-Zomba area and the Lower Shire, were already doing door-to-door witnessing before the revival that set the groundwork for the revival meetings. This to some extent made men and women equal as they ministered together. Occasionally men gave women the opportunities to lead in singing and preaching in church worship services, an involvement that attracted more people to join the church. The numbers of women becoming members of BACOMA churches did so because other women witnessed to them, one to one. In some villages members of the same family who were married women but living in their villages according to matrilineal custom became Baptists following each other. Some of the husbands later became Christians. Other women moved from other denominations because they had been feeling spiritually dry, and their joining BACOMA women's groups was a search for spiritual revival. They then witnessed to their spouses and family who also joined the church. The change of life has been attributed to the women's faithful prayers for a revival in the families. In a way they were pastors of their families, a responsibility that has been common in many homes.

Not all women went out, but others showed their acquaintances the way to deal with family problems. Both Christian and non-Christian families can experience internal problems. Christian women, who sensed that their fellow women were going through very difficult times, would ask if they could be of assistance. Many turned to Jesus as others witnessed that he was the only answer. Life began to change when they began to attend church evangelism meetings, and, after several such encounters, they would profess faith in Christ which they later would share with their spouses and children. Many families have been restored as women share with those whose lives are in a mess, the result being increased church membership. Some of these have become family counsellors and teachers and church leaders in their own right because others had shown concern for them.

God's movement was also evidenced by mass repentance of mostly young people. A few young people who were already believers impacted the society of youths. These youths led in the singing that was mainly choruses. They were energetic and sang very loud; some could only sing for hours, but there were others who sang for the whole time the crusades were on without losing their voices. The music was simple and repetitive. Choruses were indigenous. They carried a straightforward message to the listener that salvation is through Jesus Christ only.

Home Missionaries

The desire on the part of BACOMA to establish more churches in some parts of the country as a result of the crusades and the revival necessitated the introduction of Malawian home missionaries. In 1976 BACOMA sent

13: Post-Classical Missions' Missionary Affair in Malawi   227

its first home missionary to Karonga. Towards the end of the 1980s there were churches at Chitipa, Songwe, Karonga and Chilumba. By 1982 there was another home missionary at Balaka. Due to financial constraints, BACOMA discontinued the position of home missionary in the early 1990s, but it was reintroduced about six years later.

European Baptist Mission (EBM) introduced the idea of some cooperation in which the EBM would not send and support German missionaries to these countries; instead it would give financial and moral support to home missionaries. Thus, the Home Mission Project came into existence. The project was from 1998 to 2000 initially. EBM would support three missionaries per year. The support would cover salary, rent, travelling, and medical expenses. By the beginning of 1998, BACOMA sent a missionary to Ntaja/Machinga area, another to Dedza and the third to Rumphi. The home missionary project is still continuing (2020).

The Crusaders

While several individual Convention Baptists were instrumental in the beginning of many churches, Baptist groups working in teams were also responsible for the beginning of a number of churches throughout the country. These were a result of the spirit of revival that swept the country. Lilongwe Baptist Crusaders, as they were first known, represent successful voluntary team evangelistic efforts that have no parallel in the history of BACOMA. They became another tool of evangelism within BACOMA. They were later known as the Baptist Crusade, or simply the Crusaders. They were an organization of young evangelists who went out to different areas during the month of December preaching the Good News of Jesus Christ. Their story begins at Lilongwe Baptist Church where a handful of young evangelists banded together in the cause of spreading the Good News. It started as the mission of one person who later took the lead to make this vision come true.

In 1979 one of the co-founders discerned God's call to preach and to begin churches where there were no Convention Baptist churches. Towards the end of 1980 two young people officially co-founded the Lilongwe Baptist Crusade with the aim of bringing people to Christ. The emphasis was on ministry to the world that Jesus died for. The Crusaders were responding to that responsibility of making themselves expendable for those whom Jesus identified as "the least of these." Members used part of their annual leave from employment for evangelism. It became a yearly campaign over the Christmas period. Although they got some help from local congregations and other individual Baptists, the members of the Crusaders paid for the major part of their transport, lodging and food expenses, and any other items they needed for their ministry.

The Crusaders travelled mainly on public transport that included buses and water motor vessels. On board MV Ilala they sang and preached many times to over 200 people who also received tracts. One would think that the Crusaders would only visit places in and around Lilongwe, but no. Apart from Lilongwe, they covered Chipoka, Salima, Nkhotakota, Ntcheu and Balaka. In December 1981 the Crusaders were in Zomba District where they held meetings at Nsanama, Jali, Nzerera, Mwembere, Gunde and Zomba Town. In all the places they visited, they preached at public places such as markets, witnessed in residential areas and visited the sick in hospitals. They prayed for healing, and they were able to witness to patients, many of whom were very willing to hear God's Word. During the evening they held meetings in halls where people sang songs of praise and ended with preaching. In some places Baptist congregations in the area hosted the Crusaders and co-planned for the activities. Some members who needed their family members to hear the Word gathered people at their homes.

Many people were surprised at the young people, several of whom were small in stature. Some didn't think that anything good could come out of these unqualified, rather weak people. Despite their assumptions, they let the Crusaders take the centre stage. They witnessed and preached and some gave their lives to Jesus Christ. Others became members of BACOMA. Several Convention churches were revived. Several of these young people later became pastors of outstanding qualities.

The culture in which BACOMA works is male dominated, as a result, the Crusaders were placed under Baptist Men's Committee that excluded women from the Crusaders. The reasons that were given and are still being presented against women's participation in such ministries viewed as men only are not biblical. Women may not have been in the first group of Crusaders, but definitely they were involved as they supported and let go of their spouses, and some were directly involved in the evangelistic efforts of the group. It is true that humans will always be men and women, and there are many things women and men can both do. One does not need to be a man in order to preach or teach. Some women are even better than men in some of the areas, just as men are to women in some responsibilities.

1970s and 1980s Revivals

An alliance of para-church organizations and churches, both Evangelical and Pentecostal, was instrumental for the 1970s revival that advocated the message of a personal relationship with Christ by being "born-again." Among the para-church organizations were Scripture Union, Students Christian Organization of Malawi (SCOM), and the Evangelical Association of Malawi (EAM). The two para-church organizations together with the Church of Central Africa Presbyterian (CCAP), Zambezi Evangelical Church, Nyasa Mission, Southern Baptist Convention, Africa Evangelical Church, Churches of Christ, and Assemblies of God believed that the antidote to liberal theology was aggressive evangelism through which men and women were changed by the power of the Holy Spirit. Thus, the annual week-long Blantyre Keswick Convention began in 1962 with speakers from outside of the country. 1967 was a defining moment when the annual conventions adopted a national character by bringing together church representatives from across the country, making it the nation's biggest interdenominational fellowship.[14]

EAM adapted an evangelism programme developed in Latin America, 'Evangelism in Depth', where each Church member was expected to be a witness for Christ. Because churches felt that the word 'evangelism' would turn off Muslims from being interested, they instead suggested to name the programme New Life for All (NLFA). Almost every Protestant denomination leader was invited to a sensitization retreat in 1969 for the programme, where most of them agreed to implement it in their churches.

---

[14] Brighton Kawamba, *The Blantyre Spiritual Awakening and its Music*, Mzuzu: Luviri Press, 2018, pp. 32ff.

Congregational leaders spent a month in prayer seeking God's guidance as to how to do evangelism, another month to sensitize the congregations and their satellite prayer-houses on the evangelistic programme, and then three months of weekly Bible studies and Scripture memorization to ensure that members were "born-again." The idea of being born again was not new to Baptists, but it supported their belief and teaching about the personal relationship between a believer and Jesus Christ. That also saw many Baptist pastors and missionaries being used as speakers and teachers during interdenominational meetings. The Bible studies and Scripture memorization also made sure that members had an adequate knowledge of Scripture to witness to others and be filled with the power of the Holy Spirit for effective witnessing according to Luke 24:49 and Acts 1:8. They then spent five months of house-to-house, open-air, and EAM gospel tract distribution outreaches, a month of following-up on interested contacts and converts to connect them to other regenerated believers, and finally a month of evaluation by the leaders to review the programme and plan for the next twelve-month cycle.

New Life for All influenced not only many individual Convention Baptists, but also many lives in Malawi and beyond. The results of its work may not be officially accredited by the Convention, but local Convention churches used some NLFA ideas for evangelism, applying them during revivals that brought large increases in membership. Convention churches like New Jerusalem and Soche took advantage of the NLFA teaching that saw prayer as the hub of any ministry. These churches also used Christian literature, which was not only important in evangelism, but also in the work of building up converts into mature Christians.

One of the churches that played a pivotal role was St. Columba CCAP, which opened its doors in 1962. The minister was open to other pastors ministering at the church so that the church had a steady flow of evangelists from Dorothea Mission, the main speakers at the Keswick Conventions, and other visiting preachers. Perhaps the most strategic church cooperation for revival in Blantyre at that time was that between St. Columba and the Kanjedza Assemblies of God. The ministers would invite each other to preach in the other's church. Each church would invite the other to its conferences or "revival meetings." It was during such revival meetings that Pentecostal phenomena such as speaking in tongues started in St. Columba.

By 1970, the Evangelical Association of Malawi initiated open-air outreaches in strategic locales in Blantyre such as the Blantyre Market, Limbe Market, and Ndirande Market at Chinseu. The city-wide outreaches were very successful. Two years later, EAM member churches prioritized street evangelism. They intensified open-air outreaches in Blantyre so that the revival reached its climax in 1978. The preaching of the gospel – "you must be born-again" – was characterized by a call to immediate response, miracles, power encounters, and deep conviction of sin.

EAM evangelistic groups set up preaching points in various parts of the city which later became lunch-hour fellowships in commercial centers and prayer groups in the townships. Lunch-hour fellowships proliferated in the city from around 1974. In the townships, school-teachers, vendors, and others who could not access the lunch-hour meetings in the city began to meet as fellowships. Initially these groups were formed to provide the prayer-cover for the EAM evangelistic efforts in the city-centre, but they evolved into evangelistic teams that proclaimed the gospel in their neighbourhoods and also met for prayer. There was such camaraderie amongst the members that when a fellowship member was bereaved or died, the other fellowships would also come to the member's assistance. From the fellowships and evangelistic zeal of the 1970s came ministries that would begin as followers gathered around a resilient leader with a specialized ministry call. Though the ministries did not meet on Sunday mornings to ensure every member remained a part of the local church, soon local congregations were organized around the ministry founders.

Another group that contributed to the proliferation of fellowships all over the country was Every Home Crusade (EHC), an affiliate of World Literature Centre in the USA. This ministry in 1973 distributed gospel tracts from house to house and began prayer groups in homes. After tract distribution, EHC would host a seeker's meeting at a community centre ground, district community hall, or local soccer ground. Such meetings would be followed by the formation of prayer partner groups in particular districts. Every Home Crusade reached out to towns, villages, prisons, colleges, and hospitals throughout the country. Every Home Crusade also served alongside local churches offering free gospel tracts and also personnel and some limited financial assistance towards the cost of evangelistic meetings. In many incidences the results of the partnership were tremendous. One example is the relationship between Every Home Crusade and Mzuzu Baptist Church that later saw two soldiers become pastors, and the other two, one a church leader and another a traditional leader of influence.

The Gospel on Tape

Apart from working in partnership with parachurch organizations, BACOMA began using tape recorders. It was a realization that pastors and other church members together could not meet the great need for Bible teaching in the country. Very few people were readers, and the use of radio was limited. BACOMA introduced a portable assistant that seemed to work: a small cassette tape recorder. They prepared a total of five hours of tape recordings with half-hour segments including Scripture reading, hymns and lessons for use with the first group of seven recorders.

They made the recorders available to lay preachers for use in their own areas. After ten hours of use the batteries would begin to fade. The recorders would be returned to the Media Centre in Blantyre where technicians would clean and maintain the recorders and replace the batteries. Although the response was that of excitement and the opportunities seemed endless, it was not an easy way for many leaders to borrow, use and return the recorder for maintenance, and go through the same process again. Those who were close to Blantyre and others who had means to get the recorders to and from Blantyre benefited from the use of these portable assistants. Nonetheless, the tape recorders had a very limited success.[15]

---

[15] Hany Longwe, *Christians by Grace - Baptists by Choice*, p. 205.

Music as an Evangelistic Tool

From the early days of the 1970s revival, music played a crucial part in the evangelistic meetings, not only as an attraction in a society where entertainment was inadequate, but also as a tool of evangelism. The revival produced music groups such as Kuunika Choir of St Columba CCAP Church in Blantyre in 1974, the legendary Come to Jesus Choir in 1976,[16] Tembenukani Duet from Zomba in 1979, Two Brothers in Christ in 1979, and the Jesus for All Outreach Band in 1981. The consequence of music can be observed from the fact that three of the earliest ministries that transformed into Neocharismatic churches began as outreach bands. Living Waters Band became Apostle Stanley Ndovie's Living Waters Church; Mustard Seed Band became Apostle Willy Chaponda's Mustard Seed Church; and All for Jesus Band became Apostle Felix Zalimba's All for Jesus Church.

It is no wonder that not only many Neocharismatic churches, but also various post-classical churches that includes Capital City Baptist Church in Lilongwe, have praise or worship teams. Many of those who serve on the worship or praise teams are women. Some of the musicians release albums and perform gospel concerts, especially in the cities and towns. Gospel concerts are normally held over the weekends offering a form of family entertainment in a land where such is rare. One cannot deny that contemporary gospel music has contributed to a cultural renewal of Malawian music. Hip-hop gospel is the latest variation of the gospel genre that is popular amongst the young population. These music forms, alongside Christian radio stations that play only gospel music such as African Bible College Radio, Trans-World Radio, Channel for All Nations, and Calvary Family Church Radio and TV, contribute to the rich assortment of Malawian music in which the gospel genre dominates.

In addition, many churches have effectively used singing as an evangelistic tool. For example, BACOMA quickly adopted chorus singing as a liturgical tool for evangelism and worship, and there has not been a let up in their

---

[16] For a picture see the cover of Brighton Kawamba, *The Blantyre Spiritual Awakening and its Music*, Mzuzu: Luviri Press, 2018.

use. Congregations love to sing choruses (*makorasi*) more than adopted Western hymns because it is the singing that embraces the aspirations of the membership. Much singing has been and still is accompanied with hand clapping, dancing and ululating, and in many churches, drumming. Some songs employ certain tribal gestures, movements, dance, handclapping and whistling. Some local churches freely use available traditional instruments, the commonest instrument being the drum (*ng'oma*), which is also associated with traditional dances.

Makorasi are different from hymns because they are up tempo songs that combine simple texts and repetitions. The texts reflect spiritual experiences or emphases that came up with local revivals. The 1970 revival choruses emphasized the aspect of being "born again." Many Evangelicals in the country benefited from *makorasi* because they revealed the interpretation of peoples' faith as they saw it. The choruses covered areas such as atonement and deliverance from sinful acts that included consumption of alcohol and immoral behaviour. Some songs are by choirs or individuals. In some areas, such as Blantyre and Lilongwe, choirs featured highly in the 1970s and the 1980s. Now choirs are found in many local churches throughout the country. Some churches have more than one choir. Be that as it may, choirs have been used as tools for both worship and evangelism.

Analysis of the 1970 – 1980 Revivals

The 1970s may be described as the best times for many post-classical churches. They planted many congregations. The small beginnings abruptly gave way to a surge of growth that can be traced back to the crusades of the 1970s. By the end of the 1970s, many churches had doubled their membership. Apart from producing some of its fine leaders, many churches grew and reproduced themselves. Due to evangelistic meetings that were held towards the end of the 1980s many people were added to the churches. In addition, there were many preaching point mission churches not included in the count because the people in these "daughter churches" had not yet been recognized as members.

Many decisions to follow Christ in churches did not start with the individual church's witness. There were those who went through a lot of bending and shaping through other Christian organizations before they chose to serve God through a particular church. Some did not profess Christ in these organizations, but they did so when they joined a particular church. It was during times of partnership when some would profess faith in Jesus Christ as Lord and Saviour of their life. Then they began to participate in different fellowship groups, at the same time inwardly shopping for a church.

Another example of the influence of para-church organizations on Christian life is seen in evangelism and leadership training partnerships between churches and the para-church organizations. Instead of the churches doing it alone, there were times the local congregations or a particular denomination partnered with some para-church organization in evangelism and leadership training. In many incidences the results of the partnership were tremendous.

One major result of the 1970 – 1980 revival was the beginning of many Neocharismatic churches that Klaus Fiedler considers religious diversification. In arguing against opinions that say there is no need for more churches, he perceives such diversification positively as an indicator of a "strong religiosity."[17] Such diversification shows the religious choice of the people. The growth of middle and upper class Neocharismatic churches proves that religious diversity is not just a preferred option of the poor. Klaus Fiedler further states that such diversification shows that Neocharismatic churches are Malawian initiatives and prove that Malawian Christians value mutual respect and cooperation over highly centralized ecclesiastical structures.[18]

The leaders of Neocharismatic churches are committed to pioneering or overseeing a church planting movement. They believe their offices are linked with opening new work as in church planting, raising up new leaders

---

[17] Klaus Fiedler, "The Process of Religious Diversification in Malawi: A Reflection on Method and a First Attempt at a Synthesis," in Klaus Fiedler, *Conflicted Power in Malawian Christianity. Essays Missionary and Evangelical from Malawi*, Mzuzu: Mzuni Press, 2015, p. 192.

[18] Klaus Fiedler, "The Charismatic and Pentecostal Movements in Malawi in Cultural Perspective," in Klaus Fiedler, *Conflicted Power in Malawian Christianity. Essays Missionary and Evangelical from Malawi*, Mzuzu: Mzuni Press, 2015, pp. 323-349.

for the work, and organizing a structure for continuity. They think of church leaders who have strong gifting in preaching and teaching so that believers are grounded in the Word of God. Some claim they plant churches after the leadership hears from God, when a member volunteers, and at times, though rarely, when approached by groups interested in coming under their oversight. In cases where members or leaders relocate to new areas, they start Bible study or prayer groups that culminate into local churches. This has been a most important foundation of church planting within Living Waters. On the other hand, Revival Life Ministries (RLM) churches are usually planted by sending from the Lilongwe church a person who would have been trained in ministry or when members relocate to a place where no RLM church exists. An apostle, at least in the RLM case, has a ministry that not only transcends his denomination or network but is also of global scope.

Neocharismatic churches are finding expression of their diversity in the proliferation of church planting efforts abroad. Increasingly they are locating Malawian Neocharismatic congregations in localities that have Malawian populations abroad. Living Waters Church has a branch in South Bend, Indiana in the United States of America, and another in Johannesburg, South Africa. There is a Malawian church also in South Bend, Indiana called Winners' Praise Church. There is the Calvary Family Church in the United Kingdom. Many Neocharismatic churches in Malawi have branches in Mozambique and Zambia, such as Evangelistic New Exodus Church of God and Missions.. there are also several missions to the West, but they have not actually resulted in impacting Western cultures because most migrant churches tend to be inward-looking and ethnic based.

Mission to Mozambique through Refugees[19]

From the beginning of 1988, some churches in Malawi took advantage of the civil war to evangelize Mozambican refugees in the country, followed by the introduction of missionary work in Mozambique. The Free Methodist Church student pastors began churches in their areas among the

---

[19] The character of this book of assembled essays creates an overlap here with pp. 82ff of this book. It also makes it possible to find more details there.

refugees. After having received permission from the relevant authorities, they found places to hold revival or public worship services. In the process, they founded fellowships that developed into organized churches. Several of these churches continued for a time under the supervision of Malawian pastors. At the end of the civil war in 1994, the Malawi Conference transferred 25 of these churches with a membership of about 750 in the Zambezia and Tete Provinces to the Mozambique Conference.[20] In the same year, a Malawian minister felt God calling him to be a missionary to Mozambique or Zambia. The conference of 1995 appointed him as the first Malawi FMC missionary to serve in Mozambique. Some individual FMC members from Malawi and Mozambique planted branches near the Southwest Malawi-Mozambique boundary.

The Baptist Convention of Malawi also planted churches in Mozambique among the refugees from Ntcheu and Dedza and Lilongwe. During the Mozambican civil war, BACOMA had Malawian missionaries working amongst refugees in camps in Malawi along the border in Dedza and Ntcheu districts. The ministry at Ngalande Village produced a leader who later became a pastor in Mozambique. He became a Baptist whilst in that camp. He accepted God's call to fulltime ministry, and from 1991 to 1992 he and his wife studied at the Baptist Bible School in Lilongwe. They were the first couple from this side of Mozambique to study at the Bible School in Lilongwe. Several pastors from Mozambique have since studied at the Baptist Bible School. Their training has contributed to Malawian missionary efforts in Mozambique.

In Villa Milanje, Zambezi Province, BACOMA missionary work in the region started as a result of three Mozambican Christians seeking to understand more about what was "true baptism," questioning the validity of their baptism. During the war they found refuge in Migowi and Zomba areas where they became Baptists. After the civil war, like many, they returned to Mozambique where they established churches. In 1996 one of the leaders was at the Bible School in Lilongwe. After his return, he began a couple more mission churches in the Villa Milanje area. At first the

---

[20] Henry Church, *Theological Education that Makes a Difference: Church Growth in the Free Methodist Church in Malawi and Zimbabwe,* Zomba: Kachere, 2002, p. 117.

churches were part of the voluntary association of Baptists in Migowi. Nonetheless, not all churches remained Baptist. One church joined the Four Square Gospel Church because it was said that the Four Square Gospel Church gave its members some financial support.

From 1982, a Baptist from Nkhotakota began a church in Niassa Province, Mozambique. Later there was a follow-up from Likoma Baptists. During the civil war many people were killed and others scattered. Those who remained in Mozambique continued to meet in homes. Many of the refugees went back to Mozambique after the cease-fire in October 1992. In 1997, the church sent one of its leaders to Lilongwe and he became the first Baptist leader from the Nyasa Province to study at the Bible School. By the end of the following year, there were three Baptist churches in the Nyasa province.[21]

In 1995, Capital City Baptist Church (CCBC) had the idea of sending a missionary to Mozambique. It was only in 1997 that the church missions committee sent a couple as missionaries to Villa Ulongwe. Since they could not get residence permits, CCBC rented a house for the missionaries at Dedza from where they operated into Angonia. In 1999 Bible school courses were held at Ntcheu, which also attracted leaders from Mozambique. By 2000, only Villa Ulongwe and Magwai churches survived out of the several churches the couple had started in Angonia. Due to some error the church has since stopped its missionary work in Mozambique.

International Denominational Partnerships in Evangelism

Some local churches have taken advantage of their relationships with foreign missionary churches of similar faith and persuasion. The partnership has either been because of the local church or the foreign missionary church's initiation. Some partnerships have been between African and Western ministries with local churches or individuals. Whichever is the case, the results have been mixed according to the impression of each party. Nevertheless, numbers of converts have been added to the Christian family.

---

[21] Hany Longwe, *Christians by Grace - Baptists by Choice*, pp. 224-227.

One such partnership was between BACOMA and the Baptist Union of Southern Africa (BUSA), in pioneer evangelism amongst the Muslim Yao of the Southern Lake Malawi area. Though Mangochi is a famous tourist attraction in Malawi with a large population of Muslims, it didn't immediately attract BACOMA missionary work. The partnership began with the arrival of a couple from Randburg Baptist Church and was sealed with the coming of a Malawian couple who not only served as language facilitators and translators, but as guides through delicate contacts and negotiations with village, district and government.

The team began with a Bible study that the village chief tried to stop. Despite that, several people declared their trust in Jesus during Bible study sessions. The period was characterized by daily requests to "explain" the Gospel of Christ. Some backslidden individual Christians living among Muslims in the area returned with renewed zeal to Jesus Christ as they noticed changes in the lives of their neighbours. The first baptism took place in November 1985 at which time a delegation from Randburg was present. Three more baptismal services were conducted in 1986. Some people came out of curiosity, and others had burdens that needed off-loading. BACOMA established a few churches, but several did not grow strong because they lacked established leadership to give the church the sustenance it needed in an area in which the sheer numbers of committed Muslims were very large. One or two churches had to move to new areas because they could not stand the challenge they received from the Muslims in the area. These churches needed leaders in evangelism to Muslims to withstand Muslims' counter-actions and win them to Jesus Christ. Muslim teachers had decided to do everything in their power to get rid of the missionary team and its followers and to put an end to Christianity in the area.

BACOMA missionary work in the Muslim stronghold of Southern Lake Malawi did not grow fast due to the lack of leadership development. The Malawian missionary, the South African missionary and later BUSA missionaries, fought single-handedly to keep BACOMA churches alive. He later received assistance from his disciples who became co-workers. They witnessed to and established Bible study groups among Muslims in the area and among Mozambiquean refugees. The majority of the BACOMA membership, be it individuals or churches, did not catch the vision to reach the Muslim communities. Consequently, mission to Muslims was not as effective as it should have been.

In 1987 the Far East Broadcasting Association (FEBA) made a proposal to reach the Yao people of Malawi using primarily the radio. By 1990 the Baptist Convention of Malawi was one of the participating denominations in the Yao Project. One Baptist and one Anglican went through some training in Harare. In 1991, FEBA introduced a 15-minute Yao language programme over the radio and subsequent follow-up for a period of two years in order to evangelize the unreached Yao Muslims. BACOMA prepared and recorded Scripture songs in Yao through its studios in Blantyre. In addition, the missionary team produced the first book for the Yao designed in such a way that it would fall within the evangelism, follow-up and discipleship plans of the Yao Project.

During the 1990s many Yao people wrote to the programme, and several people announced that they had trusted Jesus in the process. BACOMA through its missionary visited some villages in Machinga, Mangochi and Zomba on radio programme promotion and/or recording trips. They paid courtesy visits to the chiefs and the villagers and recorded Yao stories and music. There was also question and answer time. Many questions were about God. Some answers brought division and that sometimes led to more discussions or hate/love for Christianity.

BACOMA, in partnership with other churches, the Free Methodist Church, the Nazarene Church and Seventh Day Baptist Church in Mangochi and the surrounding areas, formed the Yao Outreach Ministry. The committee visited many churches of all Christian denominations in the area and talked to them about their vision and objectives and what was required of the churches to be part of the movement. They taught congregations that identified with the cause how to minister among Muslims and gave tracts written in Yao for use in the ministry. That resulted in an increase of new converts from Islam and church attendance. BACOMA also began work among the refugees and was further strengthened by the Baptist Bible Way

Correspondence School. They encouraged refugees who could read and write to study with Bible Way as one tool of discipleship.

Another international partnership in evangelism has been between BACOMA and the General Baptist Convention of Oklahoma, which involved people in many parts of the country. The basic plan was for a church in Oklahoma to work with the same church in Malawi for three years: the first year for evangelism, the second for discipleship, and the third for leadership training. This basic plan was carried out in Rumphi, Chintheche, Mthabuwa, Mponela, Dwangwa, and Lunzu. In some twenty to twenty-five other places, teams came once or twice but did not complete the three-year cycle. In addition to the six places where volunteers completed the three-year cycle, teams came for one or two more years to at least twenty other places doing evangelism and discipleship training. In some areas where the partnership ministered, preaching points were established. Where the converts were taught Good News for You and the Gospel of John, people were baptized. Many hundreds of volunteers served in Malawi since 1998. Almost all of them did personal evangelism using the *Good News for You* book as follow up. Many people made professions of faith. In addition, some teams did special meetings. They brought teams for four years that also did medical, evangelism, and construction work.

Challenges for Post-Classical Mission Churches

Klaus Fiedler has mentioned several challenges that are also applicable to post-classical churches. One of the challenges is that of the un-reached. For the Achewa Providence Industrial Mission (Achewa PIM), as a Baptist-type church, one would have expected it to grow in numbers since Baptists have been characterized by evangelism. It has remained very much close to the Chewa culture such that it has not copied anything from the Baptist Convention of Malawi (BACOMA) and other Evangelicals. By keeping the church "Achewa," they were not able to send missionaries to people of other tribes. Christianization by means of a group movement was not the perfect answer to the evangelization of the people. The "Achewa" did not only separate themselves from Providence Industrial Mission of John

Chilembwe, they also separated themselves from people who were different from them; people they were expected to evangelize as a church.

Although Pentecostal missions and churches are still strong in their rural base, some have shown themselves more adaptable to the cities than most post-classical churches. An example is the Assemblies of God that is still the largest Pentecostal church in Malawi. On the other hand, the urban, educated Charismatic churches have been making serious efforts to the poorer environs of the urban and rural areas. Some churches, such as Baptist Convention, have remained practically rural though they have in towns and cities a few churches that are of international nature and attract attendees from many countries. The Free Methodist Church, though it has churches in Lilongwe City for example, is still rural and has little impact on educated and international city dwellers. Many post-classical churches have in the main neglected the unreached millions in towns and cities. It is as if they have been influenced by successive Malawi governments that declared that their main concern for development is the rural masses at the expense of those in the cities. Many people are moving to the cities, and churches should make a deliberate effort to follow them with the Word. Although there are several denominations with churches in Muslim areas, the challenge is that the percentage of Christians is relatively low there. Several ex-Muslim congregations have been and are being established, or have plateaued. Nevertheless, it is still a huge challenge to reach out to Muslims.

Conclusion

Malawians have and are spreading the Christian faith amongst Africans. It has taken them a long time, but when it has succeeded, the faith becomes truly indigenous, as opposed to being foreign. Mission work has not been in vain. The success can be attributed to the missionary vision of Malawian churches whose members have been crossing cultural and, in some cases, national boundaries making disciples of Jesus Christ. This is the Malawian post-classical churches' missionary affair as Klaus Fiedler would say.

Chapter 13

Zimbabwe, Zambia and Malawi[1]

During the second half of the nineteenth century, white traders, concession seekers and missionaries arrived in Zimbabwe, Zambia and Malawi in small parties. Before long, missionaries became agents in a complex transformation process of the region that was closely related to the extensive transformations that followed the impact of capitalism and colonialism. Each missionary organization entering the region chose a specific area in which to begin its work. At the end of 1859, the London Missionary Society (LMS) established a mission at Inyati in Zimbabwe, though the evangelistic efforts were not to bear fruit for many years.[2] It was the first permanent European outpost that also provided a home for travellers. In Zimbabwe, as in Zambia and Malawi, missionary presence both eased and critiqued the colonial advance.

The missionary work also demonstrates the speed and shape of the ecclesiastical scramble. In mid-1861, the Anglican Church's Universities' Mission to Central Africa (UMCA) started work at Magomero in Malawi, only to withdraw to Zanzibar due to several difficulties. It was back in Malawi in 1882.[3] In the meantime, the Scottish Presbyterian Livingstonia Mission established itself in northern Malawi. Its area of influence included central Malawi and north-eastern Zambia. Its success owed much to the work of Zulu evangelists, including Shadrach Ngunana and William Koyi.[4] In 1889, Livingstonia transferred central Malawi to the Dutch Reformed Church Mission from South Africa. Blantyre Mission, also Scottish

---

[1] First published as "Zimbabwe, Zambia and Malawi" in Kenneth R. Ross, J. Kwabena Asamoah-Gyadu & Todd M. Johnson (Eds), *Edinburgh Companion to Global Christianity: Christianity in Sub-Sahara Africa*, Edinburgh University Press, 2017.
[2] John Weller and Jane Linden, *Mainstream Christianity to 1980 in Malawi, Zambia and Zimbabwe*, Gweru: Mambo, 1984, pp. 16, 17.
[3] John Weller and Jane Linden, *Mainstream Christianity*, p. 36.
[4] John Weller and Jane Linden, *Mainstream Christianity*, p. 43.

Presbyterian, took southern Malawi, which left the lakeshore areas for the UMCA. After an abortive attempt to establish a mission in southern Malawi in 1889-1891, the Catholics returned to Malawi only in 1901. In the comity of missions in Malawi there was no place for the Catholics, whom the Presbyterians viewed as intruders into a country already divided up.[5] That has since changed. The comity agreement between Nkhoma Synod (formerly the Dutch Reformed Mission) and Livingstonia Synod has also ended, with Livingstonia starting congregations in Nkhoma's territory in central Malawi.

It was not until the founding of the Zambezi Industrial Mission at Blantyre in 1892 that the challenge to the Scottish missions' hegemony began in earnest.[6] The next nine years saw the founding of four smaller missions: Nyasa Industrial Mission (NIM) in 1893 (now Evangelical Church of Malawi); the Scottish Baptist Industrial Mission (BIM) at Gowa in 1896; the Providence Industrial Mission (PIM) of John Chilembwe in 1900; and the Seventh Day Baptist (SDB) Mission at Malamulo in Makwasa in 1901, which two years later became Seventh-day Adventist (SDA). The BIM became the Churches of Christ in 1929. It also opened the door into Malawi for other Baptist individuals and mission organizations.[7]

In 1885, the LMS was the first to establish a mission station in Zambia, based at Niamikolo, close to Lake Tanganyika; and it was followed by other missions throughout Zambia. One of the reasons for the rapid spread of mission stations was that smaller tribes in the area believed that the missionaries would provide protection from their attackers, such as the powerful Bemba. The Paris Mission established itself in 1892,[8] and achieved considerable success among the Lozi, largely due to the Sotho evangelists on its team. In the same year, the Primitive Methodists settled among the Illa. The Scottish Presbyterians settled at Mwenzo in 1894. The four

---

[5] Klaus Fiedler, "Africa's Evangelical Turn," p. 359. See also Hubert Reijnaerts, Ann Nielsen and Matthew Schoffeleers, *Montfortians in Malawi*, pp. 4, 17.

[6] John McCracken, *Politics and Christianity in Malawi 1875-1940*, p. 216.

[7] Harry Langworthy, *'Africa for the African': The Life of Joseph Booth*, Blantyre: CLAIM, 1996, p. 31.

[8] John Weller and Jane Linden, *Mainstream Christianity*, p. 32.

missions were to merge their work in 1965 and become known as the United Church of Zambia (UCZ).[9]

The Catholics established a mission among the Bemba in 1895. As a result, the Catholic Church later became by far the most influential denomination in Zambia. Catechists played an important part in the rapid proliferation of Catholic stations. In 1899, the LMS started work in the north-east of Zambia. In 1905, the NIM opened a mission station at Kafulafuta,[10] south-east of Ndola, which later became the nucleus of the Zambia Baptist Association. In 1911, Leonard Kamungu, a priest from Malawi, established the first Anglican mission at Msoro, near Chipata, under the UMCA,[11] which held to a strict Anglo-Catholic theology.

Tradition	2015 Population	%
Christians	12,740,000	81.7
Roman Catholics	1,983,000	12.7
Orthodox	5,400	0.0
Independents	6,516,000	41.8
Protestants	3,338,000	21.4
Anglicans	420,000	2.7
Pentecostals	6,944,000	44.5
Evangelicals	1,191,000	7.6
Total	15,603,000	100.0

Table 1: Christianity in Zimbabwe 2015. Source: Todd M. Johnson and Gina A. Zurlo (eds), World Christian Database, Leiden, Boston: Brill, [March 2016]

The Catholics offended the LMS by starting a mission near the LMS station in the north-east. The Catholics strongly opposed the spheres of influence, though they did not like other missions to come close to 'their' area.

---

[9] John Weller and Jane Linden, *Mainstream Christianity*, p. 152.
[10] Reinhard Ludwig Frey, *History of the Zambia Baptist Association 1905-2005*, p. 38.
[11] John Weller and Jane Linden, *Mainstream Christianity*, p. 169.

They opposed the Anglicans who wanted to open a mission in Bangweulu. The Anglicans also found resistance in eastern Zambia from the Reformed Mission. Later, however, the Catholic, Anglican and Adventist missions rejected the allocation of land to different missions, which was loosened in the 1930s because of the growth of towns and of labour migration, whereby people 'brought' their church and denominational identifications to their new locations. Among missions such as Baptist, there existed mutual agreements that if one church was already established in a place, other churches would not start new work there. That also later changed.

In Zimbabwe, the white settler regime gave missionary groups land, half of which went to the Catholics, who had returned to the country in 1890. Catholics selected land for stations and for mission farms. The Anglicans established themselves at Penhalonga in Manicaland. The mission was successful in evangelizing the Shona because it used mainly catechists, including Bernard Mizeki. Together with one of his converts, Shoniwa Kapuya, Mizeki was also involved in translations of the Scriptures and liturgy. Mizeki was later martyred, and he is officially an Anglican saint.[12] Anglicans experienced most acutely the tensions arising from the encounter of races and cultures because they had a sizable portion of whites who were either practicing or lapsed members. Due to the comparative independence of the Anglican missions, the white members met the bulk of the Church's expenses without the need for large subsidies from missionary societies. That solved some problems but raised others.

In 1891 the Salvation Army, the (British) Wesleyan Methodists, and the Dutch Reformed Church of South Africa arrived, each occupying part of the central province. In 1893 the American Board of Commissioners for Foreign Missions of the Congregational Christian Churches established a mission in the south-east. The Seventh-day Adventists arrived in Matabeleland in 1894. The Methodist Episcopal Church (MEC), also known as the American Methodists, arrived in Manicaland and began work

---

[12] John Weller and Jane Linden, *Mainstream Christianity*, pp. 66-69.

in the east around Mutare, in 1897.¹³ The British Methodists and MEC made a territorial agreement in order not to be in each other's way.

Tradition	2015 Population	%
Christians	13,858,000	85.5
Roman Catholics	5,339,000	32.9
Orthodox	7,700	0.0
Independents	2,924,000	18.0
Protestants	5,144,000	31.7
Anglicans	294,000	1.8
Pentecostals	3,676,000	22.7
Evangelicals	2,939,000	18.1
Total	16,212,000	100.0

Figure 1: **Christianity in Zambia 2016.** *Source: Todd M. Johnson and Gina A. Zurlo (eds), World Christian Database, Leiden, Boston: Brill, [March 2016].*

These territorial agreements, or spheres of influence or comity, played a large role in the spread of churches.[14] Although they were not meant to restrict people's faith, the agreements could be seen as narrowing their religious freedom. Comity agreements also meant leaders felt no need to settle doctrinal differences between the missions. It is therefore no surprise that some ethnic or language groups identified themselves with a particular mission or church in their area. Speaking against another denomination, consequently, could be seen as being hostile toward another ethnic group.[15]

Throughout the region, although white missionaries served well by staying for a long time at some mission stations, very soon African missionaries were doing most of the missionary work. The involvement of local people in mission work perhaps reflects an aspect of Christianity that sets it apart

---

[13] John Weller and Jane Linden, *Mainstream Christianity*, p. 85.
[14] Klaus Fiedler, *The Story of Faith Missions*, p. 188.
[15] Reinhard Ludwig Frey, *History of the Zambia Baptist Association*, p. 46.

from many of the other structures of colonialism (which severely limited the ability of the local population to participate in what was basically for the white people). In addition to African involvement in evangelism, the participation of the Bemba people and the use of their language throughout the country helped a Zambia-wide growth of Roman Catholicism. Political and economic considerations did, and still do, play a major role in the response to Christianity.

The early missions followed the typical mission station approach in which the mission constructed buildings to house church, school and dispensary. The principal aim was to attract the local people to a central place. The later missions took a different approach. Evangelical missions, in particular, began by teaching the Bible in the areas where people lived.[16] The idea of a personal relationship with Jesus became attractive for many people. The message about a new birth struck a chord with many who were adapting to new circumstances. Some members from mainline churches have founded other churches because they felt their churches did not focus enough on 'being born again.'

Apart from spiritual formation, missions and churches have been providing social welfare, including education and health care. Biblical principles of care for the weak and provision of alternative medical care to traditional healing motivated the churches' provision of health care. Through health care, churches have generally tried to change or discourage cultural practices that are contrary to Christian beliefs. Schools were often associated with mission stations and they retained the ethos of their parent denomination. Mission schools soon became centres where the aspiration for national independence was nurtured.

Pentecostal and Charismatic Churches

Over the years, many Pentecostal-type denominational missions established themselves in this region. Pentecostalism has also contributed to the birth of some major Zionist African Indigenous Church movements. Some have understood the 'messianic' leadership among the Shona African Instituted

---

[16] Hany Longwe, *Christians by Grace – Baptists by Choice*, pp. 36, 69.

Churches in Zimbabwe, for example, as a 'translation and interpretation of Christ' and, within the processes of fragmentation and fission of independent church groups, they have seen seeds for Christian unity. The result was the founding of the Conference of Shona Independent Churches, popularly known as Fambidzano, in 1972. Prophetic-healing churches have a mythical understanding of biblical Zion (believed to have come from heaven) in their own Zion mountain-top centres. Samuel Mutendi founded Mutendi Zion Church in Zimbabwe. Other famous Zimbabwean Zion Church leaders include Yohane Masowe and Yohane Maranke.[17]

In Malawi, Pentecostal churches established themselves rather late, in the mid-twentieth century. After they started, they progressed slowly for at least two decades. The beginnings were all attributable to returning matchona (migrant workers). The Apostolic Faith Mission and the Assemblies of God came from Tanzania, Zimbabwe and South Africa. After 1960 the Pentecostal section of Malawian Christianity experienced a major expansion. The 'old' Pentecostal matchona churches started to grow much faster and new missions came in, like the Pentecostal Assemblies of Canada, the Foursquare Gospel Church and the Apostolic Faith Church.[18]

In contrast to the earlier missions, the Charismatic churches often came into existence after a period of germination in the form of interdenominational fellowships or within interdenominational para-church movements. Counter to all the earlier denominational families that had a rural base in Africa, the Charismatic movement began its ministry in the cities and in institutions of higher learning. There is no doubt that its success has been great, especially among the urban population, and that most of those who join come from mainline or from other Evangelical denominations.[19]

---

[17] Steven Paas, *The Faith Moves South*, p. 148. For a detailed study see M.L. Daneel, *Quest for Belonging*. For Malawi see Kenneth R. Ross and Klaus Fiedler, *A Malawi Church History 1860 – 2020*, Mzuzu: Mzuni Press, 2020, p. 160.

[18] Klaus Fiedler, "Africa's Evangelical Turn", p. 365.

[19] Klaus Fiedler, "Africa's Evangelical Turn," pp. 357-358.

Charismatic piety is in high demand among the better-off urban people, and it gives convincing answers to the deep traditional African quests for power, wealth and health. Although most Charismatic churches are still predominantly urban and wealthy, they have started to spread to the poor suburbs of the cities and to the rural areas.[20] On the other hand, the Charismatic movement spans both traditional and modern socio-cultural elements. Charismatic ministries address issues such as witchcraft and spirit possession while simultaneously responding to modern issues, with street children ministries, electronic music or entrepreneurial seminars.[21] This sensitivity to the African worldview is evident in the Charismatic movement's concern with issues of witchcraft, prosperity, and healing.[22] Furthermore, modernization has not eradicated ancient beliefs, as is evident from witchcraft stories that constantly feature in the media.

With many people living with HIV/AIDS and malaria infections and dysfunctional health care systems, the need for healing has never been greater. This is aggravated by the grinding poverty in which many people find themselves. Consequently, the Charismatic practice of deliverance from evil spirits, curses, sicknesses and poverty finds an audience ready to receive a solution. The Charismatic influence is such that many non-Charismatic churches have adopted the Charismatic style of worship.

Church and State

Up until national independence, churches usually took the middle of the road by ministering to the needs of the people without antagonizing the colonial administration, although at times they became a means through which to oppose colonial rule.[23] As the demand for political independence

---

[20] Klaus Fiedler, "Africa's Evangelical Turn," pp. 368-369.

[21] See Rhodian Munyenyembe, *Christianity and Socio-Cultural Issues. The Charismatic Movement and Contextualization in Malawi*, Mzuzu: Mzuni Press, 2011, esp. pp. 72ff.

[22] For problems with healing in some branches of the Charismatic Movement see: Klaus Fiedler, *Fake Healing Claims for HIV and AIDS in Malawi: Traditional, Christian and Scientific*, Mzuni Press, 2016, pp. 24-35.

[23] See John McCracken, "Church and State in Malawi: The Scottish Presbyterian Missions, 1875 – 1965", pp. 181-188.

deepened, supporters of independence looked to the church as a welcome ally. Church sympathy for the nationalist cause aroused strong resentment among some white Christians and the governments. To achieve their goal, the churches made use of their para-church agencies or organizations to engage the state on economic, political and social issues.

After independence, the established churches faced widespread suspicion due to their association with the former colonial regimes. For this reason, churches generally sought legitimacy through endorsing state-directed development at the expense of promoting multi-party democracy. The established churches embarked on a policy of appeasement due to the fear

Tradition	2015 Population	%
Christians	13,735,000	79.8
Roman Catholics	5,901,000	34.3
Orthodox	3,600	0.0
Independents	2,406,000	14.0
Protestants	4,972,000	28.9
Anglicans	331,000	1.9
Pentecostals	3,711,000	21.6
Evangelicals	3,045,000	17.7
Total	16,212,000	100.0

Figure 2: **Christianity in Malawi 2015**. *Source: Todd M. Johnson and Gina A. Zurlo (eds), World Christian Database, Leiden, Boston: Brill, [March 2016].*

that their compromised relationship with colonial powers would cause the new government to prefer independent churches at their expense.

In Zimbabwe, for example, after independence in 1980, the protection of an individual against the excesses of the state received inadequate attention and the democratic role of civic organizations was ignored. More recently, however, the churches have stood as a voice of morality by condemning political violence and lack of political tolerance. The democratic space for association has been at the centre of conflict between the churches and the government.

Whereas some politicians rebuked the dissenting voices of the clergy, and sought to limit the church to prayers and offering guidance on moral issues, the leaders of the national Catholic bishops' conferences, the national Evangelical Fellowships and the National Council of Churches, including the Public Affairs Committee in Malawi, embarked on a strategy to give dialogue a chance. The churches have been strong in issuing periodic criticism of the government on various issues. Not only have the churches been prominent as one of the key actors in the transition process from one-party state to multiparty political governance, they have also continued to be vocal politically. Even when they have held divergent and conflicting views on some issues, they have avoided division. The churches have also played a leading role in empowering and coordinating civil society.

Since many people identify with the Christian faith, this gives the churches legitimacy in their advocacy role. The joint working of the churches' national councils and associations, the Catholic Commissions for Justice and Peace, and the ecumenical Public Affairs Committee in Malawi, gives weight to the voice of the churches and therefore increases their influence. Although ecumenical bodies have played very important advocacy roles, they face a common dilemma in the need to expend a great deal of energy to reach consensus, a process often complicated by their own cumbersome structures. Despite the difficulties, joint work of the churches has been effective in advocating political change.[24]

Whereas nationalist movements played a major role in the decolonization process, and mainline church leaders were deeply involved in the democratization efforts of the 1990s, more recently the Pentecostals and Charismatics have become increasingly important political actors. Pentecostals speak of praying for and electing Christians into power so that government and society should be transformed into a 'Christian nation.' Zambian President Frederick Chiluba, an avowed Pentecostal, after taking

---

[24] For a detailed study see Matembo S. Nzunda & Kenneth R. Ross (eds), *Church, Law and Political Transition in Malawi 1992-94*.

office invited a group of Pentecostal ministers to 'cleanse' the presidential palace of evil spirits and publicly dedicated Zambia and its government to 'the Lordship of Jesus Christ.' Chiluba's declaration of Zambia as a 'Christian nation' was not only anti-democratic but was also soon discredited.[25]

Zimbabwean President Robert Mugabe, facing deepening political crises and increasing criticism from mainline church leaders, turned to Pentecostals for religious and moral legitimization, which some Pentecostal leaders were eager to provide. Despite being a Roman Catholic, he sought closer ties to some Charismatic and Pentecostal leaders, in which he was assisted by the fact that his wife and sister were members of the Zimbabwe Assemblies of God Africa (ZAOGA). On 26 June 2006, Mugabe presided at a Zimbabwe National Day of Prayer in Harare. The event was boycotted by prominent Catholic and Anglican leaders but it included representatives of the Evangelical Fellowship of Zimbabwe and the Zimbabwe Council of Churches, because both include Pentecostal members. In Malawi, the current Malawi Congress Party President, Dr Lazarus Chakwera, the former president of the Assemblies of God in Malawi and founding pastor of the International Christian Assembly in Lilongwe, is aiming to be the next president of the country.[26] Although the church does its best to provide effective leadership in a heavily divided political environment, this has not had the desired impact. Divisions within the church and lack of radical theologies have compromised the church's efforts.

The Inculturation of the Faith

The missions and churches have been able to make the Bible accessible to the people by translating it into many of the local languages, though there are still some smaller ethnic groups lacking a Bible in their own languages. For almost all churches, translations of religious instruction material into local African languages were done from the missions' catechisms with little

---

[25] See Austin Cheyeka, *Church, State and Political Ethics in a Post-Colonial State: The Case of Zambia*, Zomba: Kachere, 2008, pp. 83- 123.

[26] *Since the article was first published, Lazarus Chakwera has become President of Malawi in 2020, after the Constitutional Court had declared invalid the 2019 election.

or no adaptation. This is an area that requires more indigenizing effort. There is a need for African theological writers to produce instruction material that replaces the Western methodology of questions and answers with one of stories and proverbs. Unless theological teaching becomes rooted in African culture, the African church will not be able to develop its own theology. It will not be able to respond to its own context. Non-Christian contexts will remain unchallenged and the theology taught will be of marginal relevance to African issues. If the African church is to develop indigenous roots, then written theology in local languages needs to be encouraged to reflect the oral theologizing already going on.

Of late, the Catholic Church has promoted the idea of the church as the family of God, an ecclesiastical structure that is more African. The model of 'family' tends to promote interpersonal relationships between people in the church.[27]

This allows for shared responsibilities, rather than leaving all initiative with the clergy or lay leaders. Some churches want to see full involvement of all members and this finds expression particularly in strengthening the role of women. Women's organizations are a strong branch of many churches. Their visibility and strong character have caused them to be seen as 'the face' of the church or 'a church within a church'. In the context of a patriarchal society, the church has proved to be a sphere in which women find liberation and engage themselves actively in religious and social life. In Malawi churches began establishing these organizations around 1940. They blossomed from sewing clubs and Bible study and prayer groups to become national organizations. Through their evangelistic programmes, pastoral care and social work, churches have expanded tremendously.[28]

For a long time, churches have tended to place the youth and the children under the wings of the women's organizations, but that is changing. Churches have developed children's Bible study programmes and youth

---

[27] See Maximian Khisi, *The Church as the Family of God and the Care for Creation*, Mzuzu: Mzuni Press, 2018.

[28] See Isabel Apawo Phiri, *Women, Presbyterianism and Patriarchy*. Also Hany Longwe, *Christians by Grace*, pp. 242-278; Rachel NyaGondwe-Banda, *Women of Bible and Culture*, pp. 18-88.

groups in churches, schools and colleges. There are denominational as well as interdenominational materials and groups. Subjects being discussed include femininity and masculinity, love and marriage, gender-based violence, the importance of education in relation to the Bible and how to apply biblical teaching in an African context. Churches that do not prepare their youth spiritually and mentally through such programmes lose them to other churches or non-Christian groups. With such support and as their lives are shaped by the gospel, Christian young people can exercise great influence on their peers. In many churches, the youth have moved from being the driven to being the drivers. The issue of gender, however, remains very significant. When it comes to decision-making, power is in the hands of men, and therefore decisions tend to benefit men more than women. Many girls have internalized a sense of inferiority and therefore do not aspire to leadership. As a result, their avenue of service tends to be through women's organizations, which offer a space where they can develop and exercise their gifts.

A major concern for the churches in these three countries is that Christians live in two worlds. When they are within the church premises, they behave in one way, but when they are out of the premises their behaviour is quite different. There is a need to develop integrity of faith and life rather than looking on Christianity as a list of things to do and not to do. There is a great need in this region for the churches to proclaim the Christian message to people from within the perspective of their culture, in order for them to live a Christian life that is grounded in their own context. Many claim to be Christians, but much of their life does not portray their faith. The problem is compounded by the high number of church members per minister and the high number of prayer houses (chapels) for a minister to visit. It becomes difficult for the clergy to apply appropriate methods of evangelism that would ground members in biblical teaching for them to be true representatives of Christ in their way of life.

One area where considerable progress has been made is inculturation of the liturgy. Mainline churches have tolerated dancing or even tried to integrate it into the liturgy of a congregation. The Catholic Church recognized from the beginning that most of its converts, who were unschooled and from an oral culture, sought a literal embodiment of religion in song, word and gesture. Liturgy was their most powerful tool and means by which the community would live and express its own history and faith experience.[29] African music and styles of worship permeate even English-language services in the urban context.

One prominent champion of inculturation is the former Catholic Archbishop of Lusaka, Emmanuel Milingo. He argued for the development of an authentic African Christianity growing out of African values, including spiritual ones, and challenged Western control of African Christianity. Controversially, Milingo insisted that people of colour are not inferior but that they have wisdom that the West neither possesses nor acknowledges. The Catholic Church hierarchy criticized Milingo for exorcism and faith-healing practices not approved by the church. It was also disturbed by his argument that Catholic priests should be allowed to marry, and he was eventually deposed.

One way of indigenizing the faith has been through theological education. This started with denominational Bible schools and colleges, but then interdenominational and non-denominational colleges were founded. The universities also introduced Theology and Religious Studies (TRS) departments. Recently a number of Christian universities have been opened. The great majority of theology students have been men. Because clericalism empowers the pastor over the laity, it also dis-empowers women in theological education. That has created a shortage of theologically trained women in the churches.

Theology

Theological issues are apparent in the popular experience of the Christian faith. Christology is one area where there is active discussion. Many Christians struggle to defend the belief that Jesus was not only human but divine as well. Others stress Christ's divinity and tend towards the view that Jesus only appears to have taken on our human condition. Stressing the

---

[29] Hubert Reijnaerts, Ann Nielsen and Matthew Schoffeleers, *Montfortians in Malawi: Their Spirituality and Pastoral Approach*, p. 120.

difference between Jesus's humanity and ours can be a way of limiting the ethical demands of the faith. Many also find it hard to believe in the Trinity and this is further complicated by the African belief in spirits.

Marriage and family life are another common area of concern. Most churches hold to a biblical theology of marriage that regard polygamy as a violation of God's norm of a monogamous and indissoluble marriage. Very few attempts have been made to baptize converted polygamists without their first divorcing the 'surplus' wives.[30] A combination of Western missionary theology and loyalty to some African traditional cultural values has tended to create a male-dominated church and society. Only ordained men were recognized as clergy and church leaders. Women were expected to play supportive roles. Although many churches believe in the priesthood of all believers, historically they have not accepted the ordination of women as clergy. Since the 1990s, however, a growing number of Protestant mainline and Pentecostal and Charismatic churches have begun ordaining women – a significant development for the theology of gender.

The interface of church and society is another area that attracts theological reflection. Most churches' theology does not exclude cooperation with the government, provided that enough distance is being kept. It is believed that if the church, corporately and individually, is to impact a nation, Christian values must permeate the nation, including the political terrain. There is evidence of tension, however, between an 'ecumenical' approach that is oriented to social liberation and favours political activism and an 'evangelical' approach that is oriented to the spiritual dimension and stresses the personal salvation of individual souls and individual social involvement.

Since the 1980s the challenge of publishing local theologies has been taken up by Mambo Press in Zimbabwe and by Kachere Series and Mzuni Press in Malawi. Much theological research is done by the university TRS departments and theological colleges. MA and PhD dissertations produced in the universities and theological colleges form a basis for the development of local theology. Pioneering scholars, such as Ezra Chitando and Paul

---

[30] See Moses Mlenga, *Polygamy in Northern Malawi: A Christian Rethinking*, Mzuzu: Luviri Press, 2015.

Gundani in Zimbabwe, and Patrick Kalilombe, Augustine Musopole and Isabel Apawo Phiri in Malawi, have offered theological analysis that is engaged with local cultural and social issues.

Innovative approaches to theology have been promoted by women affiliated to the Circle for Concerned African Women Theologians, such as Isabel Apawo Phiri, Francisca Chihanda and Fulata Moyo.[31] They have argued that inherited forms of theologizing are patently inadequate to respond meaningfully to the present crises, including HIV/AIDS, poverty and gender injustice, that plague continental Africa. The work of women theologians on such issues is marked by its collaborative character and its inter-disciplinary nature. This creative movement is promoting women's self-expression, leadership skills and spiritual development, and space for ecumenism.

The Church and Other Faiths

Malawi, in contrast to Zambia and Zimbabwe, has a sizable Muslim minority. Islam attracted the Yao more than any other tribe in Malawi because they had been in constant touch with the Arabs and Swahili since before the 1800s. The Yao felt Islam seemed more suited to Africans than did Christianity because it did not oblige Africans to give up traditional practices such as polygamy. By incorporating certain Islamic elements into the traditional puberty ceremony, they made the revised version an entrance to both Yao adulthood and Islam, and thereby made a significant contribution to the identification of the Yao with Islam that has long been characteristic in Malawi.

Although the numbers are rather small, there are conversions from Islam to Christianity. The Baptist Convention of Malawi has three Yao Muslim-background congregations. The Assemblies of God and the Roman Catholic Church also have members who converted from Islam. However, most converts from Islam join Evangelical churches. There are also conversions from Christianity to Islam, particularly through marriage of

---

[31] For the history of the Circle see: Rachel NyaGondwe Fiedler, *The History of the Circle of Concerned African Women Theologians, 1989-2007*, Mzuzu: Mzuni Press, 2016.

Christian women to Muslim men. In some cases, such women return from Islam to their original church, such as Anglican or Catholic, following divorce or the death of their Muslim husbands.

There has rarely been real friction between Christians and Muslims in Central Africa. In 2003, some Muslims torched Christian churches in Mangochi, a strongly Muslim district in Malawi. Christians retaliated by burning some mosques in several towns. The government downplayed the episodes and called the two groups to settle their differences and agree to work alongside each other. In Zambia, Pentecostals organized public evangelistic campaigns to counter the perceived ascendancy of Muslims. They organized an effort to promote Christianity and contain Islam in the eastern part of the country.

African Traditional Religion (ATR) does not exist any longer as an organized entity in the region. Nonetheless, in school textbooks on religious education it is given equal weight with Christianity and Islam. Many practicing Christians or Muslims incorporate elements of ATR into their daily lives. Since ATR as such is difficult to find, traditional customs and institutions, such as chieftainship, are used to represent ATR.[32] However, in reality chiefs are either Christians or Muslims.

One can also note the presence of Judaism, Hinduism, Sikhism and the Baha'i faith in several towns and cities throughout Central Africa. Here and there one can also meet members of marginal Christian groups such as Jehovah's Witnesses, Bible Believers, the Unification Church and the Church of Jesus Christ of Latter-day Saints. So far there is no generally agreed method for engaging with people of other faiths. Different missiological approaches create tensions and a degree of competition. This is an area that is ripe for deeper consideration.

Protestant and Catholic missions produced an African Christianity that was mainly shaped by the respective European traditions. That changed when waves of revival brought greater diversification to the missionary effort and to the emergent churches. Pentecostals gave birth to the Zionist family of

---

[32] Jessica O. Jarhall, *A Look at Changes in Primary Religious Education in Malawi from a Swedish Perspective*, Linköping: Linköping University Electronic Press, 2001.

African Indigenous Churches, while inter-denominational fellowships produced Charismatic churches. The remarkable growth of Christianity in the three countries is attributable not only to evangelism but also to the high level of African religiosity and to population growth. Despite divisions, the churches have made a huge contribution to national development in such areas as education, health care, political governance and the economy. Despite belief in the priesthood of all believers, in practice women are excluded from leadership positions. Christian-Muslim relations remain a delicate issue especially in Malawi.

Chapter 14

A Pictorial Essay on the Early Life of the Baptist Convention of Malawi

The Southern Baptist Convention (SBC) began operating in Malawi in July 1959 with the arrival in Limbe of William and Blanche Wester, and LeRoy and Jean Albright who had been missionaries in Zimbabwe.

Bible Study versus the Traditional Mission Station Strategy

Baptist Mission in Malawi (BMIM) deliberately did not start by establishing the traditional mission station, but rather Bible study groups.

Figure 3: Bible Study. The picture was on the 1969 BACOMA calendar which emphasized family Bible study. Abusa Steven Galatiya, with Amayibusa Mary Galatiya, and their little children are seen studying the Bible together

The First BACOMA Church: Ndalama

Steven Galatiya was instrumental in the transformation of an African Instituted Church (AIC) that was led by Thomas Kachaso Gama at Ndalama Village in Zomba District into the first BACOMA church.

Figure 4: The first BACOMA Church at Ndalama Village, Zomba 1962. Notice how the people set in rows, with children close to the speaker, followed by women ('amayi' – mothers) immediately behind them. Men set on higher ground or stools of some sort.

The Second BACOMA Church

Figure 5: Cliccord House (from Gene & Beverly Kingsley's letter to friends Feb 1962.

14: A Pictorial Essay: The Early Life of the Baptist Convention   263

On 28 October 1962, Limbe Baptist Church was officially organized. The church later moved to Chichiri, and then in 1969, to the new BMIM premises off-Makata Road where they constructed their own sanctuary. They chartered the building for their own use and also for the Chichewa-speaking congregation which had developed from its ministry.

Figure 6: Blantyre Baptist Church. The church has since moved to their new spacious and modern building near the Independence Arch at Chichiri.

Baluwa Baptist Church

McDonald W. Kaduya, and his wife, Agnes, a Tswana from Francistown in Botswana, were instrumental in the beginning and development of another BACOMA church at Baluwa Village in Chiradzulu. The church began sometime in 1962.

Figure 7: Abusa Kaduya and missionary Wester

Figure 8: Sunday school at Baluwa Church

Figure: 9 The Kaduya Family. Amayibusa and her two daughters entertaining Mary Ann Chandler and a volunteer. In the

Soche Community Centre

On 4 November 1962 services began in the chapel-reading room at Kamba. The centre became a BACOMA church on 12 November of the same year. Rev. Leonard C. Muocha represented PIM at the ceremony.

Figure 10: Soche Church in 1962

Lilongwe Baptist Church: the First BACOMA Church in Central Malawi

The development of BACOMA congregations in Central Malawi was due to the relationship between LeRoy Albright and Achewa Providence Industrial Mission (PIM). Some PIM members helped Albright in the first BMIM public meeting which was held at the Lilongwe Community Centre Ground. They included Henry Kafulatira, Z.B. Sakhula and Kampangire. These men had been to Nkhoma and PIM schools.

Figure 11: Albright speaking to Aaron Kamkalamba, leaders of the Achewa PIM. This was during the construction of the Achewa PIM main church at Nyanje across Nanjiri River, on the left off M1 road towards Blantyre. Albright bought steel door frames and roofing material.

Figure 12: Kadango's Grocery Store. Falls Estate Bible study fellowship met in this building before moving into the Baptist Bible School campus which was bought behind this store.

14: A Pictorial Essay: The Early Life of the Baptist Convention

For a while those who had declared faith in Jesus met at the Lilongwe Community Centre, and later in a rented room at Kadango's grocery store. The fellowship met for Bible study and it had no name attached to it.

Figure 13: Lilongwe Baptist Church. This is when the church was meeting at the Baptist Bible School Administration Block courtyard.

Figure 14: Lilongwe Baptist Church Film Night. This is at the Baptist Bible School. Some of the members were coming from as far as Area 25. The choice of Kawale as the home of Lilongwe Baptist Church was because a good proportion of the membership came from there.

The First Lay-Pastors' Training Institute

Between April and May 1992 the first pastors' school was held for approximately four weeks in one of the rented rooms behind Kadango's grocery shop.

Figure 15: The first Bible School Class. Some of the students in the picture were (from left to right) Seated: Dafren Makhaya, and Chikuse from Balaka; Crouching: Stephen Galatiya (second), Ruben Nkhata (3rd not a student), Makorija (6th) from Zomba, and Gresham

Construction of the Would-be Leadership Training Centre at Kawale

As a way of developing more church leaders, Albright bought five plots in a row on the road south of Kawale Post Office with the idea of developing the plots into a leadership training centre. For a while all leadership training sessions were carried out there until the construction of the BBS campus at Falls Estate

14: A Pictorial Essay: The Early Life of the Baptist Convention   269

Figure 16: Pastors' Training School. The pictures show some of the teachers and students outside the building, and inside the sleeping quarters. Note Ruben Nkhata (top picture standing 4th from left).

Baptist Bible School

In 1965 the first permanent buildings were completed. Classes used short term courses of six to eight weeks.

Figure 17: People waiting for the official opening of the Baptist Bible School "picture by Gerald S. Harvey".

Figure 18: Bible School Class in Session. The courses were "between crops' to allow the students who were mainly subsistence farmers to attend classes. BACOMA has remained mainly a rural church ever since in spite of its efforts to reach people in the urban areas.

14: A Pictorial Essay: The Early Life of the Baptist Convention 271

Figure 19: Abusa and Amayibusa Stephen and Mary Galatiya, and McFarron Njolomole and Elizabeth Phiri. Because he was an outstanding student at the Bible School, Steven and Mary Galatiya were the first to be sent for further theological training in Gweru.

Figure 20: A Class of Women at the Bible School in the 1960s

Figure 21: BBS 1978 Graduates. Standing left to right: G. Kamtunda, D. Malikebu, McFerron Njolomole Phiri and William Mallungo (teachers), Kitely Chirwa, A. Dulana and Seven Dzimbiri. Front row l to r: F. Mtsinje, Benderson Eraton, Mvula, Maunda Phiri, Booker P. Kapalamula, Mikeka Bauleni and R.D. Dzadyela Milazi

Publishing and Printing Ministry

The completion of the first BBS buildings also opened the way to the first attempt at a publishing and printing ministry. In 1966 a small press was purchased and installed in one of the rooms in the Bible School. To meet the needs of the literature programme of the growing ministries, a bigger press was bought and put into operation in the Bible School in 1969.

Figure 22: Trimming BACOMA hymnal and tracts ready for distribution. In the picture above, Albright is showing missionary visitors some of the work from a new printing press. Note: Abusa Ruben Nkhata, as a young man, trimming some of the literature.

Figure 23: Abusa Makhaya and missionary Albright operating the small printing press

A bookstall in the open market in Lilongwe as well as a small bookshop in Limbe proved very effective ways of distributing literature.

Figure 24 A Bookstall in the Open Market in Lilongwe

Bible Way Correspondence School (BWCS)

It was only in 1964 that the BWCS got off the ground in Malawi.

Figure 25: Bible Way Correspondence School. Re¬becca Phifer, (missionary ad¬vi¬sor), W.A.C. Chisi (the Director), and Elizabeth Chirombo who was the Secretary of Bible Way Correspondence School which was housed at the Baptist Bible School campus.

Baptist Christians from all over the country on Friday ended a three day Bible Way Correspondence School training seminar, at the Baptist Bible School in Lilongwe. According to the missionary adviser of the bible school, Mrs. R. Phifer, the purpose of the seminar was to train people from each of the 17 Baptist Association of Malaŵi centres. Bible Way Correspondence School started in Zambia in 1962. The school now operates in 20 African countries with over 300,000 students. The seminar was conducted by the director of the Malaŵi Bible Way School, Rev. W.A. Chisi, assisted by Rev. W. Malungo Nkhoma. Pictured, the seminar participants with the course conductors.

Figure 26: Bible Way Leadership Seminar. A Caption from a Local Newspaper

Radio Ministry

Figure 27: Radio Drama

Figure 28: In picture on the left, Josamu Sankhani, MBC Mema studio director, interviews a lay preacher at a village in Lilongwe District. In the second picture missionary Gene Kingsley and Josamu Sankhani setting up a tape recorder

The Baptist Building at Chichiri also housed an emerging radio ministry. Soon after independence, the government of Malawi, as was in many countries, controlled radio programming. There were no local radio stations. No radio time was for sale. Programmes were produced at government expense. Nevertheless, the Christian Council of Malawi (CCM) built a recording studio in Lilongwe.

Figure 29: Gospel on Tape. A group of villagers at Tsabango in the Lower Shire listening to messages on tapes. This was in 1971.

This was the only avenue through which BACOMA was able to have programme time. By providing their members some special training in radio speech, radio preaching, script writing, and radio drama, BACOMA was able to play an active role in the production of religious programmes in connection with MCC.

The Dawn of BACOMA as an Organization

Due to continued friction between them and the missionaries, the local leadership, with the help of some missionaries, discussed the formation of a separate body that was to be called Baptist Convention of Malawi.

"Employer-employee" Relationship

Disagreements between Roy Davidson and Stephen Galatiya over support, led to Blantyre Baptist Church split into black Africans and white groups. The Black Africans, led by Galatiya, formed a new church at Newlands, Limbe, where they met for some time as a church in Galatiya's home.

Figure 30 Proclaiming the Word. Abusa Galatiya was forced to leave preaching from the Blantyre Baptist pulpit to a make-shift pulpit outside his house at Newlands. People came and heard him preach, and a church was formed.

Figure 31: Mary and Stephen Galatiya seen in the "Jerusalem Gospel Hall".

14: A Pictorial Essay: The Early Life of the Baptist Convention 279

Figure 32 : Jerusalem Baptist Church. Abusa and Amayibusa Galatiya (3rd and 4th standing from right) proudly display their church building and membership of Jerusalem Baptist Church, which included S. Malabwanya, J.M. and Helen Ng'oma, and Sweet Chikanga.

Later they moulded bricks and built a building they named "Jerusalem Gospel Hall," later known as Jerusalem Baptist Church. The new church building was dedicated on 17 June 1979.

The Organization of BACOMA

The tension within Baptist Mission in Malawi (BMIM) and between the Mission and BACOMA led to BMIM to encourage the African leaders to follow a legal process to have the local churches registered with the government as a separate organization from the BMIM.

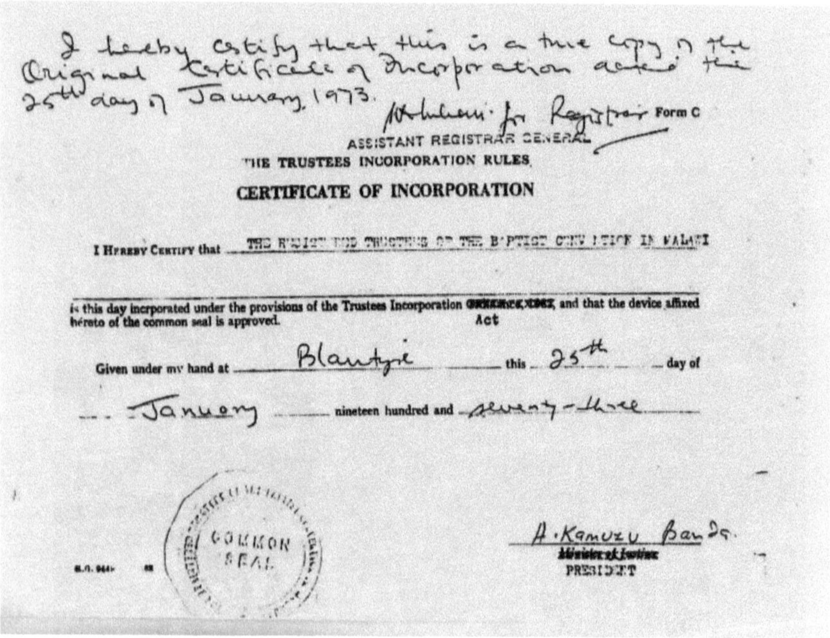

I hereby certify that this is a true copy of the Original Certificate of Incorporation dated the 25th day of January, 1973.

... for Registrar

Form C

ASSISTANT REGISTRAR GENERAL

THE TRUSTEES INCORPORATION RULES

CERTIFICATE OF INCORPORATION

I HEREBY CERTIFY that THE REGISTERED TRUSTEES OF THE BAPTIST CONVENTION IN MALAWI

is this day incorporated under the provisions of the Trustees Incorporation Act, and that the device affixed hereto of the common seal is approved.

Given under my hand at Blantyre this 25th day of January nineteen hundred and seventy-three

COMMON SEAL

H. Kamuzu Banda
PRESIDENT

Figure 33: A Copy of the Certificate of Incorporation

Ordinances: Baptism

Baptists retain the New Testament rite of baptism for individual response of faith to the Good News of Jesus Christ, and have not extended this rite to those who are yet unconscious of the meaning of individual responsibility.

Figure 34: Baptism in a River or Stream

Ordinances: The Lord's Supper

In many congregations, baptism is followed with the communion of the Lord's Supper. This is a sign that the baptized are then part of the local congregation. The Convention does not have a prescribed form of Communion Service, as they have none for baptism or for worship in general. Some guide of course is given in the "*Buku Lothandiza Atsogoleri a Mpingo wa Baptist.*"

Figure 35: Women Participating in Holy Communion

Evangelism and Church Growth

The period 1970 to 1989 was characterized by evangelism as it was also a time of teething troubles for the newly formed BACOMA.

Figure 36: Banner. Chidzaoneka nchiani (what will be seen or happen 1968, 1969, 1970?)

Figure 37: Baptist Crusade. Many churches were started through evangelistic meetings organized by individuals, mainly by groups such as the Baptist Crusaders, as they became to be known. The group has its origins in Lilongwe Baptist Church in Kawale.

The first Church in Northern Malawi

The first church in Northern Malawi began in a village under Chief Kabunduli near the junction of Nkhata Bay/Mzuzu Road and the Lakeshore Road

Figure 38: The First BACOMA Church in the North in Nkhata Bay District

A Result of Evangelism: Senga Bay Baptist Clinic

Figure 39: Official Openning of Senga Bay Clinic

Figure 40: The first building for Senga Bay Baptist Clinic in Salima District

The Beginning of "Umodzi wa Amayi Abaptist ku Malawi"

"Umodzi was Amayi Abaptist ku Malawi" commonly known as "Umodzi wa Amayi" traces its beginning back to an assembly held on 8 May 1967 at the campus of the Baptist Bible School.

Figure 41: Sewing Class being Taught by Missionary Wives.

Figure 42: Home Bible Study Group

14: A Pictorial Essay: The Early Life of the Baptist Convention   286

Figure 43: Liddah Kalako and Nellie Phiri Witnessing

Figure 44: Helen Ng'oma was instrumental in starting Area 23 Baptist Church in her home

14: A Pictorial Essay: The Early Life of the Baptist Convention

The development of Umodzi wa Amayi is related to the evangelistic revivals of the 1970s and the 1980s.

In 1973 Helen Ng'oma and her husband arrived in Area 23 and immediately opened their home for a church to meet there.

Figure 45: First "Umodzi wa Amayi" Leadership. From left to right: Amayibusa Maya (treasurer), Amayibusa Elizabeth Phiri (youth adviser), Amayibusa Mallungo (chair), and Amayibusa Mary Galatiya (secretary). The concern to have women wear uniforms became a serious issue.

Women and Theological Training

Many early and even recent women seminary candidates went for training on their husbands' tickets. They attended separate classes.

Figure 46: Seven Women and their Husbands at Gweru Seminary. From left to right: George Mwase, Martha Chirwa, Akim Chirwa, Fletcher Kaiya, Joramu Nyirenda (single man), Clara Kaiya, Peter Maseko, Harriet Misinde, Misinde Phiri, Charity Gunya, Sonny Gunya, Joyce Mwase, Emma Maseko, Pigot and Dorah Makhuwira

Figure 47: Seminary Class at Gweru Zimbabwe. In the picture is Amayibusa Chisi, Amayi Mponya, Amayi Thuwe (Teacher, a Zimbeabwean), amayi Kanyemba, Amayibusa Kandawe (behind the teacher) in class in 1973.

14: A Pictorial Essay: The Early Life of the Baptist Convention 289

BACOMA Youth

Figure 47: Lilongwe Association Girls' Conference of 1978. There were conferences for girls only probably for two reasons: first, "chinamwali," and second, there had not been an effort by the local churches to integrate girls and boys into a single youth group.

Figure 48: Lilongwe Association Youth Conference in 1983. By this time there was a deliberate effort by the youth leadership team which was led by Beverly Kingsley (standing far right) to bring boys and girls together into one group, the youth.

Figure 49: Youth: National Coordinators. Beverly Kingsley, Abusa Kapalamula Banda, Helen Ng'oma.

Ordination

By Baptist understanding, it is the local congregation which is the highest ordaining authority. Since local churches are interdependent, they cooperate with each other in ordination as a commissioning for ministry. Earliest BACOMA ordination of pastors was done during the Annual General Meeting (AGM).

14: A Pictorial Essay: The Early Life of the Baptist Convention 291

Figure 50: Ordination of Deacons. Falls Baptist Church ordained its first deacons in August 1983. They were assisted by Abusa Galatiya (in dark suit shaking hands, and is followed by Abusa Mallungo and Abusa Chisi. The deacons were: George Mwase (by the by the doorway) followed by Harry Tambuli, Paulina Chigwe and Mike Chiomba. Also present were Rebecca Phifer and Abusa Kapalamula Banda.

BACOMA Congregations

BACOMA has basically been more rural although its churches started in urban areas of Blantyre, Lilongwe, and Zomba.

Figure 51: Some met on designated pieces of land, in church buildings, or rented classrooms, some without desks and chairs.

14: A Pictorial Essay: The Early Life of the Baptist Convention

Figure 52: A Local Congregation

Bibliography

Oral Sources

Agnes Kaduya, Baluwa, Chiradzulu, 9.4.2002.

Aidane Chaotcha, church leader, Mambere Baptist Church, Nyasa Province, Mozambique, 17.3.1998.

Angela Maseko, Salima, 7.8.2018.

Christopher Chimtengo, deacon, Baluwa 1 Village, Chiradzulu, 9.4.2002.

D.M. Makonyola, pastor, Migowi Baptist Church, 12.9.1999.

Fernando Malei, Lilongwe, 18.3.1998.

Foulger Kafulatira, PIM Mangoni leader, Majondo, 21.5.1999.

Frank Muhosa, Baptist Bible School student, Lilongwe, 24.3.1998.

Gary K. Swafford, former SBC missionary to Malawi, Montgomery, Alabama, 17.10.2001.

George Mwase Baptist Bible School Director, Lilongwe, 18.3.1998.

Grace Kachere, pastor, Sigerege Baptist Church, Blantyre, 18.10.2010.

Gusto'nio Sumaine, Lilongwe, 16.3.1998.

Helen Ng'oma, Lilongwe, 1998.

John Moses, Lilongwe, 25.5.1998.

Joyce Tenewa, member, Baluwa Baptist Church, Chiradzulu, 9.4.2002.

July Maya, Pastor Mombe Baptist Church, Liwonde, 28.8.2003.

Liddah Kalako, member, Lilongwe, 15.11.1997.

Mary Kagwa, Mangochi, 2.4.2018.

Nazare Luciano Phiri, Lilongwe, 9.11.2004.

Paulo Tsabola, Milanje, Mozambique, 24.3.1998.

Rachel Fiedler, Zomba, 5.4.2004.

Ruben Nkhata, pastor, Lilongwe, 18.11.1997. BACOMA Minutes, 24.5.1973.

Stephen Galatiya, Baptist pastor Lilongwe, 13.06.1997.

Stephen Galatiya, Lilongwe, 13.4.1997.

Stephen Galatiya, Lilongwe, 15.4.2003.

Stephen Galatiya, Lilongwe, 16.4.2003.

Timothy Simango, missionary to Mozambique, Dedza, 15.9.2003.

Timothy W. Kandawe, pastor, Lilongwe, 29.8.1997.

W.J.H. Kalenga, Baptist pastor, Nsomo Village, pastor, 12.11.1997.
W.J.H. Kalenga, Nsomo Village, pastor, 12.11.1997.
Yosofati Ndege, Bishop of Achewa PIM, Kakwere, 5.7.1999.

Dissertations, Modules and Unpublished Articles

"Ministry of Hope to Persons Infected and Affected with HIV & AIDS" module, 2005.

Baptist Mission and Baptist Convention of Malawi, "Report and Proposals of the Seminary Feasibility Study Committee," 1988.

Baptist Mission of Central Africa Annual Report, Gweru, April 1963.

Baptist Theological Seminary of Zambia Handbook, 1985.

Baptist World Alliance, 2008 Yearbook.

Day, Rendell, "From Gowa to Landmark Missionary Baptists: One Hundred Years of Baptist Churches in Malawi," PhD module, Kachere Document no. 52, Zomba: Kachere, 2008.

Fiedler, Klaus, Chairperson Board of Governors, Baptist Theological Seminary of Malawi, Meeting Minutes, Lilongwe, 9.7.2006.

Kalenga, Rustin, "Compromising the Baptist Heritage: The Re-defining the Qualifications of and the Place of Ministry for a Pastor in the Baptist Convention of Malawi (BACOMA)," BA, Baptist Theological Seminary of Malawi, 2012, p. 23.

Kingsley, Gene, a note to Hany Longwe, Fort Worth, nd.

Klaus Fiedler, reminiscences to Hany Longwe, Zomba, August 2003.

Mastern, John, Baptist Convention General Secretary, email to Hany Longwe, Lilongwe, 7.8.2018.

Michael Canady – Baptist Mission in Malawi, 12.12.1998.

Minutes BACOMA, 10.6.1975.

Mwamdaza, Amess, "The Relationship between the Baptist Convention of Malawi (BACOMA and the Baptist Mission in Malawi (BMIM) and the Nationalization of the Baptist Theological Seminary of Malawi (BTSM)," BTh, Baptist Theological Seminary of Malawi, 2012.

Nkhoma, Cesar, BTSM 4th Year Student, Christ Saves and Loves: Dowa Baptist Church - The Steps of Ladder (Achievement), Report, Baptist Theological Seminary of Malawi, February 2006.

Nyika, Felix, 'Apostleship amongst Malawian Neocharismatics,' PhD module, University of Mzuzu, 2010.

Parratt, John, "Mbombwe Revisited: Dr. Daniel Malikebu and the Second Era of the Providence Industrial Mission," a history seminar paper, University of Malawi, 29 January 1985.

Phiri, Canaan R.K., Official Opening Speech, HIV&AIDS Counseling Training organized by Ecumenical Counselling Center (ECC) Msamba and NRC, Lilongwe., 1.10.2007.

Phiri, Emmanuel Chinkwita, Lilongwe, 22.11.2011, email to Rustin Kalenga.

Report BACOMA, 1994.

Report BMIM 13.6.1986.

Report George Mwase, President of BACOMA, Annual Convention, Blantyre, 2017.

Report Patricia and Lonnie Quillen – Baptist Mission in Malawi, 1989.

Report Steve Evans – Baptist Mission in Malawi, Blantyre, 14.6.1990.

Sam Upton – Chinkwita Phiri, 9.6.1983.

Saunders, D.L., "A History of Baptists in East and Central Africa," PhD, Southern Baptist Theological Seminary, 1973, p. 27.

Southern Baptist Convention, "Resolution on Ordination and the Role of Women in Ministry," Kansas City, Missouri – 1984.

Souza, Alversonde, "A Black Heart: The Life and Work of Thomas Jefferson Bowen among Blacks in Africa and in Brazil between 1840 and 1875," MA, University of Natal, 1998.

Waruta, Douglas W., "Celebrating Christ: The Hope of Africa," All African Baptist Theological Educators' Conference, Ibadan, 2000.

W.A.C. Chisi – Baptist Theological Seminary, Rüschlikon, 3.8.1984.

Books and Published Articles

"Challenges to Christian Mission," in *Proceedings of the Summit on Baptist Mission in the 21st Century*, Fall Church: Baptist World Alliance, 2003, p. 28.

Albright, LeRoy, *Malawi: A Changing Scene*, Richmond: The Department of Missionary Education and Promotion, Foreign Mission Board, SBC, 1967.

Baker, Robert A., *A Baptist Source Book with Particular Reference to Southern Baptists*, Nashville: Broadman, 1966.

Baker, Robert A., *A Summary of Christian History*, Nashville: Broadman, 1959.

Banda [Fiedler,], Rachel NyaGondwe, *Women of Bible and Culture. Baptist Convention Women in Southern Malawi*, Zomba: Kachere, 2006.

Banks, Robert, *Paul's Idea of Community: The Early House Churches in their Historical Setting*, Exeter: The Paternoster Press, 1980.

Baptist Convention of Zimbabwe, *Programme Design*, Bulawayo: Baptist Publishing House, 1984.

Bediako, Kwame, *Christianity in Africa: The Renewal of a Non-Western Religion*, Edinburgh: University Press, 1995.

Bokundoa, Andre, and Frank Adams, "All Africa Baptist Fellowship," in *Baptist World Centenary Congress Official Report*, 2005, p. 132.

Bosch, David J., *Transforming Mission: paradigm Shifts in Theology of Mission*, Maryknoll: Orbis Books, 1996.

Brackney, William H., with Ruby J. Burke, *Faith, Life, and Witness: The Papers of the Study and Research Division of the Baptist World Alliance - 1986-1990*, Birmingham, AL: Sanford University, 1990.

Brown, Raymond E., *The Churches the Apostles Left Behind*, Ramsey: Paulist Press, 1984.

Cairns, Earl E., *Christianity through the Centuries*, Grand Rapids: Zondervan, 1996, p. 299.

Chapman, Morris H., "Local Church Autonomy," *SBC Life*, December 1997, pp. 4-5.

Cheyeka, Austin, *Church, State and Political Ethics in a Post-Colonial State: The Case of Zambia* Zomba: Kachere, 2008.

Church, Henry, *Theological Education that Makes a Difference: Church Growth in the Free Methodist Church in Malawi and Zimbabwe*, Blantyre: CLAIM, 2002.

Clinton, J. Robert, *Making of a Leader: Recognizing the Lessons and Stages of Leadership Development*, Colorado Springs: Navpress, 1992.

Crawley, Winston, *Global Mission: A Story to Tell. An Interpretation of Southern Baptist Foreign Missions*, Nashville: Broadman, 1985.

Daneel, M.L., *Quest for Belonging: Introduction to a Study of African Independent Churches*, Gweru: Mambo, 1987.

Day, Rendell, "From Gowa to Landmark Missionary Baptists: One Hundred Years of Baptist Churches in Malawi," PhD module, Kachere Document no. 52, Zomba: Kachere, 2008.

Eastwood, Cyril, *The Priesthood of All Believers*, Minneapolis: Augsburg, 1962.

Eighmy, John Lee, *Churches in Cultural Captivity: A History of the Social Attitudes of Southern Baptists*, Knoxville: University of Tennessee, 1987.

Engel, Lothar, "Funding of Theological Education," in J.S. Pobee and J.N. Kudadjie (eds), *Theological Education in Africa*, Accra: Asempa, 2000, p. 136.

Enyioha, B. Uche, "Baptist Presence in Africa," in *All Africa Baptist Theological Educators' Conference*, Ibadan: All Africa Baptist Fellowship, 2000, 69.

Fackre, Gabriel, *The Christian Story: A Narrative Interpretation of Basic Christian Doctrine*, Grand Rapids: Eerdmans, 1984.

Falk, Peter, *The Growth of the Church in Africa*, Grand Rapids: Zondervan, 1979.

Fiedler, Klaus, "Africa's Evangelical Turn," in Klaus Fiedler, *Conflicted Power in Malawian Christianity: Essays Missionary and Evangelical from Malawi*, Mzuzu: Mzuni Press, 2015, p. 364, Fn 82.

Fiedler, Klaus, "The 'Smaller' Churches and the Big Government," in Matembo S. Nzunda and Kenneth Ross (eds), *Church, Law and Political Transition in Malawi 1992-94*, Gweru: Mambo-Kachere, 1997, pp. 158-159.

Fiedler, Klaus, "The Charismatic and Pentecostal Movements in Malawi in Cultural Perspective," *Religion in Malawi*, vol. 9, Balaka: Montfort, 1999, p. 33.

Fiedler, Klaus, *Baptists and the Ordination of Women*, Zomba: Lydia Print, no. 5, 2008.

Fiedler, Klaus, *Fake Healing Claims for HIV and AIDS in Malawi: Traditional, Christian and Scientific*, Mzuni Press, 2016.

Fiedler, Klaus, *Interdenominational Faith Missions in Africa. History and Ecclesiology*, Mzuzu: Mzuni Press, 2018.

Fiedler, Klaus, *The Making of a Maverick Missionary. Joseph Booth in Australasia*, Zomba: Kachere, 2008.

Fiedler, Klaus, *The Story of Faith Missions*, Oxford: Regnum; Sutherland: Albatross, 1994.

Fiedler, Rachel NyaGondwe, *The History of the Circle of Concerned African Women Theologians, 1989-2007*, Mzuzu: Mzuni Press, 2016.

Foster, John, *Setback and Recovery: Church History 2: AD 500-1500*, London: SPCK, 1991.

Frey, Richard Ludwig, *History of the Zambia Baptist Association 1905-2005*, Zomba: Kachere, 2009.

Gerstenberger, Erhard S., *Yahweh the Patriarch: Ancient Images of God and Feminist Theology*, Minneapolis: Fortress Press, 1996.

Gibellini, Rosino (ed), *Paths of Africa Theology*, London: SCM, 1994.

Goerner, H. Cornell, "Africa," in Baker J. Cauthen et al. (eds), *Advance: A history of Southern Baptist Foreign Missions*, Nashville: Broadman, 1970, p. 165.

Grenz, Stanley J., and Roger E. Olson, *Who Needs Theology? An Invitation to the Study of God*, Downers Grove: Inter-Varsity, 1996.

Grudem, Wayne, *Systematic Theology: An Introduction to Biblical Doctrine*, Leicester: InterVarsity, 1994.

Hastings, Adrian, *The Church in Africa, 1450-1950*, Oxford: Clarendon, 1994.

Haus, Fritz, *Carl Hugo and Mary Gutsche and the "German" Baptists of the Eastern Cape*, Mzuzu: Luviri Press, 2018.

Hay, Denys, *Europe in the Fourteenth and Fifteenth Centuries*, New York: Longman, 1989.

Herr, Friedrich, *The Medieval World*, New York: Mentor, 1963.

Hildebrandt, Jonathan, *History of the Church in Africa: A Survey*, rev., Achimota: African Christian Press, 1990.

Irvine, Cecilia, *The Church of Christ in Zaïre. A Handbook of Protestant Churches, Missions and Communities, 1878-1978*, Indianapolis: Christian Church (Disciples of Christ), 1978.

Jarhall, Jessica O., *A Look at Changes in Primary Religious Education in Malawi from a Swedish Perspective*, Linköping: Linköping University Electronic Press, 2001.

Kaiser, Walter C. Jr., "Israel's Missionary Call," in Ralph D. Winter & Steven C, Hawthorne (eds), *Perspectives on the World Christian Movement: A Reader*, Pasadena: William Carey Library, 1981, pp. 29-30.

Kalilombe, Patrick, *Doing Theology at the Grassroots: Theological Essays from Malawi*, Gweru: Mambo, 1999 (Mzuzu: Luviri Press, 2018).

Kastener, Patricia Wilson-, *Faith, Feminism, and the Christ*, Philadelphia: Fortress Press, 1983.

Kawamba, Brighton, *The Blantyre Spiritual Awakening and its Music*, Mzuzu: Luviri Press, 2018.

Khisi, Maximian, *The Church as the Family of God and the Care for Creation*, Mzuzu: Mzuni Press, 2018.

Kholowa, Janet and Klaus Fiedler, *Mtumwi Paulo ndi Udindo wa Amayi mu Mpingo*, Blantyre: CLAIM-Kachere, 2001.

Kombo, James, "Role and Relevance of Theology for the Future of African Christianity," in Isabel Apawo Phiri and Dietrich Werner, Chammah Kaunda and Kennedy Owino (eds), *Anthology of African Christianity*, Oxford: Regnum, 2016, p. 1225.

Kretzschmar, Louise, "Authentic Baptist Leadership in Africa," in *All Africa Baptist Theological Educators' Conference*, Ibadan: All Africa Baptist Fellowship, 2000, pp. 43-44.

Kretzschmar, Louise, "The Ethos and History of the Baptist Convention of South Africa's Winter Schools of Theology, *Winter School 1998*, Johannesburg: Baptist Convention College, 1998, p. 12.

Kretzschmar, Louise, *Privatization of the Christian Faith: Mission, Social Ethics and the South African Baptists*, Legon: Legon Theological Studies Series, 1998.

Langworthy, Harry, *'Africa for the African': The Life of Joseph Booth*, Blantyre: CLAIM, 1996.

Latourette, Kenneth Scott, *A History of Christianity*, Vol. II, New York: Harper & Row, 1975.

Leonard, Bill J., "Southern Baptists and the Laity," in the *Review and Expositor*, vol. LXXXIV, no. 4, 1987, p. 633.

Longwe, Hany, "Zimbabwe, Zambia and Malawi," in Kenneth R. Ross, J. Kwabena Asamoah-Gyadu & Todd M. Johnson (eds), *Edinburgh Companion to Global Christianity: Christianity in Sub-Sahara Africa*, Edinburgh University Press, 2017.

Longwe, Hany, *Christians by Grace – Baptists by Choice: A History of the Baptist Convention of Malawi*, Mzuzu: Mzuni Press; Zomba: Kachere, 2011.

Longwe, Hany, *Identity by Dissociation - A History of Achewa Providence Industrial Mission*, Mzuzu: Mzuni Press, 2013.

Longwe, Molly, "Engendered Theological Education: A Case of Women Theological Educators in the Baptist Convention of Malawi," in Isabel Apawo Phiri (ed), *Journal of Constructive Theology*, Pietermaritzburg: Centre for Constructive Theology, 2010, p. 85.

Lotz, Denton, "Paradigm Shifts in Missiology, in *Proceedings of the Summit on Baptist Mission in the 21st Century*, Falls Church: Baptist World Alliance, 2003, p. 62-64.

Makondesa, Patrick, *Moyo ndi Utumiki wa Mbusa ndi Mai Muocha wa Providence Industrial Mission*, Blantyre: CLAIM-Kachere, 2000 (Mzuzu: Luviri Press, 2020).

Makondesa, Patrick, *The Church History of Providence Industrial Mission*, Zomba: Kachere, 2006.

Matemba, Yonah, *Matandani. The Second Adventist Mission in Malawi*, Zomba: Kachere, 2004.

McBeth, H. Leon, *The Baptist Heritage: Four Centuries of Baptist Witness*, Nashville: Broadman, 1987.

McCracken, John, "Church and State in Malawi: The Scottish Presbyterian Missions, 1875 – 1965" in Holger Bernt & Michael Twaddle (eds), *Christian Missionaries & the State in the Third World*, Oxford: James Currey, 2002, pp. 181-188.

McCracken, John, *Politics & Christianity in Malawi 1875-1940: The Impact of Livingstonia Mission in Northern Province*, Zomba: Kachere, 2008.

McGavran, Donald A., *Effective Evangelism: A Theological Mandate*, Phillipsburg: Presbyterian and Reformed Publishing Co, 1988.

Means, Frank K., *Advance to Bold Mission Thrust: A History of Southern Baptist Foreign Missions 1970-1980*, Nashville: Southern Baptist Convention, 1981.

Messer, Donald E., *Contemporary Images of Christian Ministry*, Nashville: Abingdon, 1991.

Michael Green, *Freed to Serve: Training and Equipping for Ministry*, London: Hodder and Stoughton, 1988.

Mid-America Baptist Theological Seminary Catalog 2000-2002, pp. 53-54.

Mijoga, Hilary, *Separate but Same Message*, Blantyre: CLAIM-Kachere, 2000.

Milne, Bruce, *Know the Truth: A Handbook of Christian Belief*, Nottingham: InterVarsity Press, 1998, 2006.

Mlenga, Moses, *Polygamy in Northern Malawi: A Christian Rethinking*, Mzuzu: Luviri Press, 2015.

Mtewa, Mekki, "Tribute to Dr Malikebu," *The Enquirer*, Vol. 1 No. (6 September 1993), p. 5.

Munyenyembe, Rhodian, *Christianity and Socio-Cultural Issues. The Charismatic Movement and Contextualization in Malawi*, Mzuzu: Mzuni Press, 2011.

Norman, R. Stanton, *The Baptist Way: Distinctives of a Baptist Church*, Nashville: Academic, 2005.

Nzunda, Matembo S., and Kenneth R. Ross (eds), *Church, Law and Political Transition in Malawi 1992-94*, Gweru: Mambo, 1994.

Osei-Mensah, Gottfried, *Wanted Servant Leaders: The Challenge of Christian Leadership in Africa Today*, Achimoto: African Christian Press, 1990.

Phiri, D., *"Let Us Die for Africa": An African perspective on the life and death of John Chilembwe of Nyasaland/Malawi*, Blantyre: Central Africana Limited, 1999, p. 24.

Phiri, Isabel Apawo, "Introduction and Survey on Recent Research in African Christianity," in Isabel Apawo Phiri and Dietrich Werner, and Chammah Kaunda and Kennedy Owino (eds), *Anthology of African Christianity*, Oxford: Regnum, 2016, p. 10.

Phiri, Isabel Apawo, "Marching Suspended and Stoned: Christian Women in Malawi 1995," in Kenneth Ross (ed), *God, People and Power in Malawi: Democratization in Theological Perspective*, Blantyre: CLAIM-Kachere, 1996, pp. 63-105.

Phiri, Isabel Apawo, "Stand up and be Counted: Identity, Spirituality and Theological Education in my Faith Journey," in Denise Ackermann, Eliza Getman, Hantie Kotze and Judy Tobler (eds), *Claiming our Footprints: South African Women Reflect on Context, Identity and Spirituality*, Stellenbosch: EFSA Institute for Theological & Interdisciplinary Research, 2000, pp. 152, 153.

Phiri, Isabel Apawo, and Dietrich Werner, Chammah Kaunda and Kennedy Owino (eds), *Anthology of African Christianity*, Oxford: Regnum, 2016.

Phiri, Isabel Apawo, and Dietrich Werner, *Handbook for Theological Education in Africa*, Oxford: Regnum, 2013.

Phiri, Isabel Apawo, *Women, Presbyterianism and Patriarchy: Religious Experience of Chewa Women in Central Malawi*, Blantyre: CLAIM, 1997.

Pobee, John S., "Theological Trends in Africa Today," in J.S. Pobee and J.N. Kudadjie (eds), *Theological Education in Africa: Quo Vadimus?* Accra: Asempa, 1990, p. 60.

Rakoczy, Suzan I.H.M., *In Her Name: Women Doing Theology*, Pietermaritzburg: Cluster, 2004.

Reijnaerts, Hubert, Ann Nielsen and Matthew Schoffeleers, *Montfortians in Malawi: Their Spirituality and Pastoral Approach*, Blantyre: CLAIM-Kachere, 1997

Renwick, A.M., *The Story of the Church*, Guilford: Billing & Sons, 1958.

Richardson, Cyril C. (ed), *Early Christian Fathers*, New York: Touchstone, 1996.

Robinson, H. Wheeler, *The Life and Faith of the Baptists*, London: The Kingsgate, 1946.

Sanford, Don A., *A Choosing People: The History of Seventh Day Baptists*, Nashville" Broadman, 1992.

Selfridge, Jack, *Jack of all Trades Mastered by One*, Fearn: Christian Focus, 1996.

Shepperson, G., and T. Price, *Independent African*, Edinburgh: University Press, 1987, [reprinted Blantyre: CLAIM-Kachere, 2000].

Shepperson, George, and Thomas Price, *Independent African: John Chilembwe and the Origins, Setting and Significance of the Nyasaland Native Rising of 1915*, Blantyre: CLAIM-Kachere, 2000.

Snook, Stewart G., *Developing Leaders through Theological Education by Extension: Case Studies from Africa*, Wheaton: The Billy Graham Center, 1992.

Steven, Paas, *The Faith Moves South: A History of the Church in Africa*, Zomba: Kachere, 2006.

Stott, John, *The Cross of Christ*, Leicester: Inter-Varsity Press, 1989, p. 263.

Strohbehn, Ulf, *Pentecostalism in Malawi: A History of the Apostolic Faith Mission in Malawi*, Zomba: Kachere, 2005.

Sundkler, B.G.M., *Bantu Prophets in South Africa*, 2nd ed., London: Oxford, 1961.

Swartley, Willard M., *Slavery, Sabbath, War and Women: Case Issues in Biblical Interpretation*, Scottdale: Herald, 1983.

Tengatenga, James, "Religious Pluralism in Malawi: A Challenge to the Church," *Religion in Malawi*, no. 8, April 1998.

Tengatenga, James, "Early African Christianity," in Isabel Apawo Phiri and Dietrich Werner, and Chammah Kaunda and Kennedy Owino (eds), *Anthology of African Christianity*, Oxford: Regnum, 2016, p. 16.

The South African Baptist Journal of Theology, vol. 19, 2010, pp. 141-149.

The Times, 27.3.1972.

Thomas, George F., (ed), *The Vitality of the Christian Tradition*, New York: Harper & Brothers, 1945.

Tucker, Ruth A., "Women in Missions" in Joel A. Carpenter and Wilbert R Shenk (eds), *Earthen Vessels: American Evangelicals and Foreign Mission, 1880-1980*, Grand Rapids: William B. Eerdmans, 1990, p. 279.

Tucker, Ruth A., and Walter Liefeld, *Daughters of the Church: Women and Ministry from New Testament Times to the Present*, Grand Rapids: Academie Books, 1987.

Turner, Sam, *Baptist Beliefs and Customs*, Nairobi: International Publications, 2004.

Walls, Andrew F., *The Missionary Movement in Christian History: Studies in the Transmission of Faith*, Maryknoll: Orbis, 2000.

Weller, John, and Jane Linden, *Mainstream Christianity to 1980 in Malawi, Zambia and Zimbabwe*, Gweru: Mambo, 1984.

Winter, Ralph D. and Steven C. Hawthorne (eds), *Perspectives on the world Christian Movement: A Reader*, Pasadena: William Carey Library, 1981.

Wright, Gerald, "Theological Education as Ministerial Formation: A Response," in *Theological Education Consultation*, Cisurua: Foreign Mission Board, 1990, p. 2.

Internet Sources

"Who are the Baptists? – Africa," www.bwa-baptist-heritage.org/hst-afr.htm.

All Africa Baptist Fellowship, Mission Statement, www.aabfellowship.org/aabf/index.php/items/3-vision-mission.

Baptist Press, "Ebola Kills 6 in Baptist Woman's Family," www.bpnews.net/bpnews?id=43477.

Baptist World Alliance – Statistics, https://www.bwanet.org/about-us2/statistics.

Baptist World Alliance Heritage and Identity Commission, "Who are the Baptists? – Africa," www.bwa-baptist-heritage.org/hst-afr.htm.

Cupit, Tony, "Religious Freedom and the Baptist Perspective," www.bwanet.org/Ministries/Human%20Rights/rfreedom.htm.

www.baptisthistory.org/baptistorigins/priesthood.html [13.6.2018].

https://www.aacu.org/publications-research/periodicals/religious-studies-major-and-liberal-education [17.12.2018].

Longren, Trudie, "Baptist Beliefs on Women in the Ministry,". https://classroom.synonym.com/baptist-beliefs-on-women-in-the-ministry-12087385.html [12.11.2019].

Mount Meru University, Arusha, Tanzania, http://emica.org/projectEAhighlight_9066.shtm [4.7.2007].

Mount Meru University, www.mmu.ac.tz, [4.7.2007].

Strauch, Alexander, *Biblical Leadership: An Urgent Call to Restore Biblical Church Leadership*, Littleton: Lewis and Ruth Publishers, 1995, pp. 51-66.

What Presbyterians Believe, www.pcusa.org/believe/past/mar04/priesthood.htm, [10.12.2007].

www.aacu.org/publications-research/periodicals/religious-sttudies-major-and-liberal-education [17.12.2018].

www.researchgate.net/publication/265634000_Why_Study_Theology_and_Religious_Studies [4.6.2018].

Index

A

Abelard, Peter · 56f
Abraham · 136, 160f
Accountability · 49f, 52f
Admonition · 203
Affiliation · 202
African Bible College · 20f, 121, 233
African Christianity · 24, 54f, 256, 259, 301
African Culture · 70, 254
African Theological Fellowship (ATF) · 24
Agape Life Church · 209
Aggressive · 133, 201, 205, 215, 229
Akrofi-Christaller Memorial Centre for Mission Research and Applied Theology · 24
Alaniz, Dr. Anne · 18
Albright, LeRoy · 11, 147
All Africa Baptist Fellowship (AABF) · 47, 107, 195
All for Jesus Band · 233
Anabaptist · 187f
Anselm · 56
Anti-women · 158
Apartheid · 31, 190f
Apostolic Faith Mission · 93, 95, 209, 249
Aquinas, Thomas · 56-58
Arusha · 13, 21, 37, 42, 107
Assemblies of God · 19, 100, 140, 209, 229f, 242, 249, 253, 258
Australia · 20, 180

Authority · 9, 28, 58f, 65, 130, 135, 149, 150f, 153, 155f, 163f, 169f, 172, 182, 188-190, 207, 290
Autonomy of the local Church · 28, 49, 129, 172

B

Baduya, Elestina · 13
Banda, Jande · 20
Banda, Kamuzu · 8, 65f, 103
Banda, Kapalamula · 15, 113
Banda, Marrie · 21
Banda, Rachel ·[Fiedler] 20, 23f, 180
Banda, Rutherford · 21
Baptist Beliefs and Practice · 9, 33
Baptist Bible School · 12, 30, 81f, 86, 107, 113, 237, 269, 287
Baptist Missionary Society · 184, 208
Baptist Seminary in Lusaka · 13
Baptist Theological Seminary of Rüschlikon · 13
Baptist Witness · 187
Baptist World Alliance · 107, 109, 134, 184f, 195, 295-297, 300, 303
Bediako, Dr Kwame · 24
Believer's baptism · 141, 188
Bible study · 9, 32f, 76, 97, 108, 142, 203, 217-219, 223f, 236, 239, 254, 261, 267
Bible Way Correspondence School · 12, 112, 241
Biblical approach · 116
Biblical fidelity · 130
Bishop · 9, 56, 58, 60, 64f, 132, 134f

Index

Blantyre Baptist Church · 13, 23, 25, 98, 105, 172, 278
Board of Governors · 119, 295
Bone of contention · 168
Booth, Joseph · 8, 146f, 186, 209, 244
Born Again · 10, 27, 75, 189, 200, 202, 225, 230, 234, 248
Bowen, Thomas · 183
Breadwinners · 116
BTh · 16, 20f, 295
Bunda College of Agriculture · 20, 62, 196
Butao, Christopher · 15, 19
BWUA · 106, 109, 113, 174

C

Calvinism · 187
Cape Town Baptist Seminary · 23
Capital City Baptist Church · 21-23, 87, 120, 233, 238
Capitalism · 243
Carey, Lott · 183
Carey, William · 208, 299
CCM · 14, 141, 277
Chakwera, Emmanuel · 253
Challenge · 32f, 46-48, 68f, 95, 122, 131f, 136, 144, 150, 160, 171, 179, 192, 211, 216, 239, 242, 244, 257
Chakwera, Lazarus · 253
Challenged · 119, 123, 126, 256
Chaotcha, Aidane · 84-86
Charismatic · 24, 165, 196f, 200, 204f, 208, 242, 249f, 253, 260, 298
Chewa culture · 136, 138, 146, 241
Chewa speaking · 114
Chichiri Baptist Church · 77
Chififitini · 135
Chigede, Isaac · 108

Chikanga, H. Sweet · 100
Child abuse · 190
Chilembwe, John · 8, 74, 127, 141, 146f, 197f, 211, 242, 244
Chilokoteni, Samuel · 80
Chiluba, Frederick · 252
Chimbalanga Village · 95
Chimombo, Napolo Alexander · 16
Chinguwo, Robert · 95
Chipande, Agnes · 14
Chipande, Graham · 14, 22, 175
Chiradzulu · 11, 100, 108-110, 127-131, 144, 264
Chirwa, Akim · 13, 18f, 24, 206
Chirwa, Martha · 14, 19f
Chirwa, Vincent · 23
Chisi, Nellie · 78
Chisi, W.A.C. · 15, 296
Chitando, Ezra · 257
Christian Council of Malawi (CCM) · 14, 141, 277
Christian Education · 22
Christian Missionary Alliance College · 20
Christian radio stations · 233
Christianization · 24, 143, 145, 241
Christocentric · 141
Church Government · 156
Church Planting · 9, 12, 35, 67, 95, 170, 218, 235f
Church Reformation · 150, 153
Churches of Christ · 136, 146, 209, 229, 244
Civic Organizations · 251
Classical Mission · 208
Clergy · 9, 26, 56, 59f, 141, 149-156, 159f, 162-166, 182, 189, 216, 224, 252, 254f, 257
Clericalism · 163
Cliccord House · 98, 262

Colonial · 8f, 54, 66, 75, 92f, 103, 184, 186, 191, 243, 250f
Come to Jesus Choir · 233
Comity · 244, 247
Community · 10, 26, 35, 41, 43, 48, 67, 71, 73, 102, 116f, 120, 126, 131, 138, 149-154, 163f, 169, 186f, 194, 205, 216, 218, 220, 231, 256
Concern · 13, 42, 72, 120, 124, 174, 190, 207, 226, 242, 250, 255, 257
Contemporary issues · 46, 73
Corruption · 72, 190
Counselling · 27, 73, 117, 119, 169, 192
Covenant · 154, 160, 189, 215
Covington, Victor · 23
Crusades · 202, 225f, 234
curriculum · 29, 33, 39, 48, 105

D

Day, Rendell · 23, 83
Decentralized Theological Education (DTE) · 15
Decision Making · 171, 188, 210, 218
Decolonization · 191, 252
DeLaney, Emma · 8
Democratic · 14, 150f, 155, 206f, 251, 253
Denominational · 27, 34, 45, 48f, 91, 100, 133, 135, 156, 164, 201f, 205, 208, 246, 248f, 255f, 260
Diaconate · 160
Diakonhjemmet University College · 21
Dictatorship · 67
Dignity · 157, 165
Direction · 116, 165, 205, 223
Distinct · 114

Distinction · 7, 9, 26, 41, 149-154, 160, 163, 167, 189
DTE · 15, 38

E

Eastern and Southern African Management Institute · 21
Ebola · 193
Ecclesiology · 163, 188
Egalitarian · 154
Empowered · 149, 152
Empowerment · 25, 152, 190, 206
English speaking · 99, 114
Episcopate · 132
Equal partners · 7
Equality · 152, 154, 167, 171
Equip · 16, 32, 34, 36, 41, 46, 48, 118
Ethnocentrism · 145
Evangelical Association of Malawi (EAM) · 17, 116, 197, 229
Evangelical conversion · 155
Evangelism · 9f, 13, 33- 35, 49, 75, 95, 105, 113, 132, 142f, 157, 162, 170, 180, 191, 201-203, 212-216, 220-235, 239-241, 248, 255, 260, 283
Exploitation · 189

F

Faith · 7, 9-11, 19, 27, 29, 32, 35, 45-47, 55, 57f, 64, 69, 80, 91, 95f, 101f, 112, 118, 126, 132, 141f, 147, 150, 153f, 157, 165, 169, 190-192, 194, 202, 206, 208f, 211, 214, 216-221, 224-226, 234f, 238, 241f, 247, 252, 255-257, 259, 267, 282
Falls Estate · 11, 106, 268

Fatherhood · 198
Fear · 88, 115, 119, 181, 251
FEBA · 89, 240
Fellowship · 9, 35, 78, 94, 98, 108, 130, 132f, 136, 140f, 146, 151, 170-172, 177, 181, 183, 189, 196f, 199-207, 217, 224, 229, 231, 235, 267
Feminist · 71f
Fiedler, Klaus · 17, 20, 23f, 68, 99, 119, 158, 164, 168, 174, 176f, 182, 185, 192f, 196f, 200, 204f, 208f, 211, 217, 235, 241f, 244, 247, 295, 298
Fiedler, Rachel NyaGondwe · 25, 120, 174-176, 180
FMB · 133f
Free Church Movement · 159
Free Methodist Church · 87, 91, 95, 209, 216, 222, 236f, 240, 242, 297
Freedom · 30f, 45, 49, 99, 104, 112, 115, 131, 139, 142, 155, 158, 171, 175, 181, 187, 189f, 192, 211, 221, 247

G

Galatiya, Mary · 11f, 95f, 99f, 105-107, 110, 181, 185
Galatiya, Stephen · 11f, 79f, 95, 97-107, 110, 113, 278
Gama, Kachaso · 11, 97, 146, 262
Gender · 20, 64, 70, 72, 117, 136f, 152, 167, 171f, 176, 255, 257f
General Baptist Convention of Oklahoma · 241
German Baptists · 185
Gifting · 26, 170, 173, 236
Girgis, Seddick W. · 187

Goal · 143, 175, 251
God Called Men and Women for Christian Ministry · 16
Gordon-Conwell Theological Seminary · 22
Govati, Alex · 174
Government · 9, 14, 31, 61f, 65-67, 70, 72f, 79, 126, 128, 131, 134f, 139, 148, 155f, 162, 172, 183, 188f, 191, 193, 196f, 239, 251-253, 257, 259, 277, 280
Great Awakening · 208
Group Movement · 145, 241
Guilds · 58
Gweru · 12-15, 18f, 37, 76-78, 92, 97, 99, 108, 176, 192, 243, 295, 297-299

H

Haggai Institute · 178
Heritage · 30, 51, 55, 130, 184, 187, 190f, 200, 216
Hierarchy · 65, 130, 153f, 256
Hip-hop Gospel · 233
HIV/AIDS · 64, 72, 115-122, 125, 250, 258
Holy poverty · 134
Homogeneity · 143
Homosexuality · 139
Hughes Baptist Church · 180
Human Resources · 73, 116, 222
human rights · 67, 139, 172

I

Ignorance · 125
Immorality · 93

Impact of religion · 64
inculturation · 66, 255f
Independence · 59, 62, 66f, 99, 132, 139, 155, 188, 207, 246, 248-251, 277
Indigenous · 38, 51, 99, 134f, 143, 200, 210f, 214, 226, 242, 254
Indigenous Church Principle · 99, 210f
Individualism · 143, 188, 191, 207
Infected · 115, 119-121
Inferiority · 165, 255
Infrastructure · 115
Institute of Public Administration · 62
Interdenominational · 89, 98, 146, 184-186, 200f, 204, 229f, 249, 255f
Interdependence · 188f, 207
Involvement · 11, 13, 65, 69, 100, 120f, 191, 215, 218, 223, 225, 247f, 254, 257

J

Jerusalem Baptist Church · 99, 110, 129, 279
Johannesburg · 78f, 103, 118, 138, 236, 299
Johnson, H.H. · 93

K

Kachere, Grace · 174f, 177
Kaduya, Agnes · 107-109
Kaduya, McDonald 11, 107, 109, 264
Kagwa, Mary · 17, 180f
Kagwa, Milward · 180
Kaiya, Fletcher · 13, 19, 89, 173
Kaiya, Grenna · 21
Kaiya, Malla · 21

Kalako, Liddah · 16f, 102f, 178f
Kalemba, Peter · 23, 127, 130, 198, 211
Kalenga, Jim · 80, · 100
Kalenga, Rustin · 16, 100, 174f, 296
Kalonga, Fenias (Peter) · 11, 133
Kalumbu · 128, 131, 133
Kamanga, Dickson · 15
Kamkalamba, Aaron · 11, 131, 133
Kamungu, Leonard · 245
Kamuzu Central Hospital · 120
Kamwana · 104
Kandawe, Timothy · 80, 113f
Kanowa, Bamusi ·13, 76, 107
Kanowa, Martha · 76
Kanyama, Alice · 21
Kanyama, Aubrey · 21
Kasiya, Howard · 116
Kato, Byang H. · 201
Kawale · 11, 102, 268
Kawamba, Bright · 24
Kingsley, Gene · 11, 98f, 108
Koyi, William · 243
Kuunika Choir · 233
Kuzalo, Ethel · 101
Kuzalo, Nelson · 101

L

Labour Migration · 91f, 217, 246
Lack of knowledge is death · 115
Laity · 9, 26, 33, 64, 140, 149-156, 159-166, 182, 189, 216, 221, 224, 256
Leadership Roles · 43, 169, 172, 194
Legacy · 9, 55, 127
Liberation · 8, 66, 72, 138, 254, 257
Liberty · 169, 183, 188, 190
Lichapa · 78, 177

Index

Light House · 120f, 125
Likoma · 83, 84f, 238
Living Waters · 209, 233, 236
Livingstone, David · 199
Livingstonia Mission · 92, 199, 243, 300
Liwembe, E. · 83
Localized Bible Schools · 12
Lombard, Peter · 56f
Lomwe · 128
Longwe, Hany · 3, 23, 25, 75, 96-98, 108f, 111, 113, 127-129, 147, 176, 178f, 186, 197-199, 202f, 223, 232, 238, 248, 254f
Longwe, Molly · 13-16, 24f, 118, 168, 176
Lord's Supper · 133, 141, 196, 282
Lusaka · 13, 15, 18-20, 76f, 99, 103, 256
Lusaka Seminary · 14, 77
Lydia Project · 120, 180

M

Mafuleka, Funwayo · 21f, 175
Magisterial Reformers · 188
Makhaya, Joanna · 12
Makina, Mellia · 177, 219
Makorasi · 234
Malabwanya, Samuel · 99, 107
Malawi Cluster of Theological Institutions · 69
Malawi Congress Party · 98, 111, 253
Malawi Council of Churches · 117f
Malawi Journal of Biblical Studies · 69
Malawi Polytechnic · 62
Malei, Real Fernando · 81
Malikebu, Dr Daniel · 8, 127, 134, 198, 296

Malikebu, Flora · 9
Mallungo, Hilda · 106f
Mandala · 92
Mandevu · 77
Mangochi · 17, 89, 180f, 239f, 259
Mangoni · 127-130, 143f, 211
Martha, Kanowa · 13, 76
Maseko, Emma · 8, 18
Maseko, Peter · 13, 18f
Master of Divinity in Theology · 23
Mastern, John · 21, 22
Matandani · 96, 97, 212, 300
Matchona · 91, 95, 106, 114, 249
Matupi, Grace · 20
Maya, Agnes · 76f, 109, 219, 264
Maya, July · 76f
Mbombwe · 107f, 127, 130, 133f, 144, 147, 296
Meharry Medical College · 8
MEMA · 105, 203
Mhango, Daina · 17
MIAA · 118
Milanje District · 81, 82
Milingo, Emmanuel · 256
Minority · 110, 187, 192, 208, 258
miphakati · 64f
Missionaries of Africa · 64
Missionary vision · 166, 209, 210f, 242
Mizeki, Bernard · 246
Mkandawire, Annie · 17
Mkandawire, Francis · 17, 116
Mkandawire, Owen · 24
Module · 117, 120, 200, 295, 297
Moises, Augusto · 81
Morality · 67, 251
Mozambique · 83f, 88, 237
Mpakati, Attati · 65
Mpatuko · 84, 128, 130f, 134, 143, 198
Mpingo · 132

Index 311

Mpombwe, Joseph · 174f
Mpulumutsi · 103f
Msiska, Sandress · 22
Mugabe, Robert · 253
Muhosa, Frank · 82, 85
Music · 13, 43, 59, 89, 206, 226, 233, 240, 250, 256
Musopole, Augustine · 258
Mustard Seed Band · 233
Mutendi, Samuel · 249
Mwale, Linesi · 14
Mwale, Samuel · 99
Mwamdaza, Amess · 17
Mwase, George · 13, 21, 79, 86, 296
Mwenefumbo, Bridget · 176

N

Nairobi Graduate School of Theology · 22
Nasimango, Sellina · 177f, 219
National Baptist Convention (NBC) Inc · 129
National Black American Baptists · 185
Nazarene Church · 209, 240
Ndalama · 11f, 97, 262
Ndege, Yosofati · 11, 132
Neocharismatic · 233, 235, 236
New Apostolic Church · 209
Ngaunje, E.N. · 83
Ng'oma, Helen · 100, 110-113, 287
Ng'ombayera, P. · 84
Ngwata, Peacewell · 77
Nikoroma, Bizwick · 174
Nkhata, Raika · 13, 77
Nkhata, Ruben · 13, 15, 18, 77
Nkhata, Titus · 21
Nkhoma, Christopher T. · 25
Nkhoma, Francis · 89

Nkhota Kota · 83f
Norway · 21
Nyangu, Anderson · 127
Nyanja · 77, 78, 94, 97
Nyanje · 131, 133, 135
Nyasa College · 61
Nyasa Industrial Mission · 186, 209, 244
Nyasaland Rising of 1915 · 198
Nyathi, Joan · 109

O

Oppression · 69, 71, 171, 189, 192
Orthodoxy · 153

P

Pandemic · 115, 122, 124
Paris · 57, 59f, 244
Parratt, Dr J. · 62
Partners in Hope · 120, 122-124
Partnerships · 43, 120, 235, 238
Paternalism · 200
Patriarchal Society · 254
Pentecostal and Charismatic · 67, 208, 248, 257
Pentecostal Holiness Association · 209
PhD · 22f, 25, 43, 65, 200, 257, 295-297
Phiri, Amos · 89
Phiri, Canaan R.K. · 118
Phiri, Elizabeth · 12, 106f
Phiri, Emmanuel Chinkwita · 13f, 17, 79, 173f, 180, 203, 296
Phiri, Isabel Apawo · 69, 71f, 254, 258, 300
Phiri, Jimmy · 21f

Phiri, Luciano · 80f, 86f
Phiri, Lydia Chinkwita · 17, 180
Phiri, MacFerron Njolomole · 12, 106
Phiri, Moses · 95
Phiri, Nellie · 17, 179f
Phiri, Patricia · 81, 86
Phoebe · 158, 167
PLWA · 118, 126
Political Issues · 190
Political Reform · 67
Post-Classical Missions · 208
Potent Source · 63
Pothawira · 18
Presbyterian · 67, 69f, 94, 110, 139, 162, 202, 229, 243, 300
Priesthood of all Believers · 9, 26f, 29, 44, 149, 151, 153f, 161, 163-165, 168, 175, 189f, 257, 260, 297
Priestly · 151f, 165, 189
Professional · 28, 41, 89, 121f, 164f
Prominence · 99, 136, 206
Prophets · 146, 181
Providence Industrial Mission · 9, 127f, 134, 186, 197f, 212, 241, 244, 265, 296, 300
Public Affairs Committee · 67, 252
Publishing · 68f, 73, 257, 273

Q

Quadrivium · 59f
Queen of the Sciences · 40, 59

R

Racism · 70, 99
Randburg Baptist Theological Seminary · 21

Refugees · 80, 84, 113, 236f, 238, 240f
Regenerate church membership · 27, 35, 97, 129
Religion in Malawi · 69, 141, 196, 298
Religious Diversification · 235
Religious Traditions · 63
Research · 25, 41, 71-74, 117, 257
Respect · 64, 138, 158, 171, 173, 177, 206, 235
Revivalism · 157
Roman Catholic Church · 139, 258
Royden, Agnes Maude · 159

S

Salima · 18, 228
Salvation Army · 209, 246
Scripture · 29, 57, 89, 130, 132, 153, 167, 169, 229f, 232, 240
Segregation · 137, 140f, 156, 171, 203
Separation · 31, 94, 131, 143, 190-192, 208
Servitude · 151
Seventh Day Baptists · 191
Seventh-day Adventists · 209, 246
Sexism · 70
Sexual · 71, 121, 193
Sexually transmitted diseases · 193
Sigerege Baptist Church · 174f
Simango, Timothy · 76
Soche Hill College of Education · 62
Social Gospel · 191
Social justice · 67
Social reform · 190
Social well-being · 191
Social witness · 191, 194
Solidarity · 71, 99, 169
Sosole, Ollen Khumbo · 21
South Africa General Mission · 79, 209

Index

Status · 99, 116, 124, 150, 161f, 165, 175, 185, 192, 206
Stigma and Discrimination · 115f
Struggle · 70, 151, 196, 256
Subordination · 172, 194
Sumaine, Gusto'nio · 81f
Sunday school · 9, 12, 33, 50, 103, 108, 156, 203, 220, 222, 224

T

TB · 123-125
Team · 76, 80, 101, 110, 131, 142, 184, 227, 239f, 244
TEE · 38f, 223f
Tembenukani Duet · 233
Tension · 35, 52, 149, 156, 163, 257, 280
The Study of TRS · 64
Theological Training · 7, 9-12, 20, 23, 26, 29f, 34, 49-51, 53, 98, 106, 165, 177, 222f
Theology and Religious Studies · 256
Tolbert, Victoria · 109
Transformation · 40, 67f, 201, 243, 262
Transmission · 91, 117, 121
Trivium · 59f
Tsabola, Paulo · 82f

U

University of Bologna · 60
University of KwaZulu Natal · 24
University of Malawi · 16-20, 23-25, 62, 66-68, 71f, 134, 196, 209, 296

V

Villa Ulongwe · 87f, 90, 238
Violence · 71f, 152, 251, 255
Visibility · 172, 254
Vision · 42, 47, 51, 144, 152, 191, 198, 207, 227, 240, 303
Vizara, Mario · 80
Vocation · 10, 27, 150, 153, 159
Voiceless · 162
Voluntarism · 155

W

WCC · 118, 201
Wenela · 92
Wester, Bill · 11, 97f
Western Missionary Theology · 257
Women in Ministry · 159, 167, 172
World Relief in Malawi · 22, 117f

Y

Yao · 88f, 91, 128, 180, 239f, 258
Yao Project · 89

Z

Zambezi Industrial Mission · 186, 209, 244
Zealous · 105, 187, 215
Zomba Theological College · 19f

www.ingramcontent.com/pod-product-compliance
Lightning Source LLC
Chambersburg PA
CBHW050858300426
44111CB00010B/1290